FACING UNPLEASANT FACTS

BY GEORGE ORWELL

FICTION
Burmese Days

A Clergyman's Daughter

Keep the Aspidistra Flying

Coming Up for Air

Animal Farm

1984

NONFICTION
Down and Out in Paris and London

The Road to Wigan Pier

Homage to Catalonia

All Art Is Propaganda: Critical Essays

FACING
UNPLEASANT FACTS

Narrative Essays

GEORGE ORWELL

Compiled and with an introduction
by George Packer

Mariner Books / Houghton Mifflin Harcourt

BOSTON   NEW YORK

First Mariner Books edition 2009
Copyright © George Orwell
Compilation copyright © 2008 by The Estate of the late Sonia Brownell Orwell
Foreword and Introduction copyright © 2008 by George Packer

For information about permission to reproduce selections from this book,
write to Permissions, Houghton Mifflin Harcourt Publishing Company,
215 Park Avenue South, New York, New York 10003.

www.hmhco.com

Essays collected from *The Complete Works of George Orwell,* edited by Peter Davison,
OBE, published in Great Britain in 1998 by Secker & Warburg. Grateful
acknowledgement is made to Peter Davison for permission to draw from his notes.

Library of Congress Cataloging-in-Publication Data
Orwell, George, 1903–1950.
Facing unpleasant facts: narrative essays/by George Orwell;
compiled and with an introduction by George Packer.—1st ed.
p.   cm.
Includes bibliographical references.
I. Packer, George, 1960–   II. Title.
PR6029.R8F33   2008
824'.912—dc22   2008014749
ISBN 978-0-15-101361-6
ISBN 978-0-15-603313-8 (pbk.)

Text set in Garamond MT
Designed by Cathy Riggs

Printed in the United States of America
DOH 10 9 8 7 6

CONTENTS

FOREWORD

BEFORE anything else, George Orwell was an essayist. His earliest published pieces were essays; so were his last deathbed writings. In between, he never stopped working at the essay's essential task of articulating thoughts out of the stuff of life and art in a compressed space with a distinctly individual voice that speaks directly to the reader. The essay perfectly suited Orwell's idiosyncratic talents. It takes precedence even in his best-known fiction: During long passages of *1984*, the novelistic surface cracks and splits open under the pressure of the essayist's concerns. His more obscure novels of social realism from the 1930s are marked, and to some extent marred, by an essayist's explaining; and his great nonfiction books, *Down and Out in Paris and London, The Road to Wigan Pier,* and *Homage to Catalonia,* continually slip between particular and general, concrete and abstract, narration and exposition, in a way that would be alien to a storytelling purist and that defines Orwell's core purpose as a writer. As soon as he began to write something, it was as natural for Orwell to propose, generalize, qualify, argue, judge—in short, to think—as it was for Yeats to versify or Dickens to invent. In his best work, Orwell's arguments are mostly with himself.

Part of the essay's congeniality for Orwell is its flexibility. All a reader asks is that the essayist mean what he says and say something interesting, in a voice that's recognizably his; beyond that, subject matter, length, structure, and occasion are extremely variable. Orwell, who produced a staggering amount of prose over the course of a career cut short at forty-six by tuberculosis, was a working journalist, and in the two volumes of this new selection of his essays you will find book, film, and theater reviews, newspaper columns, and war reporting, as well as cultural commentary, literary criticism, political argument, autobiographical fragments, and longer personal narratives. In Orwell's hands, they are all essays. He is always pointing to larger concerns beyond the immediate scope of his subject.

Orwell had the advantage of tradition: He worked in the lineage of the English essay dating back to the eighteenth century, whose earlier masters were Samuel Johnson, Charles Lamb, and William Hazlitt, and whose last great representative was Orwell himself. Within this tradition it was entirely natural for a writer to move between fiction and nonfiction, journalism and autobiography, the daily newspaper, the weekly or monthly magazine, and the quarterly review; and between the subjects of art, literature, culture, politics, and himself. This tradition hasn't thrived in the United States. Our national literature was born with the anxieties and ambitions of New World arrivistes, and Americans have always regarded the novel as the highest form of literary art; if we recognize essays at all, it's as the minor work of novelists and poets (and yet some of the greatest modern essayists—James Baldwin and Edmund Wilson, to name two—have been Americans). As for journalism of the kind that Orwell routinely turned out, the word itself has suggested something like the opposite of literature to an American reader. The English essay comes out of a more workmanlike view of what it means to be a writer: This view locates the writer squarely within the struggles of his historical time and social place, which is where the essayist has to live.

A tradition in which the line between writer and journalist is hard to draw allows plenty of room for the characteristic qualities of the Orwell essay: his informal, direct prose style; his interest in sociological criticism that takes in both high and popular culture; his penchant for overstatement and attack; his talent for memorable sentences, especially his openings, which a journalist would call the lede: "In Moulmein, in Lower Burma, I was hated by large numbers of people — the only time in my life that I have been important enough for this to happen to me"; "Saints should always be judged guilty until they are proved innocent"; "There is very little in Eliot's later work that makes any deep impression on me"; "Dickens is one of those writers who are well worth stealing." The American critic Irving Howe wrote in his autobiography *A Margin of Hope* that when he set out to learn to write essays in the 1940s, he turned to Orwell: "How do you begin a literary piece so as to hold attention? George Orwell was masterful at this, probably because he had none of the American literary snobbism about doing 'mere journalism.'"

Orwell lived in and wrote about interesting times: war, ideological extremism, intellectual combat, dilemmas over the role of the writer in a period of partisanship and upheaval. "In a peaceful age I might have written ornate or merely descriptive books, and might have remained almost unaware of my political loyalties," he speculates in "Why I Write." "As it is I have been forced into becoming a sort of pamphleteer." If it's true, then we can be grateful for the timing of Orwell's birth, since his talent was never going to lie in updating the nineteenth-century naturalistic novel. The work Orwell started doing to pay the bills while he wrote fiction — his reviews, sketches, polemics, columns — turned out to be the purest expression of his originality. "Pamphleteer" might suggest a kind of hack, but in Orwell's case it's an essayist with a cause.

Our times are interesting in similar ways and have opened up a space for writers who are similarly capable of thinking clearly about history as it's unfolding without surrendering their grip on permanent standards of artistic judgment, political idealism, and moral decency. In other words, our age demands essayists. So it's an odd fact that even readers who know *1984* well and have read one or two of Orwell's other books are likely to be unfamiliar with the most essential Orwell. Aside from "Politics and the English Language" and perhaps "Shooting an Elephant," none of his essays are widely read, and some of the best remain almost unknown. Those American readers who have read the essays are likely to have encountered only the single-volume *A Collection of Essays,* which includes just fourteen wonderful but somewhat randomly chosen pieces—not enough to give a sense of Orwell's growth as a writer, the range and evolution of his interests.

How should one conceive a more generous edition of Orwell's essays? A strictly chronological version would function as a kind of autobiography; a division by subject matter—Socialism, the Spanish civil war, England—would offer a historical primer. But for contemporary readers, the particular content of Orwell's life and times can sometimes seem dated and remote, whereas the drama of a great writer mastering a form in countless variations is always current. The two volumes of this new edition are organized to illuminate Orwell as an essayist—to show readers how he made the essay his own. In them, you'll find Orwell engaged in two different modes of writing: The essays in *Facing Unpleasant Facts* build meaning from telling a story; the essays in *All Art Is Propaganda* hold something up to critical scrutiny. The first is based on narrative, the second on analysis, and Orwell was equally brilliant at both. He wrote more narrative essays early in his career, in the 1930s, when he was drawing on his personal encounters with imperialism, poverty, and war; and more critical essays later on, in the 1940s, when his most important experiences were behind him. But he never stopped writing either kind; one of his last essays was the posthumously published account of his schooldays, "Such, Such Were the Joys." The literary problems raised and the demands imposed by these two types of essay are sufficiently different that they distinguish the essays written across Orwell's career in a more fundamental way than subject, period, or publication.

This division shows the technical difficulties of the essay in especially sharp relief. Essays seem to offer almost limitless room to improvise and experiment, and yet their very freedom makes them unforgiving of literary faults: sloppiness, vagueness, pretension, structural misshapenness, an immature voice, insular material, and the nearly universal plague of bad thinking are all mercilessly exposed under the spotlight in which the essayist stands alone onstage. There are no props, no sets, no other actors; the essayist is the existentialist of literature, and a mediocre talent will wear out his audience within a couple of paragraphs. Orwell was a technical master whose essays are so clear and coherent that they act as guides to how they were put together. You can learn most of what you need to know about the steps by which a narrative essay arrives at a larger truth out of personal experience from "Shooting an Elephant," and about the way close reading in a critical essay can open up literary and philosophical commentary from "T. S. Eliot." Orwell's essays demonstrate how to be interesting line after line. The emphasis in these collections on the two kinds of essay he wrote is directed not just at readers who want to discover or rediscover his work, but at writers who want to learn from it.

Certain essays don't fit my scheme, such as the "As I Please" columns, which appeared in the weekly *Tribune,* and Orwell's short commentaries on English cooking, sports, toads, and coal fires.

I've included these partly for the sake of their obscurity, to satisfy the aficionado along with the amateur, and partly because they show how much of life interested him. He could savor and mine the trivial and become partisan about things that have nothing to do with politics. On every subject he took up, Orwell quickly hit the target of something essential, making an insight that would occur to no other writer and would still resonate over half a century later. And it's often a short step from these slighter works to the themes of his most famous books. For example, "As I Please, 16," which sentences to death certain overused political terms, is the germ of the great essay "Politics and the English Language," which in turn crystallizes much of the intellectual content behind the nightmare vision of *1984*. Seeing the development of a writer's obsessions through his work is just one reason to read these two volumes of essays together.

A generation of students has gone to school on the banal truth that all literature is "constructed," and learned to scoff at the notion that words on the page might express something essentially authentic about the writer. The usefulness of this insight runs up against its limits when you pick up Orwell's essays. Open these books anywhere and you encounter the same voice. Orwell always sounds like Orwell: readier to fight than most writers, toughened but also deepened by hard, largely self-inflicted experience, able to zero in on what's essential about a poem or a politician or a memory, unsurprised without being cynical, principled without being priggish, direct and yet slightly reserved. It is not a clever or inventive voice, and occasionally it can sound a bit pedestrian. It doesn't seduce and exhaust you with literary dazzle; it persuades you with the strength of its prose and the soundness of its judgment. Exactly what relation this voice has to the private individual born with the name Eric Arthur Blair is unknowable. Within the confines of these pages, its integrity is consistent and enduring.

A career like Orwell's would be difficult to undertake today. There is too much specialization in writing, too little genuine independence, and not much room in the major newspapers and magazines for strongly individual essays. It was hard enough to make a living as an essay writer when Orwell was alive — in 1944, one of his most prolific years as an essayist, he earned less than six hundred pounds for his one hundred thousand words — and much harder now. Yet for any young writer willing to try, these essays don't merely survive as historical artifacts and literary masterpieces. In his openness to the world and his insistence on being true to himself, Orwell's essays show readers and writers of any era what it means to live by the vocation.

—GEORGE PACKER

INTRODUCTION
By George Packer

ORWELL's writing began with essays, and his essays began with experience. Before *Burmese Days* there was "A Hanging," and before "A Hanging" there were "five boring years within the sound of bugles" as a colonial policeman in Burma. Before *Down and Out in Paris and London* there was "The Spike," and before "The Spike" there were months spent incognito as a dishwasher and tramp. In "Why I Write" Orwell reports that he wanted to be a writer from "perhaps the age of five or six," but it was only in the hard, self-inflicted experiences of his twenties and thirties—imperialism, poverty, coal mines and miners, the Spanish civil war—that his power as a writer was forged. Even after these years were behind him, and he became famous as a novelist and critic, and readers forgot or never knew his beginnings, the authority of his voice and the conviction of his vision depended on his being able to say: *I was there—I saw it—I know.*

Orwell's insistence on seeing, feeling, even—perhaps especially—smelling his subjects led him to judge harshly others who wrote from abstraction or orthodoxy or sheer wishfulness. Once, in 1937, when a left-wing review asked him to answer a list of questions for a volume to be published under the self-congratulatory title *Authors Take Sides on the Spanish War,* Orwell shot back a reply that was brutal even by his standards: "Will you please stop sending me this bloody rubbish. This is the second or third time I have had it. I am not one of your fashionable pansies like Auden and

Spender. I was six months in Spain, most of the time fighting, I have a bullet-hole in me at present and I am not going to write blah about defending democracy or gallant little anybody." Similarly, after Auden published his poem "Spain," which included the lines, "Today the deliberate increase in the chances of death, / The conscious acceptance of guilt in the necessary murder," Orwell delivered a scathing review in his essay "Inside the Whale": "It could only be written by a person to whom murder is at most a *word*. Personally I would not speak so lightly of murder. It so happens that I have seen the bodies of numbers of murdered men— I don't mean killed in battle, I mean murdered. Therefore I have some conception of what murder means—the terror, the hatred, the howling relatives, the post-mortems, the blood, the smells. To me, murder is something to be avoided." Whether or not because of this crushing rebuke, Auden later disowned "Spain," refusing to permit its publication in any of his collections. Orwell wasn't merely getting even with more famous writers by pulling rank based on his own tendency to seek out difficult experiences; it was a matter of literary principle. He was something of an empirical absolutist. He distrusted words that didn't immediately call to mind a fresh concrete image and issued a ban on them in "Politics and the English Language." He summed up his credo in "Why I Write": "Good prose is like a window pane."

Every writer is limited by his strengths, and Orwell's belief in the supremacy of sensory evidence restricted him as a novelist and a critic. His imaginative writing always stood on shaky legs (the poet William Empson called Orwell "the eagle eye with the flat feet"); he was unable to create persuasive female characters (his pigs are more convincing); in his critical essays he disparaged Yeats and despised Woolf. But he was also able to see through the heroic posing of writers "to whom murder is at most a *word*," and who "can swallow totalitarianism *because* they have no experience of anything except liberalism." The soundness of Orwell's political judgment is of a piece with the clarity of his sentences, and both were hammered out on the unyielding anvil of the life he chose to live. In a rare tribute to himself that gave away one key to his literary greatness, Orwell once wrote that he had "a power of facing unpleasant facts." They were, first and most important, facts on the ground where he stood.

The first essays in this collection were written before there was a George Orwell, and they aren't really even essays. "The Spike" was published under Orwell's real name, Eric A. Blair, and "Clink," an account of an attempt to get thrown in jail, was never published at all. These are pieces from his down-and-out period in the late twenties and early thirties, after his return to England from Burma, when, driven by some inner necessity born of guilt and rage, Orwell went "native in his own country," in V. S. Pritchett's phrase. Unlike the often awkward and overwritten fiction that Orwell was composing at the same time, these descriptions of the submerged life of shelters and prisons show early signs of the frank, colloquial exactness that became Orwell's stylistic trademark: "It was a disgusting sight, that bathroom. All the indecent secrets of our underwear were exposed; the grime, the rents and patches, the bits of string doing duty for buttons, the layers upon layers of fragmentary garments, some of them mere collections of holes held together by dirt." But these sketches have no purpose other than to record. The conclusions they reach are no larger than the confines of the experiences that produced them.

Something new happens in "A Hanging." It was also published under his real name, in August 1931, in a pacifist English monthly called *Adelphi*. The twenty-seven-year-old, entirely unknown Eric Blair, upon arriving at the magazine's offices, described himself to its editor, Richard Rees, as a "Tory anarchist" and admitted to using copies of *Adelphi*, which he had once

considered a "damned rag," for target practice in his garden outside Rangoon when he was a colonial policeman. Though Orwell
remained a democratic Socialist until his death, his sympathies and
manners were complex and provocative from the start.

"It was in Burma, a sodden morning of the rains": "A Hanging" begins abruptly, like "The Spike," without explanation or
context, in precise but unreflective description. Who is telling
this story? Why is he one of "a party of men walking together"
through a prison courtyard in Burma during the rainy season?
What does he think of the deed they're about to do? Is the account based in fact, or is it made up? Brief and open ended, "A
Hanging" also seems more a story than an essay—until its mid-
point, when the Burmese prisoner being led to the gallows steps
aside to avoid a puddle. Prompted by this apparently trivial detail,
the narrator says: "It is curious, but till that moment I had never
realised what it means to destroy a healthy, conscious man."

In a sense, the whole of Orwell's nonfiction is contained in
"that moment" and the paragraph that follows. This move recurs
in essays throughout this volume, and it always signals, in Orwell's
deceptively casual style ("It is curious"), that what follows will be
essential—his reason for telling the story. Something very similar appears at the climax of his other, more famous Burma essay,
"Shooting an Elephant": "I perceived in this moment that when
the white man turns tyrant it is his own freedom that he destroys."
A version of it precedes an anecdote from "Looking Back on the
Spanish War," about the unexpected aftermath of a false accusation: "I ask you to believe that it is moving to me, as an incident
characteristic of the moral atmosphere of a particular moment in
time." And another version follows the scene of bedwetting and
punishment that opens his memoir of his schooldays, "Such, Such
Were the Joys":

I had fallen into a chair, weakly snivelling. I remember that
this was the only time throughout my boyhood when a beating actually reduced me to tears, and curiously enough I was
not even now crying because of the pain. The second beating had not hurt very much either. Fright and shame seemed
to have anaesthetised me. I was crying partly because I felt
that this was expected of me, partly from genuine repentance, but partly also because of a deeper grief which is
peculiar to childhood and not easy to convey: a sense of desolate loneliness and helplessness, of being locked up not only
in a hostile world but in a world of good and evil where the
rules were such that it was actually not possible for me to
keep them.

In these moments, Orwell takes a step that's as short, as apparently easy, and yet as significant as that of the prisoner who
evades the puddle and establishes his humanity. He moves from
observation to thought, from a painful detail to some broader, re-
demptive understanding. It's the most important journey an essay
can make, and the hardest. It requires the essayist to be equally
good at rendering experience and interpreting it—to be a character and a narrator, a sensitive consciousness and a dispassionate
philosopher. "A Hanging" sets the precedent: Out of the smallest
incidents come the deepest recognitions, whether "that moment"
occurs on the path to the gallows or years later at the writer's desk.
So the ideas that form the core of Orwell's essays are not the product of abstract thinking; there is no disembodied mind working
through its material. They come directly out of recollected experience, and between the act and the idea there's always the con-
nective tissue of emotion.

———

Five years after "A Hanging," in 1936, Orwell was asked to contribute to a magazine of antifascist writing. He replied, with the defensive aggression that was habitual in his struggling early years, that he was thinking of writing "a sketch (it would be abt 2000–3000 words), describing the shooting of an elephant. It all came back to me very vividly the other day & I would like to write it, but it may be that it is quite out of your line. I mean it might be too low brow for your paper & I doubt whether there is anything anti-Fascist in the shooting of an elephant!" As it turned out, there was. "Shooting an Elephant" is probably Orwell's most perfect essay, and a crucial advance beyond "A Hanging." This time, the narrative and reflective elements are woven together, and the "I" is no longer a camera eye but a character, with a past, prejudices, feelings, judgments, self-judgments. This is no opaque fragment or sketch: Its structure is transparent and entirely built around the passage through experience to understanding and self-knowledge.

"One day something happened which in a roundabout way was enlightening," Orwell (now publishing under his pseudonym) writes after two pages of prelude. "It was a tiny incident in itself, but it gave me a better glimpse than I had had before of the real nature of imperialism—the real motives for which despotic governments act." If Orwell presented "Shooting an Elephant" in a writing workshop today, his teacher and classmates, followers of the rigid ideology known as "show, don't tell," would have him cut these sentences and the two pages that precede them as unnecessary and start the piece with the next sentence: "Early one morning the sub-inspector . . ." But Orwell, by showing and telling—often, showing *then* telling—gives this tale a personal and historical context that makes it more than just vivid. Telling deepens its emotional effect and widens its intellectual reach. And because Orwell's self-exposure, though not at all exhibitionistic, is merciless, it wins the reader over. As he later wrote in criticizing

Salvador Dalí's memoirs, "Autobiography is only to be trusted when it reveals something disgraceful."

Here's a troubling thought: There's no way of knowing whether the events in the essay ever happened. Orwell's biographers haven't been able to prove them either factual or false, although Emma Larkin, in her book *Finding George Orwell in Burma,* comes close to establishing the existence of something like this incident. Does it matter? Would the essay be any less powerful if Orwell never actually shot an elephant? If you're a literary sophisticate, the correct answer is obvious: of course not. All we have are Orwell's words; they are what they are regardless of his life story, and only a naive reader demands that they reflect factual truth. If anything, an invented incident would show that Orwell's imaginative writing is underrated.

But I think in this case the naive reaction is the right one. Writers always use their imaginations in reconstructing the past, but if central incidents are going to be invented out of nothing, an essayist's authority to say that this is how the world is (and that it's not the way you think) will diminish, perhaps fatally. An Orwell essay—like all his nonfiction—establishes a sort of contract with the reader. This is the writer Orwell presents himself to be: *I was there—I saw it—I know.* With another writer it would matter less to learn that an incident was made up in the name of another kind of truth than fact. If Virginia Woolf never watched a moth die on her windowpane, "The Death of the Moth" would still be a lyrical meditation on the nature of existence and death. But part of the power of an epigrammatic statement such as "When the white man turns tyrant it is his own freedom he destroys" comes from its having been hard-won out there in the world of German elephant rifles and Burmese rice paddies. "Accounts of actual happenings cast a particular kind of narrative spell," the critic Gordon Harvey says about this essay; "they give a particular pleasure that fiction doesn't give and that won't withstand the suspicion of fictiveness, depending as the pleasure does on our perception of an effort being made to preserve the integrity of past experience, from both the assaults of subsequent experience and the temptations of art." It's essential to one's sense of how Orwell thinks and writes that he *doesn't* rig the facts to fit a predigested idea or an elegant conceit. The end of that road is dishonest propaganda or art for art's sake—both of which he rejected. It would be perverse to assume that Orwell subscribed to the postmodern literary doctrine of the constructedness of reality and the unknowability of truth. A fear that facts could materialize or vanish on command lay at the heart of the totalitarian nightmare that preoccupied the last decade of his life.

Like Antaeus, Orwell drew his strength from having his feet planted on the ground. "I have a sort of belly-to-earth attitude," he confessed in a letter to Henry Miller a few months after writing "Shooting an Elephant," "and always feel uneasy when I get away from the ordinary world where grass is green, stones hard, etc." In "Why I Write," the closest thing to an Orwell literary manifesto, he declared, "When I sit down to write a book, I do not say to myself, 'I am going to produce a work of art.' I write it because there is some lie that I want to expose, some fact to which I want to draw attention." At the risk of unsophistication, it's better to take Orwell at his word and hold him to his own standard.

"Shooting an Elephant" established Orwell as a great essayist. In it he found a voice that was flexible and forceful: sensitive without being sentimental, sad but never surprised, matter-of-factly rendering devastating judgments, as hard on himself as on the world. It's a voice that commands trust.

Orwell tells the stories in these essays because they are good stories. He tells them, in the words of "Why I Write," with "aesthetic enthusiasm" and "[p]leasure in the impact of one sound on another, in the firmness of good prose or the rhythm of a good story." The sheer vitality of language in his descriptions of a Moroccan funeral or a Parisian charity hospital is part of what makes one return to the essays again and again. Orwell had an ability to create single images that somehow capture the moral atmosphere of a world and make it unforgettable: the cupping of patients' backs to raise blisters in "How the Poor Die," the store mannequins lying like corpses on Oxford Street in the "War-time Diary," the old woman bent double under her load of firewood in "Marrakech," the bone handle of the headmaster's riding crop breaking across Orwell's backside in "Such, Such Were the Joys," the "four sodden, debauched, loathely cigarette ends" placed in his hand at the end of "The Spike," the dead flies collecting on the tops of bookshop volumes, the dying elephant's blood flowing like "red velvet," the puddle in the prisoner's path. They are usually images of cruelty, squalor, or injustice (dirt and bad smells were among his fixations), but their power lies in their specificity, their objectivity. "I am not commenting," he says in "Marrakech," "merely pointing to a fact."

The truth is that Orwell is always commenting, whether indirectly through these revelatory details, or else directly and, indeed, unambiguously. Few writers today care to show their hand (or could if they tried) as Orwell does when he writes, for example, "People with brown skins are next door to invisible," "the long drilling in patriotism which the middle classes go through had done its work," or "A family with the wrong members in control—that, perhaps, is as near as one can come to describing England in a phrase." Propositions as blunt as these are dangerous for the writer because they invite resistance and contestation, ultimately risking the loss of that essential assent he needs from his reader. But they give Orwell's essays their tremendous intellectual liveliness, and over the course of his work they occur more and more thickly as he became surer of his views and bolder in his expression of them. He is emphatic, but he is rarely didactic; a characteristic tone of the Orwell essay is its lack of expressed outrage. Again, he is saying: "This is how things are—like it or not." Occasionally, the political purpose that animates an essay overwhelms its literary control, producing outbursts like this in the middle of an indignant passage in "Looking Back on the Spanish War": "The damned impertinence of these politicians, priests, literary men, and what not who lecture the working-class Socialist for his 'materialism'!" The exclamation mark is usually a bad sign in Orwellian punctuation. But if he didn't always live up to his own injunctions about good writing (as he was quick to admit in "Politics in the English Language"), his faults were often linked to his insistence on saying exactly what he meant as forcefully as he could, which is no fault at all.

The essays in this volume could not be farther from the kind of autobiographical writing that has been fashionable over the past ten or fifteen years, in which a writer puts the reader under the spell of pure novelistic storytelling, all emotional vibration without an insight anywhere. The narrator of this type of memoir drifts helplessly on the surface of events in an eternal present tense, which takes away the power and the responsibility of retrospection: It just happened—don't ask me what it means. Orwell's essays are the opposite—transparent and accountable. He is both character and narrator, and in the distance that comes with looking *back* at his own experience in the past tense he manages to raise it out of the narrow circle of private confession and into the sphere of universal revelation—even when the subject is bedwetting.

These essays don't invite elaborate feats of interpretation or philosophical subtlety or clever subversions of ostensible meaning. They have a puritanical bias toward clarity. This doesn't mean that they moralize under the assumption that the world is open to simple judgments. What they demand of the reader is a sort of grown-upness about life—that you accept its complexities, its refusal to provide happy endings, without losing or surrendering the ability to judge. Orwell asks that you understand how he could sympathize with the oppressed Burmese and also want to drive a bayonet through the stomach of a Buddhist monk; why it was necessary to fight fascism and yet impossible to shoot a fascist who was holding up his trousers as he ran along a trench; why revenge is sour, even in occupied Germany.

The subjects most writers turn to for autobiographical material were almost off-limits to Orwell. He was the product of a middle-class, early-twentieth-century English upbringing and tight-lipped about his feelings, but his reserve was more than merely cultural. Family, love, sex, marriage, friendship, parenthood, loss—Orwell never wrote about any of these, perhaps because they had no obvious connection to his abiding political themes. Even his late and long essay on the misery of his early schooling, "Such, Such Were the Joys," is a study of the English class system just before it began to break down. He never seems to have felt an impulse to record what it was like, for example, to adopt a son, or lose his wife to a botched hysterectomy. He wasn't interested in portraits of individuals, especially those close to him. His characters are walk-ons and types: the Arab-looking militia boy in "Looking Back on the Spanish War"; Flip and Sambo, the headmistress and headmaster of his grammar school; his fellow tramps. He lavishes more descriptive attention on an elephant, a toad, and England than on any single person. His abiding subject is human society, not isolated human beings.

This is true even when he was writing about his one constant character—himself. Reflecting on one's own life is an astringent endeavor that requires the opposite of self-indulgence. This most autobiographical of writers believed that "one can write nothing readable unless one constantly struggles to efface one's own personality." And yet Orwell is felt everywhere in these essays. The facts they record are registering on a particular storyteller: an independent-minded one, who is usually writing *against* something. The pressure of subjectivity—Orwell's biases, concerns, obsessions, turns of mind—is what gives the prose its vividness.

After Orwell entered his forties in the 1940s, autobiography dwindled from his writing. It didn't disappear: Two of his greatest essays, "How the Poor Die" and "Such, Such Were the Joys," were written in his last years. But by then his major experiences were behind him, and he suffered the fate of any serious writer, which was to spend most of his time alone in a room—a subject that Virginia Woolf could transform into literature but Orwell could not. Even as he began to produce his great critical essays and his output of narrative essays declined, he didn't stop writing this type altogether. It took on different forms. There were his lengthy wartime studies of his own country, such as "England Your England," which appeared in a small 1941 volume called *The Lion and the Unicorn: Socialism and the English Genius,* a call for an egalitarian revolution at home as part of the fight against fascism abroad. There were his shorter, lighter, but always pointed pieces on quotidian subjects ranging from coal fires to the return of spring. There were the weekly columns that he published under the headline "As I Please" in the left-wing paper *Tribune,* beginning in late 1943 and continuing for three and a half years, covering miscellaneous topics, two or three per column, that often drew on daily observations of wartime London (a sort of print prototype of blogging). And there was his "War-time Diary," a remarkable journal that he kept intermittently from the evacuation of Dunkirk in May 1940 until the victory in Egypt in November

1942, containing some of his best descriptive writing and filling a strange gap in Orwell's work—for he never wrote a novel or non-fiction book about the most historically important event of his life (his tubercular lungs kept him out of uniform; instead, he spent "two wasted years" as a producer in the Eastern Service of the BBC). The entries from 1940 are included here almost in their entirety, for the picture they give of history unfolding day by day, and of Orwell taking it all in without blinking.

These are not narrative essays in the conventional sense, as "Shooting an Elephant" is. Several essays in this volume, such as "In Front of Your Nose," are here only because they come under no obvious categorical heading but are too good to omit. Still, diary entries, newspaper columns, and occasional pieces show Orwell using his descriptive powers in new ways. On the whole, even as the world picture grows ever darker, he becomes a lonely widower, and his health declines, there is more pleasure taken in these pieces—in nature, in common rituals, solid objects, bits of trivia, and old cultural artifacts. These small attachments become, in *1984*, essential pillars of Winston Smith's rebellion against the regime of Big Brother. No longer a struggling young writer afflicted by resentments and a chronic sense of failure, Orwell grew more fully into himself and his essay writing relaxed. He could accept and set down his loves as well as his horrors.

The first-person protagonist, with his dramatic situations and emotional resonance, is largely missing from these late essays. But in his place there is a second Orwell—not the subject, but the writer—who has learned to cut straight to the heart of everything he sees and hears with a diamond precision. The world of action has shrunk, but the world of his mind keeps growing until nothing, neither the global battlefield nor a cup of tea, seems to escape it. Observation and thought have become perfectly inextricable, without a wasted word, and there's a kind of expository poetry in sentences such as this: "The unspeakable depression of lighting the fires every morning with papers of a year ago, and getting glimpses of optimistic headlines as they go up in smoke." Or this: "[t]he earth is still going round the sun, and neither the dictators nor the bureaucrats, deeply as they disapprove of the process, are able to prevent it." Or these: "The child thinks of growing old as an almost obscene calamity, which for some mysterious reason will never happen to itself. All who have passed the age of thirty are joyless grotesques, endlessly fussing about things of no importance and staying alive without, so far as the child can see, having anything to live for. Only child life is real life."

This last is from the conclusion of "Such, Such Were the Joys," Orwell's final narrative essay, written while he was dying of tuberculosis and struggling to finish *1984,* and published after his death. Near the end of his foreshortened life he returned to childhood, and he rendered it with all the intelligence and ruthlessness and compassion in his power. The prose has the wintry wisdom of late work. In this essay Orwell shows, again and for the last time, that a great work of art can emerge from the simple act of seeing oneself and the world clearly, honestly, without fear.

The Spike

The Adelphi, April 1931

It was late afternoon. Forty-nine of us, forty-eight men and one woman, lay on the green waiting for the spike to open. We were too tired to talk much. We just sprawled about exhaustedly, with home-made cigarettes sticking out of our scrubby faces. Overhead the chestnut branches were covered with blossom, and beyond that great woolly clouds floated almost motionless in a clear sky. Littered on the grass, we seemed dingy, urban riff-raff. We defiled the scene, like sardine-tins and paper bags on the seashore.

What talk there was ran on the Tramp Major of this spike. He was a devil, everyone agreed, a tartar, a tyrant, a bawling, blasphemous, uncharitable dog. You couldn't call your soul your own when he was about, and many a tramp had he kicked out in the middle of the night for giving a back answer. When you came to be searched he fair held you upside down and shook you. If you were caught with tobacco there was hell to pay, and if you went in with money (which is against the law) God help you.

I had eightpence on me. "For the love of Christ, mate," the old hands advised me, "don't you take it in. You'd get seven days for going into the spike with eightpence!"

So I buried my money in a hole under the hedge, marking the spot with a lump of flint. Then we set about smuggling our matches and tobacco, for it is forbidden to take these into nearly all spikes, and one is supposed to surrender them at the gate. We hid them in our socks, except for the twenty or so per cent who had no socks, and had to carry the tobacco in their boots, even under their very toes. We stuffed our ankles with contraband until anyone seeing us might have imagined an outbreak of elephantiasis. But it is an unwritten law that even the sternest tramp majors do not search below the knee, and in the end only one man was caught. This was Scotty, a little hairy tramp with a bastard accent sired by cockney out of Glasgow. His tin of cigarette ends fell out of his sock at the wrong moment, and was impounded.

At six the gates swung open and we shuffled in. An official at the gate entered our names and other particulars in the register and took our bundles away from us. The woman was sent off to the workhouse, and we others into the spike. It was a gloomy, chilly, lime-washed place, consisting only of a bathroom and dining room and about a hundred narrow stone cells. The terrible Tramp Major met us at the door and herded us into the bathroom to be stripped and searched. He was a gruff, soldierly man of forty, who gave the tramps no more ceremony than sheep at the dipping pond, shoving them this way and that and shouting oaths in their faces. But when he came to myself, he looked hard at me, and said:

"You are a gentleman?"

"I suppose so," I said.

He gave me another long look. "Well, that's bloody bad luck, guv'nor," he said, "that's bloody bad luck, that is." And thereafter he took it into his head to treat me with compassion, even with a kind of respect.

It was a disgusting sight, that bathroom. All the indecent secrets of our underwear were exposed; the grime, the rents and patches, the bits of string doing duty for buttons, the layers upon layers of fragmentary garments, some of them mere collections of holes held together by dirt. The room became a press of steaming nudity, the sweaty odours of the tramps competing with the sickly, sub-fæcal stench native to the spike. Some of the men refused the bath, and washed only their "toe rags," the horrid, greasy little clouts which tramps bind round their feet. Each of us had three minutes in which to bathe himself. Six greasy, slippery roller towels had to serve for the lot of us.

When we had bathed our own clothes were taken away from us, and we were dressed in the workhouse shirts, grey cotton things like nightshirts, reaching to the middle of the thigh. Then we were sent into the dining room, where supper was set out on the deal tables. It was the invariable spike meal, always the same, whether breakfast, dinner or supper—half a pound of bread, a bit of margarine, and a pint of so-called tea. It took us five minutes to gulp down the cheap, noxious food. Then the Tramp Major served us with three cotton blankets each, and drove us off to our cells for the night. The doors were locked on the outside a little before seven in the evening, and would stay locked for the next twelve hours.

The cells measured eight feet by five, and had no lighting apparatus except a tiny, barred window high up in the wall, and a spyhole in the door. There were no bugs, and we had bedsteads and straw palliasses, rare luxuries both. In many spikes one sleeps on a wooden shelf, and in some on the bare floor, with a rolled up coat for pillow. With a cell to myself, and a bed, I was hoping for a sound night's rest. But I did not get it, for there is always something wrong in the spike, and the peculiar shortcoming here, as I discovered immediately, was the cold. May had begun, and in honour of the season—a little sacrifice to the gods of spring, perhaps—the authorities had cut off the steam from the hot pipes. The cotton blankets were almost useless. One spent the night in turning from side to side, falling asleep for ten minutes and waking half frozen, and watching for dawn.

As always happens in the spike, I had at last managed to fall comfortably asleep when it was time to get up. The Tramp Major came marching down the passage with his heavy tread, unlocking the doors and yelling to us to show a leg. Promptly the passage was full of squalid shirt-clad figures rushing for the bathroom, for there was only one tub full of water between us all in the morning, and it was first come first served. When I arrived twenty tramps had already washed their faces. I gave one glance at the black scum on top of the water, and decided to go dirty for the day.

We hurried into our clothes, and then went to the dining room to bolt our breakfast. The bread was much worse than usual, because the military-minded idiot of a Tramp Major had cut it into slices overnight, so that it was as hard as ship's biscuit. But we were glad of our tea after the cold, restless night. I do not know what tramps would do without tea, or rather the stuff they miscall tea. It is their food, their medicine, their panacea for all evils. Without the half gallon or so of it that they suck down a day, I truly believe they could not face their existence.

After breakfast we had to undress again for the medical inspection, which is a precaution against smallpox. It was three-quarters of an hour before the doctor arrived, and one had time now to look about him and see what manner of men we were. It was an instructive sight. We stood shivering naked to the waist in two long ranks in the passage. The filtered light, bluish and cold, lighted us up with unmerciful clarity. No one can imagine, unless he has seen such a thing, what pot-bellied, degenerate curs we looked. Shock heads, hairy, crumpled faces, hollow chests, flat feet, sagging muscles—every kind of malformation and physical rottenness were there. All were flabby and discoloured, as all tramps are under their deceptive sunburn. Two or three figures seen there stay ineradicably in my mind. Old "Daddy," aged seventy-four, with his truss, and his red, watering eyes: a herring-gutted starveling, with sparse beard and sunken cheeks, looking like the corpse of Lazarus in some primitive picture: an imbecile, wandering hither and thither with vague giggles, coyly pleased because his trousers constantly slipped down and left him nude. But few of us were greatly better than these; there were not ten decently-built men among us, and half, I believe, should have been in hospital.

This being Sunday, we were to be kept in the spike over the week-end. As soon as the doctor had gone we were herded back to the dining room, and its door shut upon us. It was a lime-washed, stone-floored room unspeakably dreary with its furniture of deal boards and benches, and its prison smell. The windows were so high up that one could not look outside, and the sole ornament was a set of Rules threatening dire penalties to any casual who misconducted himself. We packed the room so tight that one could not move an elbow without jostling somebody. Already, at eight o'clock in the morning, we were bored with our captivity. There was nothing to talk about except the petty gossip of the road, the good and bad spikes, the charitable and uncharitable counties, the iniquities of the police and the Salvation Army. Tramps hardly ever get away from these subjects; they talk, as it were, nothing but shop. They have nothing worthy to be called conversation, because emptiness of belly leaves no speculation in their souls. The world is too much with them. Their next meal is never quite secure, and so they cannot think of anything except the next meal.

Two hours dragged by. Old Daddy, witless with age, sat silent, his back bent like a bow and his inflamed eyes dripping slowly on to the floor. George, a dirty old tramp notorious for the queer habit of sleeping in his hat, grumbled about a parcel of tommy that he had lost on the road. Bill the moocher, the best built man of us all, a Herculean sturdy beggar who smelt of beer even after twelve hours in the spike, told tales of mooching, of pints stood him in the boozers, and of a parson who had peached to the police and got him seven days. William and Fred, two young ex-fishermen from Norfolk, sang a sad song about Unhappy Bella, who was betrayed and died in the snow. The imbecile drivelled about an imaginary toff who had once given him two hundred and fifty-seven golden sovereigns. So the time passed, with dull talk and dull obscenities. Everyone was smoking, except Scotty, whose tobacco had been seized, and he was so miserable in his smokeless state that I stood him the makings of a cigarette. We smoked furtively, hiding our cigarettes like schoolboys when we heard the Tramp Major's step, for smoking, though connived at, was officially forbidden.

Most of the tramps spent ten consecutive hours in this dreary room. It is hard to imagine how they put up with it. I have come to think that boredom is the worst of all a tramp's evils, worse than hunger and discomfort, worse even than the constant feeling of being socially disgraced. It is a silly piece of cruelty to confine an ignorant man all day with nothing to do; it is like chaining a dog in a barrel. Only an educated man, who has consolations within himself, can endure confinement. Tramps, unlettered types as nearly all of them are, face their poverty with blank, resourceless minds. Fixed for ten hours on a comfortless bench, they know no way of occupying themselves, and if they think at all it is to whimper about hard luck and pine for work. They have not the stuff in them to endure the horrors of idleness. And so, since so much of their lives is spent in doing nothing, they suffer agonies from boredom.

I was much luckier than the others, because at ten o'clock the Tramp Major picked me out for the most coveted of all jobs in the spike, the job of helping in the workhouse kitchen. There was

not really any work to be done there, and I was able to make off
and hide in a shed used for storing potatoes, together with some
workhouse paupers who were skulking to avoid the Sunday morning service. There was a stove burning there, and comfortable
packing cases to sit on, and back numbers of the *Family Herald,*
and even a copy of *Raffles* from the workhouse library. It was paradise after the spike.

Also, I had my dinner from the workhouse table, and it was
one of the biggest meals I have ever eaten. A tramp does not see
such a meal twice in the year, in the spike or out of it. The paupers
told me that they always gorged to the bursting point on Sundays,
and went hungry six days of the week. When the meal was over the
cook set me to do the washing up, and told me to throw away the
food that remained. The wastage was astonishing; great dishes of
beef, and bucketfuls of bread and vegetables, were pitched away
like rubbish, and then defiled with tea leaves. I filled five dustbins
to overflowing with good food. And while I did so my fellow
tramps were sitting two hundred yards away in the spike, their bellies half filled with the spike dinner of the everlasting bread and
tea, and perhaps two cold boiled potatoes each in honour of Sunday. It appeared that the food was thrown away from deliberate
policy, rather than that it should be given to the tramps.

At three I left the workhouse kitchen and went back to the
spike. The boredom in that crowded, comfortless room was now
unbearable. Even smoking had ceased, for a tramp's only tobacco
is picked-up cigarette ends, and, like a browsing beast, he starves
if he is long away from the pavement-pasture. To occupy the time
I talked with a rather superior tramp, a young carpenter who wore
a collar and tie, and was on the road, he said, for lack of a set of
tools. He kept a little aloof from the other tramps, and held himself more like a free man than a casual. He had literary tastes, too,

and carried one of Scott's novels on all his wanderings. He told me he never entered a spike unless driven there by hunger, sleeping under hedges and behind ricks in preference. Along the south coast he had begged by day and slept in bathing machines for weeks at a time.

We talked of life on the road. He criticised the system which makes a tramp spend fourteen hours a day in the spike, and the other ten in walking and dodging the police. He spoke of his own case — six months at the public charge for want of three pounds' worth of tools. It was idiotic, he said.

Then I told him about the wastage of food in the workhouse kitchen, and what I thought of it. And at that he changed his tune immediately. I saw that I had awakened the pew-renter who sleeps in every English workman. Though he had been famished along with the rest, he at once saw reasons why the food should have been thrown away rather than given to the tramps. He admonished me quite severely.

"They have to do it," he said; "if they made these places too pleasant you'd have all the scum of the country flocking into them. It's only the bad food as keeps all that scum away. These tramps are too lazy to work, that's all that's wrong with them. You don't want to go encouraging of them. They're scum."

I produced arguments to prove him wrong, but he would not listen. He kept repeating:

"You don't want to have any pity on these tramps — scum, they are. You don't want to judge them by the same standards as men like you and me. They're scum, just scum."

It was interesting to see how subtly he disassociated himself from his fellow tramps. He had been on the road six months, but in the sight of God, he seemed to imply, he was not a tramp. His body might be in the spike, but his spirit soared far away, in the pure æther of the middle classes.

The clock's hands crept round with excruciating slowness. We were too bored even to talk now, the only sound was of oaths and reverberating yawns. One would force his eyes away from the clock for what seemed an age, and then look back again to see that the hands had advanced three minutes. Ennui clogged our souls like cold mutton fat. Our bones ached because of it. The clock's hands stood at four, and supper was not till six, and there was nothing left remarkable beneath the visiting moon.[1]

At last six o'clock did come, and the Tramp Major and his assistant arrived with supper. The yawning tramps brisked up like lions at feeding time. But the meal was a dismal disappointment. The bread, bad enough in the morning, was now positively uneatable; it was so hard that even the strongest jaws could make little impression on it. The older men went almost supperless, and not a man could finish his portion, hungry though most of us were. When we had finished, the blankets were served out immediately, and we were hustled off once more to the bare, chilly cells.

Thirteen hours went by. At seven we were awakened, and rushed forth to squabble over the water in the bathroom, and bolt our ration of bread and tea. Our time in the spike was up, but we could not go until the doctor had examined us again, for the authorities have a terror of smallpox and its distribution by tramps. The doctor kept us waiting two hours this time, and it was ten o'clock before we finally escaped.

At last it was time to go, and we were let out into the yard. How bright everything looked, and how sweet the winds did blow, after the gloomy, reeking spike! The Tramp Major handed each man his bundle of confiscated possessions, and a hunk of bread and cheese for midday dinner, and then we took the road, hastening to get out of sight of the spike and its discipline. This was our interim of freedom. After a day and two nights of wasted time we had eight hours or so to take our recreation, to scour the roads for cigarette ends, to beg, and to look for work. Also, we had to make our ten, fifteen, or it might be twenty miles to the next spike, where the game would begin anew.

I disinterred my eightpence and took the road with Nobby, a respectable, downhearted tramp who carried a spare pair of boots and visited all the Labour Exchanges. Our late companions were scattering north, south, east and west, like bugs into a mattress. Only the imbecile loitered at the spike gates, until the Tramp Major had to chase him away.

Nobby and I set out for Croydon. It was a quiet road, there were no cars passing, the blossom covered the chestnut trees like great wax candles. Everything was so quiet and smelt so clean, it was hard to realise that only a few minutes ago we had been packed with that band of prisoners in a stench of drains and soft soap. The others had all disappeared; we two seemed to be the only tramps on the road.

Then I heard a hurried step behind me, and felt a tap on my arm. It was little Scotty, who had run panting after us. He pulled a rusty tin box from his pocket. He wore a friendly smile, like a man who is repaying an obligation.

"Here y'are, mate," he said cordially, "I owe you some fag ends. You stood me a smoke yesterday. The Tramp Major give me back my box of fag ends when we come out this morning. One good turn deserves another—here y'are."

And he put four sodden, debauched, loathely cigarette ends into my hand.

Clink[1]

[August 1932]

This trip was a failure, as the object of it was to get into prison, and I did not, in fact, get more than forty eight hours in custody; however, I am recording it, as the procedure in the police court etc. was fairly interesting. I am writing this eight months after it happened, so am not certain of any dates, but it all happened a week or ten days before Xmas 1931.

I started out on Saturday afternoon with four or five shillings, and went out to the Mile End Road, because my plan was to get drunk and incapable, and I thought they would be less lenient towards drunkards in the East End. I bought some tobacco and a "Yank Mag" against my forthcoming imprisonment, and then, as soon as the pubs opened, went and had four or five pints, topping up with a quarter bottle of whisky, which left me with twopence in hand. By the time the whisky was low in the bottle I was tolerably drunk—more drunk than I had intended, for it happened that I had eaten nothing all day, and the alcohol acted quickly on my empty stomach. It was all I could do to stand upright, though my brain was quite clear—with me, when I am drunk, my brain remains clear long after my legs and speech have gone. I began staggering along the pavement in a westward direction, and for a long time did not meet any policemen, though the streets were crowded and all the people pointed and laughed at me. Finally I saw two policemen coming. I pulled the whisky bottle out of my pocket and, in their sight, drank what was left, which nearly knocked me out, so that I clutched a lamp-post and fell down. The two policemen ran towards me, turned me over and took the bottle out of my hand.

They: "'Ere, what you bin drinking?" (For a moment they may have thought it was a case of suicide.)

I: "Thass my boll whisky. You lea' me alone."

They: "Coo, 'e's fair bin bathing in it!—What you bin doing of, eh?"

I: "Bin in boozer 'avin' bit o' fun. Christmas, ain't it?"

They: "No, not by a week it ain't. You got mixed up in the dates, you 'ave. You better come along with us. We'll look after yer."

I: "Why sh'd I come along you?"

They: "Jest so's we'll look after you and make you comfortable. You'll get run over, rolling about like that."

I: "Look. Boozer over there. Less go in 'ave drink."

They: "You've 'ad enough for one night, ole chap. You best come with us."

I: "Where you takin' me?"

They: "Jest somewhere as you'll get a nice quiet kip with a clean sheet and two blankets and all."

I: "Shall I get drink there?"

They: "Course you will. Got a boozer on the premises, we 'ave."

All this while they were leading me gently along the pavement. They had my arms in the grip (I forget what it is called) by which you can break a man's arm with one twist, but they were as gentle with me as though I had been a child. I was internally quite sober, and it amused me very much to see the cunning way in which they persuaded me along, never once disclosing the fact that we were making for the police station. This is, I suppose, the usual procedure with drunks.

When we got to the station (it was Bethnal Green, but I did not learn this till Monday) they dumped me in a chair & began emptying my pockets while the sergeant questioned me. I pretended, however, to be too drunk to give sensible answers, & he told them in disgust to take me off to the cells, which they did. The cell was about the same size as a Casual Ward cell (about 10 ft. by 5 ft. by 10 ft high), but much cleaner & better appointed. It was made of white porcelain bricks, and was furnished with a W.C., a hot water pipe, a plank bed, a horsehair pillow and two blankets. There was a tiny barred window high up near the roof, and an electric bulb behind a guard of thick glass was kept burning all night. The door was steel, with the usual spy-hole and aperture for serving food through. The constables in searching me had taken away my money, matches, razor, and also my scarf—this, I learned afterwards, because prisoners have been known to hang themselves on their scarves.

There is very little to say about the next day and night, which were unutterably boring. I was horribly sick, sicker than I have ever been from a bout of drunkenness, no doubt from having an empty stomach. During Sunday I was given two meals of bread and marg. and tea (spike quality), and one of meat and potatoes—this, I believe, owing to the kindness of the sergeant's wife, for I think only bread and marg. is provided for prisoners in the lockup. I was not allowed to shave, and there was only a little cold water to wash in. When the charge sheet was filled up I told the story I always tell, viz. that my name was Edward Burton, and my parents kept a cake-shop in Blythburgh, where I had been employed as a clerk in a draper's shop; that I had had the sack for drunkenness, and my parents, finally getting sick of my drunken habits, had turned me adrift. I added that I had been working as an outside porter at Billingsgate, and having unexpectedly "knocked up" six shillings on Saturday, had gone on the razzle.

The police were quite kind, and read me lectures on drunkenness, with the usual stuff about seeing that I still had some good in me etc. etc. They offered to let me out on bail on my own recognizance, but I had no money and nowhere to go, so I elected to stay in custody. It was very dull, but I had my "Yank Mag," and could get a smoke if I asked the constable on duty in the passage for a light—prisoners are not allowed matches, of course.

The next morning very early they turned me out of my cell to wash, gave me back my scarf, and took me out into the yard and put me in the Black Maria. Inside, the Black Maria was just like a French public lavatory, with a row of tiny locked compartments on either side, each just large enough to sit down in. People had scrawled their names, offences and the lengths of their sentences all over the walls of my compartment; also, several times, variants on this couplet—

> "Detective Smith knows how to gee;
> Tell him he's a cunt from me."

("Gee" in this context means to act as an agent provocateur.) We drove round to various stations picking up about ten prisoners in all, until the Black Maria was quite full. They were quite a jolly crowd inside. The compartment doors were open at the top, for ventilation, so that you could reach across, and somebody had managed to smuggle matches in, and we all had a smoke. Presently we began singing, and, as it was near Christmas sang several carols. We drove up to Old Street Police Court singing—

> "Adeste, fideles, laeti triumphantes,
> Adeste, adeste ad Bethlehem" etc.

which seemed to me rather inappropriate.

At the police court they took me off and put me in a cell identical with the one at Bethnal Green, even to having the same number of bricks in it—I counted in each case. There were three men in the cell besides myself. One was a smartly dressed, florid, well-set-up man of about thirty five, whom I would have taken for a commercial traveller or perhaps a bookie, and another a middle-aged Jew, also quite decently dressed. The other man was evidently a habitual burglar. He was a short rough-looking man with grey hair and a worn face, and at this moment in such a state of agitation over his approaching trial that he could not keep still an instant. He kept pacing up and down the cell like a wild beast, brushing against our knees as we sat on the plank bed, and exclaiming that he was innocent—he was charged, apparently, with loitering with intent to commit burglary. He said that he had nine previous convictions against him, and that in these cases, which are mainly of suspicion, old offenders are nearly always convicted. From time to time he would shake his fist towards the door and exclaim "Fucking toe-rag! Fucking toe-rag!," meaning the "split" who had arrested him.

Presently two more prisoners were put into the cell, an ugly Belgian youth charged with obstructing traffic with a barrow, and an extraordinary hairy creature who was either deaf and dumb or spoke no English. Except this last all the prisoners talked about their cases with the utmost freedom. The florid, smart man, it appeared, was a public house "guv'nor" (it is a sign of how utterly the London publicans are in the claw of the brewers that they are always referred to as "governors," not "landlords"; being, in fact, no better than employees), & had embezzled the Christmas Club money. As usual, he was head over ears in debt to the brewers, and no doubt had taken some of the money in hopes of backing a winner. Two of the subscribers had discovered this a few days before the money was due to be paid out, and laid an information. The "guv'nor" immediately paid back all save £12, which was also refunded before his case came up for trial. Nevertheless, he was certain to be sentenced, as the magistrates are hard on these cases — he did, in fact, get four months later in the day. He was ruined for life, of course. The brewers would file bankruptcy proceedings and sell up all his stock and furniture, and he would never be given a pub licence again. He was trying to brazen it out in front of the rest of us, and smoking cigarettes incessantly from a stock of Gold Flake packets he had laid in — the last time in his life, I dare say, that he would have quite enough cigarettes. There was a staring, abstracted look in his eyes all the time while he talked. I think the fact that his life was at an end, as far as any decent position in society went, was gradually sinking into him.

The Jew had been a buyer at Smithfields for a kosher butcher. After working seven years for the same employer he suddenly misappropriated £28, went up to Edinburgh — I don't know why Edinburgh — and had a "good time" with tarts, and came back and surrendered himself when the money was gone. £16 of the money had been repaid, and the rest was to be repaid by monthly instalments. He had a wife and a number of children. He told us, what interested me, that his employer would probably get into trouble at the synagogue for prosecuting him. It appears that the Jews have arbitration courts of their own, & a Jew is not supposed to prosecute another Jew, at least in a breach of trust case like this, without first submitting it to the arbitration court.

One remark made by these men struck me — I heard it from almost every prisoner who was up for a serious offence. It was, "It's not the prison I mind, it's losing my job." This is, I believe, symptomatic of the dwindling power of the law compared with that of the capitalist.

They kept us waiting several hours. It was very uncomfortable in the cell, for there was not room for all of us to sit down on the plank bed, and it was beastly cold in spite of the number of us.

Several of the men used the W.C., which was disgusting in so small a cell, especially as the plug did not work. The publican distributed his cigarettes generously, the constable in the passage supplying lights. From time to time an extraordinary clanking noise came from the cell next door, where a youth who had stabbed his "tart" in the stomach — she was likely to recover, we heard — was locked up alone. Goodness knows what was happening, but it sounded as though he were chained to the wall. At about ten they gave us each a mug of tea — this, it appeared, not provided by the authorities but by the police court missionaries — and shortly afterwards shepherded us along to a sort of large waiting room where the prisoners awaited trial.

There were perhaps fifty prisoners here, men of every type, but on the whole much more smartly dressed than one would expect. They were strolling up and down with their hats on, shivering with the cold. I saw here a thing which interested me greatly. When I was being taken to my cell I had seen two dirty-looking ruffians, much dirtier than myself and presumably drunks or obstruction cases, being put into another cell in the row. Here, in the waiting room, these two were at work with note-books in their hands, interrogating prisoners. It appeared that they were "splits," and were put into the cells disguised as prisoners, to pick up any information that was going — for there is complete freemasonry between prisoners, and they talk without reserve in front of one another. It was a dingy trick, I thought.

All the while the prisoners were being taken by ones & twos along a corridor to the court. Presently a sergeant shouted "Come on the drunks!" and four or five of us filed along the corridor and stood waiting at the entrance of the court. A young constable on duty there advised me —

"Take your cap off when you go in, plead guilty and don't give back answers. Got any previous convictions?"

"No."

"Six bob you'll get. Going to pay it?"

"I can't, I've only twopence."

"Ah well, it don't matter. Lucky for you Mr. Brown isn't on the bench this morning. Teetotaller he is. He don't half give it to the drunks. Coo!"

The drunk cases were dealt with so rapidly that I had not even time to notice what the court was like. I only had a vague impression of a raised platform with a coat of arms over it, clerks sitting at tables below, and a railing. We filed past the railing like people passing through a turnstile, & the proceedings in each case sounded like this—

"Edward-Burton-drunk-and-incapable-Drunk?-Yes-Six-shillings-move-on-NEXT!"

All this in the space of about five seconds. At the other side of the court we reached a room where a sergeant was sitting at a desk with a ledger.

"Six shillings?" he said.

"Yes."

"Going to pay it?"

"I can't."

"All right, back you go to your cell."

And they took me back and locked me in the cell from which I had come, about ten minutes after I had left it.

The publican had also been brought back, his case having been postponed, and the Belgian youth, who, like me, could not pay his fine. The Jew was gone, whether released or sentenced we did not know. Throughout the day prisoners were coming and going, some waiting trial, some until the Black Maria was available to take them off to prison. It was cold, and the nasty faecal stench in the cell became unbearable. They gave us our dinner at about two o'clock—it consisted of a mug of tea and two slices of bread and marg. for each man. Apparently this was the regulation meal. One could, if one had friends outside get food sent in, but it struck me as damnably unfair that a penniless man must face his trial with only bread and marg. in his belly; also unshaven—I, at this time, had had no chance of shaving for over forty-eight hours—which is likely to prejudice the magistrates against him.

Among the prisoners who were put temporarily in the cell were two friends or partners named apparently Snouter and Charlie, who had been arrested for some street offence—obstruction with a barrow, I dare say. Snouter was a thin, red-faced, malignant-looking man, and Charlie a short, powerful, jolly man. Their conversation was rather interesting.

Charlie: "Cripes, it ain't 'alf fucking cold in 'ere. Lucky for us ole Brown ain't on to-day. Give you a month as soon as look at yer."

Snouter (bored, and singing):

"Tap, tap, tapetty tap,
I'm a perfect devil at that;
Tapping 'em 'ere, tapping 'em there,
I bin tapping 'em everywhere—"

Charlie: "Oh, fuck off with yer tapping! Scrumping's what yer want this time of year. All them rows of turkeys in the winders, like rows of fucking soldiers with no clo'es on—don't it make yer fucking mouth water to look at 'em. Bet yer a tanner I 'ave one of 'em afore tonight."

Snouter: "What's 'a good? Can't cook the bugger over the kip-'ouse fire, can you?"

Charlie: "Oo wants to cook it? I know where I can flog (sell) it for a bob or two, though."

Snouter: "'Sno good. Chantin's the game this time of year. Carols. Fair twist their 'earts round, I can, when I get on the mournful. Old tarts weep their fucking eyes out when they 'ear me. I won't 'alf give them a doing this Christmas. I'll kip indoors if I 'ave to cut it out of their bowels."

Charlie: "Ah, *I* can sling you a bit of a carol. 'Ymns, too. (He begins singing in a good bass voice)—

> "Jesu, lover of my soul,
> Let me to thy bosom fly—"

The constable on duty (looking through the grille): "Nah then, in 'ere, nah then! What yer think this is? Baptist prayer meeting?"

Charlie (in a low voice as the constable disappears): "Fuck off, pisspot. (He hums)—

> "While the gathering waters roll,
> While the tempest still is 'igh!

You won't find many in the 'ymnal as I can't sling you. Sung bass in the choir my last two years in Dartmoor, I did."

Snouter: "Ah? Wassit like in Dartmoor now? D'you get jam now?"

Charlie: "Not jam. Gets cheese, though, twice a week."

Snouter: "Ah? 'Ow long was you doing?"

Charlie: "Four year."

Snouter: "Four years without cunt—Cripes! Fellers inside'd go 'alf mad if they saw a pair of legs (a woman), eh?"

Charlie: "Ah well, in Dartmoor we used to fuck old women down on the allotments. Take 'em under the 'edge in the mist. Spud-grabbers they was—ole trots seventy year old. Forty of us was caught and went through 'ell for it. Bread and water, chains—everythink. I took my Bible oath as I wouldn't get no more stretches after that."

Snouter: "Yes, you! 'Ow come you got in the stir lars' time then?"

Charlie: "You wouldn't 'ardly believe it, boy. I was narked — narked by my own sister! Yes, my own fucking sister. My sister's a cow if ever there was one. She got married to a religious maniac, and 'e's so fucking religious that she's got fifteen kids now. Well, it was 'im put 'er up to narking me. But I got it back on 'em *I* can tell you. What do you think I done first thing, when I come out of the stir? I bought a 'ammer, and I went round to my sister's 'ouse and smashed 'er piano to fucking matchwood. I did. 'There,' I says, 'that's what you get for narking me! You mare,' I says" etc. etc. etc.

This kind of conversation went on more or less all day between these two, who were only in for some petty offence & quite pleased with themselves. Those who were going to prison were silent and restless, and the look on some of the men's faces — respectable men under arrest for the first time — was dreadful. They took the publican out at about three in the afternoon, to be sent off to prison. He had cheered up a little on learning from the constable on duty that he was going to the same prison as Lord Kylsant.[2] He thought that by sucking up to Lord K. in jail he might get a job from him when he came out.

I had no idea how long I was going to be incarcerated, & supposed that it would be several days at least. However, between four and five o'clock they took me out of the cell, gave back the things which had been confiscated, and shot me into the street forthwith. Evidently the day in custody served instead of the fine. I had only twopence and had had nothing to eat all day except bread and marg., and was damnably hungry; however, as always happens when it is a choice between tobacco and food, I bought tobacco with my twopence. Then I went down to the Church Army shelter in the Waterloo Road, where you get a kip, two meals of bread and corned beef and tea and a prayer meeting, for four hours work at sawing wood.

The next morning I went home,[3] got some money, and went out to Edmonton. I turned up at the Casual Ward about nine at night, not downright drunk but more or less under the influence, thinking this would lead to prison — for it is an offence under the Vagrancy Act for a tramp to come drunk to the Casual Ward. The porter, however, treated me with great consideration, evidently feeling that a tramp with money enough to buy drink ought to be respected. During the next few days I made several more attempts to get into trouble by begging under the noses of the police, but I seemed to bear a charmed life — no one took any notice of me. So, as I did not want to do anything serious which might lead to investigations about my identity etc., I gave it up. The trip, therefore, was more or less of a failure, but I have recorded it as a fairly interesting experience.

A Hanging

The Adelphi, August 1931; reprinted in *The New Savoy,* 1946

It was in Burma, a sodden morning of the rains. A sickly light, like yellow tinfoil, was slanting over the high walls into the jail yard. We were waiting outside the condemned cells, a row of sheds fronted with double bars, like small animal cages. Each cell measured about ten feet by ten and was quite bare within except for a plank bed and a pot for drinking water. In some of them brown silent men were squatting at the inner bars, with their blankets draped round them. These were the condemned men, due to be hanged within the next week or two.

One prisoner had been brought out of his cell. He was a Hindu, a puny wisp of a man, with a shaven head and vague liquid eyes. He had a thick, sprouting moustache, absurdly too big for his body, rather like the moustache of a comic man on the films. Six tall Indian warders were guarding him and getting him ready for the gallows. Two of them stood by with rifles and fixed bayonets, while the others handcuffed him, passed a chain through his handcuffs and fixed it to their belts, and lashed his arms tight to his sides. They crowded very close about him, with their hands always on him in a careful, caressing grip, as though all the while feeling him to make sure he was there. It was like men handling a fish which is still alive and may jump back into the water. But he stood quite unresisting, yielding his arms limply to the ropes, as though he hardly noticed what was happening.

Eight o'clock struck and a bugle call, desolately thin in the wet air, floated from the distant barracks. The superintendent of the jail, who was standing apart from the rest of us, moodily prodding the gravel with his stick, raised his head at the sound. He was an army doctor, with a grey toothbrush moustache and a gruff voice. "For God's sake hurry up, Francis," he said irritably. "The man ought to have been dead by this time. Aren't you ready yet?"

Francis, the head jailer, a fat Dravidian in a white drill suit and gold spectacles, waved his black hand. "Yes sir, yes sir," he bubbled. "All iss satisfactorily prepared. The hangman iss waiting. We shall proceed."

"Well, quick march, then. The prisoners can't get their breakfast till this job's over."

We set out for the gallows. Two warders marched on either side of the prisoner, with their rifles at the slope; two others marched close against him, gripping him by arm and shoulder, as though at once pushing and supporting him. The rest of us, magistrates and the like, followed behind. Suddenly, when we had gone ten yards, the procession stopped short without any order or warning. A dreadful thing had happened—a dog, come goodness knows whence, had appeared in the yard. It came bounding among us with a loud volley of barks, and leapt round us wagging its whole body, wild with glee at finding so many human beings together. It was a large woolly dog, half Airedale, half pariah. For a moment it pranced round us, and then, before anyone could stop it, it had made a dash for the prisoner, and jumping up tried to lick his face. Everyone stood aghast, too taken aback even to grab at the dog.

"Who let that bloody brute in here?" said the superintendent angrily. "Catch it, someone!"

A warder, detached from the escort, charged clumsily after the dog, but it danced and gambolled just out of his reach, taking everything as part of the game. A young Eurasian jailer picked up a handful of gravel and tried to stone the dog away, but it dodged the stones and came after us again. Its yaps echoed from the jail walls. The prisoner, in the grasp of the two warders, looked on incuriously, as though this was another formality of the hanging. It was several minutes before someone managed to catch the dog. Then we put my handkerchief through its collar and moved off once more, with the dog still straining and whimpering.

It was about forty yards to the gallows. I watched the bare brown back of the prisoner marching in front of me. He walked clumsily with his bound arms, but quite steadily, with that bobbing gait of the Indian who never straightens his knees. At each step his muscles slid neatly into place, the lock of hair on his scalp danced up and down, his feet printed themselves on the wet gravel. And once, in spite of the men who gripped him by each shoulder, he stepped slightly aside to avoid a puddle on the path.

It is curious, but till that moment I had never realised what it means to destroy a healthy, conscious man. When I saw the prisoner step aside to avoid the puddle, I saw the mystery, the unspeakable wrongness, of cutting a life short when it is in full tide. This man was not dying, he was alive just as we were alive. All the organs of his body were working—bowels digesting food, skin renewing itself, nails growing, tissues forming—all toiling away in solemn foolery. His nails would still be growing when he stood on the drop, when he was falling through the air with a tenth-of-a-second to live. His eyes saw the yellow gravel and the grey walls, and his brain still remembered, foresaw, reasoned—reasoned even about puddles. He and we were a party of men walking together, seeing, hearing, feeling, understanding the same world; and in two minutes, with a sudden snap, one of us would be gone—one mind less, one world less.

The gallows stood in a small yard, separate from the main grounds of the prison, and overgrown with tall prickly weeds. It was a brick erection like three sides of a shed, with planking on top, and above that two beams and a crossbar with the rope dangling. The hangman, a grey-haired convict in the white uniform of the prison, was waiting beside his machine. He greeted us with a servile crouch as we entered. At a word from Francis the two warders, gripping the prisoner more closely than ever, half led half pushed him to the gallows and helped him clumsily up the ladder. Then the hangman climbed up and fixed the rope round the prisoner's neck.

We stood waiting, five yards away. The warders had formed in a rough circle round the gallows. And then, when the noose was fixed, the prisoner began crying out on his god. It was a high, re-iterated cry of "Ram! Ram! Ram! Ram!" not urgent and fearful like a prayer or a cry for help, but steady, rhythmical, almost like the tolling of a bell. The dog answered the sound with a whine. The hangman, still standing on the gallows, produced a small cotton bag like a flour bag and drew it down over the prisoner's face. But the sound, muffled by the cloth, still persisted, over and over again: "Ram! Ram! Ram! Ram! Ram!"

The hangman climbed down and stood ready, holding the lever. Minutes seemed to pass. The steady, muffled crying from the prisoner went on and on, "Ram! Ram! Ram!" never faltering for an instant. The superintendent, his head on his chest, was slowly poking the ground with his stick; perhaps he was counting the cries, allowing the prisoner a fixed number—fifty, perhaps, or a hundred. Everyone had changed colour. The Indians had gone grey like bad coffee, and one or two of the bayonets were waver-ing. We looked at the lashed, hooded man on the drop, and lis-tened to his cries—each cry another second of life; the same thought was in all our minds: oh, kill him quickly, get it over, stop that abominable noise!

Suddenly the superintendent made up his mind. Throwing up his head he made a swift motion with his stick, "Chalo!" he shouted almost fiercely.

There was a clanking noise, and then dead silence. The prisoner had vanished, and the rope was twisting on itself. I let go of the dog, and it galloped immediately to the back of the gallows; but when it got there it stopped short, barked, and then retreated into a corner of the yard, where it stood among the weeds, looking timorously out at us. We went round the gallows to inspect the prisoner's body. He was dangling with his toes pointed straight downwards, very slowly revolving, as dead as a stone.

The superintendent reached out with his stick and poked the bare brown body; it oscillated slightly. "*He's* all right," said the superintendent. He backed out from under the gallows, and blew out a deep breath. The moody look had gone out of his face quite suddenly. He glanced at his wrist-watch. "Eight minutes past eight. Well, that's all for this morning, thank God."

The warders unfixed bayonets and marched away. The dog, sobered and conscious of having misbehaved itself, slipped after them. We walked out of the gallows yard, past the condemned cells with their waiting prisoners, into the big central yard of the prison. The convicts, under the command of warders armed with lathis, were already receiving their breakfast. They squatted in long rows, each man holding a tin pannikin, while two warders with buckets marched round ladling out rice; it seemed quite a homely, jolly scene, after the hanging. An enormous relief had come upon us now that the job was done. One felt an impulse to sing, to break into a run, to snigger. All at once everyone began chattering gaily.

The Eurasian boy walking beside me nodded towards the way we had come, with a knowing smile: "Do you know, sir, our friend (he meant the dead man), when he heard his appeal had been dismissed, he pissed on the floor of his cell. From fright.—Kindly take one of my cigarettes, sir. Do you not admire my new silver case, sir? From the boxwalah, two rupees eight annas. Classy European style."

Several people laughed—at what, nobody seemed certain.

Francis was walking by the superintendent, talking garrulously: "Well, sir, all hass passed off with the utmost satisfactoriness. It wass all finished—flick! like that. It iss not always so—oah, no! I have known cases where the doctor wass obliged to go beneath the gallows and pull the prissoner's legs to ensure decease. Most disagreeable!"

"Wriggling about, eh? That's bad," said the superintendent.

"Ach, sir, it iss worse when they become refractory! One man, I recall, clung to the bars of hiss cage when we went to take him out. You will scarcely credit, sir, that it took six warders to dislodge him, three pulling at each leg. We reasoned with him. 'My dear fellow,' we said, 'think of all the pain and trouble you are causing to us!' But no, he would not listen! Ach, he wass very troublesome!"

I found that I was laughing quite loudly. Everyone was laughing. Even the superintendent grinned in a tolerant way. "You'd better all come out and have a drink," he said quite genially. "I've got a bottle of whisky in the car. We could do with it."

We went through the big double gates of the prison, into the road. "Pulling at his legs!" exclaimed a Burmese magistrate suddenly, and burst into a loud chuckling. We all began laughing again. At that moment Francis' anecdote seemed extraordinarily funny. We all had a drink together, native and European alike, quite amicably. The dead man was a hundred yards away.

Shooting an Elephant

New Writing, 2, Autumn 1936

In Moulmein, in Lower Burma, I was hated by large numbers of people — the only time in my life that I have been important enough for this to happen to me. I was subdivisional police officer of the town, and in an aimless, petty kind of way anti-European feeling was very bitter. No one had the guts to raise a riot, but if a European woman went through the bazaars alone somebody would probably spit betel juice over her dress. As a police officer I was an obvious target and was baited whenever it seemed safe to do so. When a nimble Burman tripped me up on the football field and the referee (another Burman) looked the other way, the crowd yelled with hideous laughter. This happened more than once. In the end the sneering yellow faces of young men that met me everywhere, the insults hooted after me when I was at a safe distance, got badly on my nerves. The young Buddhist priests were the worst of all. There were several thousands of them in the town and none of them seemed to have anything to do except stand on street corners and jeer at Europeans.

All this was perplexing and upsetting. For at that time I had already made up my mind that imperialism was an evil thing and the sooner I chucked up my job and got out of it the better. Theoretically — and secretly, of course — I was all for the Burmese and all against their oppressors, the British. As for the job I was doing, I hated it more bitterly than I can perhaps make clear. In a job like that you see the dirty work of Empire at close quarters.

The wretched prisoners huddling in the stinking cages of the lock-ups, the grey, cowed faces of the long-term convicts, the scarred buttocks of the men who had been flogged with bamboos—all these oppressed me with an intolerable sense of guilt. But I could get nothing into perspective. I was young and ill-educated and I had had to think out my problems in the utter silence that is imposed on every Englishman in the East. I did not even know that the British Empire is dying, still less did I know that it is a great deal better than the younger empires that are going to supplant it. All I knew was that I was stuck between my hatred of the empire I served and my rage against the evil-spirited little beasts who tried to make my job impossible. With one part of my mind I thought of the British Raj as an unbreakable tyranny, as something clamped down, in saecula saeculorum, upon the will of prostrate peoples; with another part I thought that the greatest joy in the world would be to drive a bayonet into a Buddhist priest's guts. Feelings like these are the normal by-products of imperialism; ask any Anglo-Indian official, if you can catch him off duty.

One day something happened which in a roundabout way was enlightening. It was a tiny incident in itself, but it gave me a better glimpse than I had had before of the real nature of imperialism—the real motives for which despotic governments act. Early one morning the sub-inspector at a police station the other end of the town rang me up on the phone and said that an elephant was ravaging the bazaar. Would I please come and do something about it? I did not know what I could do, but I wanted to see what was happening and I got on to a pony and started out. I took my rifle, an old .44 Winchester and much too small to kill an elephant, but I thought the noise might be useful in terrorem. Various Burmans stopped me on the way and told me about the elephant's doings. It was not, of course, a wild elephant, but a tame one which had gone "must." It had been chained up as tame elephants always are when their attack of "must" is due, but on the previous night it had broken its chain and escaped. Its mahout, the only person who could manage it when it was in that state, had set out in pursuit, but he had taken the wrong direction and was now twelve hours' journey away, and in the morning the elephant had suddenly reappeared in the town. The Burmese population had no weapons and were quite helpless against it. It had already destroyed somebody's bamboo hut, killed a cow and raided some fruit-stalls and devoured the stock; also it had met the municipal rubbish van, and, when the driver jumped out and took to his heels, had turned the van over and inflicted violences upon it.

The Burmese sub-inspector and some Indian constables were waiting for me in the quarter where the elephant had been seen. It was a very poor quarter, a labyrinth of squalid bamboo huts, thatched with palm-leaf, winding all over a steep hillside. I remember that it was a cloudy stuffy morning at the beginning of the rains. We began questioning the people as to where the elephant had gone, and, as usual, failed to get any definite information. That is invariably the case in the East; a story always sounds clear enough at a distance, but the nearer you get to the scene of events the vaguer it becomes. Some of the people said that the elephant had gone in one direction, some said that he had gone in another, some professed not even to have heard of any elephant. I had almost made up my mind that the whole story was a pack of lies, when we heard yells a little distance away. There was a loud, scandalized cry of "Go away, child! Go away this instant!" and an old woman with a switch in her hand came round the corner of a hut, violently shooing away a crowd of naked children. Some more women followed, clicking their tongues and exclaiming; evidently there was something there that the children ought not to have seen. I rounded the hut and saw a man's dead body sprawling in the mud. He was an Indian, a black Dravidian coolie, almost naked, and he could not have been dead many minutes. The people said that the elephant had come suddenly upon him round the corner of the hut, caught him with its trunk, put its foot on his back and ground him into the earth. This was the rainy season and the ground was soft, and his face had scored a trench a foot deep and a couple of yards long. He was lying on his belly with arms crucified and head sharply twisted to one side. His face was coated with mud, the eyes wide open, the teeth bared and grinning with an expression of unendurable agony. (Never tell me, by the way, that the dead look peaceful. Most of the corpses I have seen looked devilish.) The friction of the great beast's foot had stripped the skin from his back as neatly as one skins a rabbit. As soon as I saw the dead man I sent an orderly to a friend's house nearby to borrow an elephant rifle. I had already sent back the pony, not wanting it to go mad with fright and throw me if it smelled the elephant.

The orderly came back in a few minutes with a rifle and five cartridges, and meanwhile some Burmans had arrived and told us that the elephant was in the paddy fields below, only a few hundred yards away. As I started forward practically the whole population of the quarter flocked out of the houses and followed me. They had seen the rifle and were all shouting excitedly that I was going to shoot the elephant. They had not shown much interest in the elephant when he was merely ravaging their homes, but it was different now that he was going to be shot. It was a bit of fun to them, as it would be to an English crowd; besides, they wanted the meat. It made me vaguely uneasy. I had no intention of shooting the elephant—I had merely sent for the rifle to defend myself if necessary—and it is always unnerving to have a crowd following you. I marched down the hill, looking and feeling a fool, with the rifle over my shoulder and an ever-growing army of people jostling at my heels. At the bottom, when you got away from the huts, there was a metalled road and beyond that a miry waste of paddy fields a thousand yards across, not yet ploughed but soggy from the first rains and dotted with coarse grass. The elephant was standing eighty yards from the road, his left side towards us. He took not the slightest notice of the crowd's approach. He was tearing up bunches of grass, beating them against his knees to clean them and stuffing them into his mouth.

I had halted on the road. As soon as I saw the elephant I knew with perfect certainty that I ought not to shoot him. It is a serious matter to shoot a working elephant—it is comparable to destroying a huge and costly piece of machinery—and obviously one ought not to do it if it can possibly be avoided. And at that distance, peacefully eating, the elephant looked no more dangerous than a cow. I thought then and I think now that his attack of "must" was already passing off; in which case he would merely wander harmlessly about until the mahout came back and caught him. Moreover, I did not in the least want to shoot him. I decided that I would watch him for a little while to make sure that he did not turn savage again, and then go home.

But at that moment I glanced round at the crowd that had followed me. It was an immense crowd, two thousand at the least and growing every minute. It blocked the road for a long distance on either side. I looked at the sea of yellow faces above the garish clothes—faces all happy and excited over this bit of fun, all certain that the elephant was going to be shot. They were watching me as they would watch a conjuror about to perform a trick. They did not like me, but with the magical rifle in my hands I was momentarily worth watching. And suddenly I realized that I should have to shoot the elephant after all. The people expected it of me and I had got to do it; I could feel their two thousand wills pressing me forward, irresistibly. And it was at this moment, as I stood there with the rifle in my hands, that I first grasped the hollowness, the futility of the white man's dominion in the East. Here was I, the white man with his gun, standing in front of the unarmed native crowd—seemingly the leading actor of the piece; but in reality I was only an absurd puppet pushed to and fro by the will of those yellow faces behind. I perceived in this moment that when the white man turns tyrant it is his own freedom that he destroys. He becomes a sort of hollow, posing dummy, the conventionalized figure of a sahib. For it is the condition of his rule that he shall spend his life in trying to impress the "natives," and so in every crisis he has got to do what the "natives" expect of him. He wears a mask, and his face grows to fit it. I had got to shoot the elephant. I had committed myself to doing it when I sent for the rifle. A sahib has got to act like a sahib; he has got to appear resolute, to know his own mind and do definite things. To come all that way, rifle in hand, with two thousand people marching at my heels, and then to trail feebly away, having done nothing—no, that was impossible. The crowd would laugh at me. And my whole life, every white man's life in the East, was one long struggle not to be laughed at.

But I did not want to shoot the elephant. I watched him beating his bunch of grass against his knees, with that preoccupied grandmotherly air that elephants have. It seemed to me that it would be murder to shoot him. At that age I was not squeamish about killing animals, but I had never shot an elephant and never wanted to. (Somehow it always seems worse to kill a *large* animal.) Besides, there was the beast's owner to be considered. Alive, the elephant was worth at least a hundred pounds; dead, he would only be worth the value of his tusks—five pounds, possibly. But I had got to act quickly. I turned to some experienced-looking Burmans who had been there when we arrived, and asked them how the elephant had been behaving. They all said the same thing:

he took no notice of you if you left him alone, but he might charge if you went too close to him.

It was perfectly clear to me what I ought to do. I ought to walk up to within, say, twenty-five yards of the elephant and test his behaviour. If he charged I could shoot, if he took no notice of me it would be safe to leave him until the mahout came back. But also I knew that I was going to do no such thing. I was a poor shot with a rifle and the ground was soft mud into which one would sink at every step. If the elephant charged and I missed him, I should have about as much chance as a toad under a steam-roller. But even then I was not thinking particularly of my own skin, only of the watchful yellow faces behind. For at that moment, with the crowd watching me, I was not afraid in the ordinary sense, as I would have been if I had been alone. A white man mustn't be frightened in front of "natives"; and so, in general, he isn't frightened. The sole thought in my mind was that if anything went wrong those two thousand Burmans would see me pursued, caught, trampled on and reduced to a grinning corpse like that Indian up the hill. And if that happened it was quite probable that some of them would laugh. That would never do. There was only one alternative. I shoved the cartridges into the magazine and lay down on the road to get a better aim.

The crowd grew very still, and a deep, low, happy sigh, as of people who see the theatre curtain go up at last, breathed from innumerable throats. They were going to have their bit of fun after all. The rifle was a beautiful German thing with cross-hair sights. I did not then know that in shooting an elephant one should shoot to cut an imaginary bar running from ear-hole to ear-hole. I ought therefore, as the elephant was sideways on, to have aimed straight at his ear-hole; actually I aimed several inches in front of this, thinking the brain would be further forward.

When I pulled the trigger I did not hear the bang or feel the kick—one never does when a shot goes home—but I heard the devilish roar of glee that went up from the crowd. In that instant, in too short a time, one would have thought, even for the bullet to get there, a mysterious, terrible change had come over the elephant. He neither stirred nor fell, but every line of his body had altered. He looked suddenly stricken, shrunken, immensely old, as though the frightful impact of the bullet had paralysed him without knocking him down. At last, after what seemed a long time—it might have been five seconds, I dare say—he sagged flabbily to his knees. His mouth slobbered. An enormous senility seemed to have settled upon him. One could have imagined him thousands of years old. I fired again into the same spot. At the second shot he did not collapse but climbed with desperate slowness to his feet and stood weakly upright, with legs sagging and head drooping. I fired a third time. That was the shot that did for him. You could see the agony of it jolt his whole body and knock the last remnant of strength from his legs. But in falling he seemed for a moment to rise, for as his hind legs collapsed beneath him he seemed to tower upwards like a huge rock toppling, his trunk reaching skyward like a tree. He trumpeted, for the first and only time. And then down he came, his belly towards me, with a crash that seemed to shake the ground even where I lay.

I got up. The Burmans were already racing past me across the mud. It was obvious that the elephant would never rise again, but he was not dead. He was breathing very rhythmically with long rattling gasps, his great mound of a side painfully rising and falling. His mouth was wide open—I could see far down into caverns of pale pink throat. I waited a long time for him to die, but his breathing did not weaken. Finally I fired my two remaining shots into the spot where I thought his heart must be. The thick blood welled out of him like red velvet, but still he did not die. His body did not even jerk when the shots hit him, the tortured breathing continued without a pause. He was dying, very slowly and in great agony, but in some world remote from me where not even a bullet could damage him further. I felt that I had got to put an end to that dreadful noise. It seemed dreadful to see the great beast lying there, powerless to move and yet powerless to die, and not even to be able to finish him. I sent back for my small rifle and poured shot after shot into his heart and down his throat. They seemed to make no impression. The tortured gasps continued as steadily as the ticking of a clock.

In the end I could not stand it any longer and went away. I heard later that it took him half an hour to die. Burmans were arriving with dahs and baskets even before I left, and I was told they had stripped his body almost to the bones by the afternoon.

Afterwards, of course, there were endless discussions about the shooting of the elephant. The owner was furious, but he was only an Indian and could do nothing. Besides, legally I had done the right thing, for a mad elephant has to be killed, like a mad dog, if its owner fails to control it. Among the Europeans opinion was divided. The older men said I was right, the younger men said it was a damn shame to shoot an elephant for killing a coolie, because an elephant was worth more than any damn Coringhee coolie. And afterwards I was very glad that the coolie had been killed; it put me legally in the right and it gave me a sufficient pretext for shooting the elephant. I often wondered whether any of the others grasped that I had done it solely to avoid looking a fool.

Bookshop Memories

Fortnightly, November 1936

When I worked in a second-hand bookshop — so easily pictured, if you don't work in one, as a kind of paradise where charming old gentlemen browse eternally among calf-bound folios — the thing that chiefly struck me was the rarity of really bookish people. Our shop had an exceptionally interesting stock, yet I doubt whether ten per cent of our customers knew a good book from a bad one. First edition snobs were much commoner than lovers of literature, but oriental students haggling over cheap textbooks were commoner still, and vague-minded women looking for birthday presents for their nephews were commonest of all.

Many of the people who came to us were of the kind who would be a nuisance anywhere but have special opportunities in a bookshop. For example, the dear old lady who "wants a book for an invalid" (a very common demand, that), and the other dear old lady who read such a nice book in 1897 and wonders whether you can find her a copy. Unfortunately she doesn't remember the title or the author's name or what the book was about, but she does remember that it had a red cover. But apart from these there are two well-known types of pest by whom every second-hand bookshop is haunted. One is the decayed person smelling of old breadcrusts who comes every day, sometimes several times a day, and tries to sell you worthless books. The other is the person who orders large quantities of books for which he has not the smallest intention of paying. In our shop we sold nothing on credit, but we would put books aside, or order them if necessary, for people who arranged to fetch them away later. Scarcely half the people who ordered books from us ever came back. It used to puzzle me at first. What made them do it? They would come in and demand some rare and expensive book, would make us promise over and over again to keep it for them, and then would vanish never to return. But many of them, of course, were unmistakeable paranoiacs. They used to talk in a grandiose manner about themselves and tell the most ingenious stories to explain how they had happened to come out of doors without any money—stories which, in many cases, I am sure they themselves believed. In a town like London there are always plenty of not quite certifiable lunatics walking the streets, and they tend to gravitate towards bookshops, because a bookshop is one of the few places where you can hang about for a long time without spending any money. In the end one gets to know these people almost at a glance. For all their big talk there is something moth-eaten and aimless about them. Very often, when we were dealing with an obvious paranoiac, we would put aside the books he asked for and then put them back on the shelves the moment he had gone. None of them, I noticed, ever attempted to take books away without paying for them; merely to order them was enough—it gave them, I suppose, the illusion they were spending real money.

Like most second-hand bookshops we had various sidelines. We sold second-hand typewriters, for instance, and also stamps— used stamps, I mean. Stamp-collectors are a strange silent fish-like breed, of all ages, but only of the male sex; women, apparently, fail to see the peculiar charm of gumming bits of coloured paper into albums. We also sold sixpenny horoscopes compiled by somebody who claimed to have foretold the Japanese earthquake. They were in sealed envelopes and I never opened one of them myself, but the people who bought them often came back and told us how "true" their horoscopes had been. (Doubtless any horoscope seems "true" if it tells you that you are highly attractive to the opposite sex and your worst fault is generosity.) We did a good deal of business in children's books, chiefly "remainders." Modern books for children are rather horrible things, especially when you see them in the mass. Personally I would sooner give a child a copy of Petronius Arbiter than *Peter Pan,* but even Barrie seems manly and wholesome compared with some of his later imitators. At Christmas time we spent a feverish ten days struggling with Christmas cards and calendars, which are tiresome things to sell but good business while the season lasts. It used to interest me to see the brutal cynicism with which Christian sentiment is exploited. The touts from the Christmas card firms used to come round with their catalogues as early as June. A phrase from one of their invoices sticks in my memory. It was: "2 doz. Infant Jesus with rabbits."

But our principal sideline was a lending library—the usual "twopenny no-deposit" library of five or six hundred volumes, all fiction. How the book thieves must love those libraries! It is the easiest crime in the world to borrow a book at one shop for twopence, remove the label and sell it at another shop for a shilling. Nevertheless booksellers generally find that it pays them better to have a certain number of books stolen (we used to lose about a dozen a month) than to frighten customers away by demanding a deposit.

Our shop stood exactly on the frontier between Hampstead and Camden Town, and we were frequented by all types from baronets to bus-conductors. Probably our library subscribers were a fair cross-section of London's reading public. It is therefore worth noting that of all the authors in our library the one who "went out" the best was—Priestley? Hemingway? Walpole? Wodehouse? No, Ethel M. Dell, with Warwick Deeping a good second and Jeffery Farnol, I should say, third. Dell's novels, of course, are read solely by women, but by women of all kinds and ages and not, as one might expect, merely by wistful spinsters and the fat wives of tobacconists. It is not true that men don't read novels, but it is true that there are whole branches of fiction that they avoid. Roughly speaking, what one might call the *average* novel—the ordinary, good-bad, Galsworthy-and-water stuff which is the norm of the English novel—seems to exist only for women. Men read either the novels it is possible to respect, or detective stories. But their consumption of detective stories is terrific. One of our subscribers to my knowledge read four or five detective stories every week for over a year, besides others which he got from another library. What chiefly surprised me was that he never read the same book twice. Apparently the whole of that frightful torrent of trash (the pages he read every year would, I calculated, cover nearly three-quarters of an acre) was stored for ever in his memory. He took no notice of titles or authors' names, but he could tell by merely glancing into a book whether he had "had it already."

In a lending library you see people's real tastes, not their pretended ones, and one thing that strikes you is how completely the "classical" English novelists have dropped out of favour. It is simply useless to put Dickens, Thackeray, Jane Austen, Trollope, etc., into the ordinary lending library; nobody takes them out. At the mere sight of a nineteenth-century novel people say "Oh, but that's *old*!" and shy away immediately. Yet it is always fairly easy to *sell* Dickens, just as it is always easy to sell Shakespeare. Dickens is one of those authors whom people are "always meaning to" read, and, like the Bible, he is widely known at second hand. People know by hearsay that Bill Sykes was a burglar and that Mr. Micawber had a bald head, just as they know by hearsay that Moses was found in a basket of bulrushes and saw the "back parts" of the Lord. Another thing that is very noticeable is the growing unpopularity of American books. And another—the publishers get into a stew about this every two or three years—is the unpopularity of short stories. The kind of person who asks the librarian to choose a book for him nearly always starts by saying "I don't want short stories," or "I do not desire little stories," as a German customer of ours used to put it. If you ask them why, they sometimes explain that it is too much fag to get used to a new set of characters with every story; they like to "get into" a novel which demands no further thought after the first chapter. I believe, though, that the writers are more to blame here than the readers. Most modern short stories, English and American, are utterly lifeless and worthless, far more so than most novels. The short stories which *are* stories are popular enough, *vide* D. H. Lawrence, whose short stories are as popular as his novels.

Would I like to be a bookseller *de métier*? On the whole—in spite of my employer's kindness to me, and some happy days I spent in the shop—no.

Given a good pitch and the right amount of capital, any educated person ought to be able to make a small secure living out of a bookshop. Unless one goes in for "rare" books it is not a difficult trade to learn, and you start at a great advantage if you know anything about the insides of books. (Most booksellers don't. You can get their measure by having a look at the trade papers where they advertise their wants. If you don't see an ad. for Boswell's *Decline and Fall* you are pretty sure to see one for *The Mill on the Floss* by T. S. Eliot.) Also it is a humane trade which is not capable of being vulgarised beyond a certain point. The combines can never squeeze the small independent bookseller out of existence as they have squeezed the grocer and the milkman. But the hours of work are very long—I was only a part-time employee, but my employer put in a 70-hour week, apart from constant expeditions out of hours to buy books — and it is an unhealthy life. As a rule a book-shop is horribly cold in winter, because if it is too warm the win-dows get misted over, and a bookseller lives on his windows. And books give off more and nastier dust than any other class of ob-jects yet invented, and the top of a book is the place where every bluebottle prefers to die.

But the real reason why I should not like to be in the book trade for life is that while I was in it I lost my love of books. A bookseller has to tell lies about books, and that gives him a distaste for them; still worse is the fact that he is constantly dusting them and hauling them to and fro. There was a time when I really did love books — loved the sight and smell and feel of them, I mean, at least if they were fifty or more years old. Nothing pleased me quite so much as to buy a job lot of them for a shilling at a coun-try auction. There is a peculiar flavour about the battered unex-pected books you pick up in that kind of collection: minor eighteenth-century poets, out of date gazetteers, odd volumes of forgotten novels, bound numbers of ladies' magazines of the 'six-ties. For casual reading — in your bath, for instance, or late at night when you are too tired to go to bed, or in the odd quarter of an hour before lunch — there is nothing to touch a back number of the *Girl's Own Paper*. But as soon as I went to work in the bookshop I stopped buying books. Seen in the mass, five or ten thousand at a time, books were boring and even slightly sickening. Nowadays I do buy one occasionally, but only if it is a book that I want to read and can't borrow, and I never buy junk. The sweet smell of de-caying paper appeals to me no longer. It is too closely associated in my mind with paranoiac customers and dead bluebottles.

Marrakech

New Writing, New Series No. 3, Christmas 1939

As the corpse went past the flies left the restaurant table in a cloud and rushed after it, but they came back a few minutes later.

The little crowd of mourners—all men and boys, no women—threaded their way across the market-place between the piles of pomegranates and the taxis and the camels, wailing a short chant over and over again. What really appeals to the flies is that the corpses here are never put into coffins, they are merely wrapped in a piece of rag and carried on a rough wooden bier on the shoulders of four friends. When the friends get to the burying-ground they hack an oblong hole a foot or two deep, dump the body in it and fling over it a little of the dried-up, lumpy earth, which is like broken brick. No gravestone, no name, no identifying mark of any kind. The burying-ground is merely a huge waste of hummocky earth, like a derelict building-lot. After a month or two no one can even be certain where his own relatives are buried.

When you walk through a town like this—two hundred thousand inhabitants, of whom at least twenty thousand own literally nothing except the rags they stand up in—when you see how the people live, and still more how easily they die, it is always difficult to believe that you are walking among human beings. All colonial empires are in reality founded upon that fact. The people have brown faces—besides, there are so many of them! Are they really the same flesh as yourself? Do they even have names? Or are they merely a kind of undifferentiated brown stuff, about as individual

as bees or coral insects? They rise out of the earth, they sweat and
starve for a few years, and then they sink back into the nameless
mounds of the graveyard and nobody notices that they are gone.
And even the graves themselves soon fade back into the soil.
Sometimes, out for a walk, as you break your way through the
prickly pear, you notice that it is rather bumpy underfoot, and only
a certain regularity in the bumps tells you that you are walking
over skeletons.

I was feeding one of the gazelles in the public gardens.

Gazelles are almost the only animals that look good to eat
when they are still alive, in fact, one can hardly look at their
hindquarters without thinking of mint sauce. The gazelle I was
feeding seemed to know that this thought was in my mind, for
though it took the piece of bread I was holding out it obviously did
not like me. It nibbled rapidly at the bread, then lowered its head
and tried to butt me, then took another nibble and then butted
again. Probably its idea was that if it could drive me away the bread
would somehow remain hanging in mid-air.

An Arab navvy working on the path nearby lowered his heavy
hoe and sidled slowly towards us. He looked from the gazelle to
the bread and from the bread to the gazelle, with a sort of quiet
amazement, as though he had never seen anything quite like this
before. Finally he said shyly in French:

"*I* could eat some of that bread."

I tore off a piece and he stowed it gratefully in some secret
place under his rags. This man is an employee of the Municipality.

When you go through the Jewish quarters you gather some
idea of what the medieval ghettoes were probably like. Under their
Moorish rulers the Jews were only allowed to own land in certain
restricted areas, and after centuries of this kind of treatment they
have ceased to bother about overcrowding. Many of the streets

are a good deal less than six feet wide, the houses are completely windowless, and sore-eyed children cluster everywhere in unbelievable numbers, like clouds of flies. Down the centre of the street there is generally running a little river of urine.

In the bazaar huge families of Jews, all dressed in the long black robe and little black skull-cap, are working in dark fly-infested booths that look like caves. A carpenter sits cross-legged at a prehistoric lathe, turning chair-legs at lightning speed. He works the lathe with a bow in his right hand and guides the chisel with his left foot, and thanks to a lifetime of sitting in this position his left leg is warped out of shape. At his side his grandson, aged six, is already starting on the simpler parts of the job.

I was just passing the coppersmiths' booths when somebody noticed that I was lighting a cigarette. Instantly, from the dark holes all round, there was a frenzied rush of Jews, many of them old grandfathers with flowing grey beards, all clamouring for a cigarette. Even a blind man somewhere at the back of one of the booths heard a rumour of cigarettes and came crawling out, groping in the air with his hand. In about a minute I had used up the whole packet. None of these people, I suppose, works less than twelve hours a day, and every one of them looks on a cigarette as a more or less impossible luxury.

As the Jews live in self-contained communities they follow the same trades as the Arabs, except for agriculture. Fruit-sellers, potters, silversmiths, blacksmiths, butchers, leatherworkers, tailors, water-carriers, beggars, porters—whichever way you look you see nothing but Jews. As a matter of fact there are thirteen thousand of them, all living in the space of a few acres. A good job Hitler isn't here. Perhaps he is on his way, however. You hear the usual dark rumours about the Jews, not only from the Arabs but from the poorer Europeans.

"Yes, *mon vieux,* they took my job away from me and gave it to a Jew. The Jews! They're the real rulers of this country, you know. They've got all the money. They control the banks, finance — everything."

"But," I said, "isn't it a fact that the average Jew is a labourer working for about a penny an hour?"

"Ah, that's only for show! They're all moneylenders really. They're cunning, the Jews."

In just the same way, a couple of hundred years ago, poor old women used to be burned for witchcraft when they could not even work enough magic to get themselves a square meal.

All people who work with their hands are partly invisible, and the more important the work they do, the less visible they are. Still, a white skin is always fairly conspicuous. In northern Europe, when you see a labourer ploughing a field, you probably give him a second glance. In a hot country, anywhere south of Gibraltar or east of Suez, the chances are that you don't even see him. I have noticed this again and again. In a tropical landscape one's eye takes in everything except the human beings. It takes in the dried-up soil, the prickly pear, the palm-tree and the distant mountain, but it always misses the peasant hoeing at his patch. He is the same colour as the earth, and a great deal less interesting to look at.

It is only because of this that the starved countries of Asia and Africa are accepted as tourist resorts. No one would think of running cheap trips to the Distressed Areas. But where the human beings have brown skins their poverty is simply not noticed. What does Morocco mean to a Frenchman? An orange-grove or a job in Government service. Or to an Englishman? Camels, castles, palm-trees, Foreign Legionnaires, brass trays and bandits. One could probably live here for years without noticing that for nine-tenths of the people the reality of life is an endless, back-breaking struggle to wring a little food out of an eroded soil.

Most of Morocco is so desolate that no wild animal bigger than a hare can live on it. Huge areas which were once covered with forest have turned into a treeless waste where the soil is exactly like broken-up brick. Nevertheless a good deal of it is cultivated, with frightful labour. Everything is done by hand. Long lines of women, bent double like inverted capital L's, work their way slowly across the fields, tearing up the prickly weeds with their hands, and the peasant gathering lucerne for fodder pulls it up stalk by stalk instead of reaping it, thus saving an inch or two on each stalk. The plough is a wretched wooden thing, so frail that one can easily carry it on one's shoulder, and fitted underneath with a rough iron spike which stirs the soil to a depth of about four inches. This is as much as the strength of the animals is equal to. It is usual to plough with a cow and a donkey yoked together. Two donkeys would not be quite strong enough, but on the other hand two cows would cost a little more to feed. The peasants possess no harrows, they merely plough the soil several times over in different directions, finally leaving it in rough furrows, after which the whole field has to be shaped with hoes into small oblong patches, to conserve water. Except for a day or two after the rare rainstorms there is never enough water. Along the edges of the fields channels are hacked out to a depth of thirty or forty feet to get at the tiny trickles which run through the subsoil.

Every afternoon a file of very old women passes down the road outside my house, each carrying a load of firewood. All of them are mummified with age and the sun, and all of them are tiny. It seems to be generally the case in primitive communities that the women, when they get beyond a certain age, shrink to the size of children. One day a poor old creature who could not have been more than four feet tall crept past me under a vast load of wood. I stopped her and put a five-sou piece (a little more than a farthing) into her hand. She answered with a shrill wail, almost a scream, which was partly gratitude but mainly surprise. I suppose that from her point of view, by taking any notice of her, I seemed almost to be violating a law of nature. She accepted her status as an old woman, that is to say as a beast of burden. When a family is travelling it is quite usual to see a father and a grown-up son riding ahead on donkeys, and an old woman following on foot, carrying the baggage.

But what is strange about these people is their invisibility. For several weeks, always at about the same time of day, the file of old women had hobbled past the house with their firewood, and though they had registered themselves on my eyeballs I cannot truly say that I had seen them. Firewood was passing—that was how I saw it. It was only that one day I happened to be walking behind them, and the curious up-and-down motion of a load of wood drew my attention to the human being underneath it. Then for the first time I noticed the poor old earth-coloured bodies, bodies reduced to bones and leathery skin, bent double under the crushing weight. Yet I suppose I had not been five minutes on Moroccan soil before I noticed the overloading of the donkeys and was infuriated by it. There is no question that the donkeys are damnably treated. The Moroccan donkey is hardly bigger than a St. Bernard dog, it carries a load which in the British Army would be considered too much for a fifteen-hands mule, and very often its pack-saddle is not taken off its back for weeks together. But what is peculiarly pitiful is that it is the most willing creature on earth, it follows its master like a dog and does not need either bridle or halter. After a dozen years of devoted work it suddenly drops dead, whereupon its master tips it into the ditch and the village dogs have torn its guts out before it is cold.

This kind of thing makes one's blood boil, whereas — on the whole — the plight of the human beings does not. I am not commenting, merely pointing to a fact. People with brown skins are next door to invisible. Anyone can be sorry for the donkey with its galled back, but it is generally owing to some kind of accident if one even notices the old woman under her load of sticks.

As the storks flew northward the negroes were marching southward — a long, dusty column, infantry, screw-gun batteries and then more infantry, four or five thousand men in all, winding up the road with a clumping of boots and a clatter of iron wheels.

They were Senegalese, the blackest negroes in Africa, so black that sometimes it is difficult to see whereabouts on their necks the hair begins. Their splendid bodies were hidden in reach-me-down khaki uniforms, their feet squashed into boots that looked like blocks of wood, and every tin hat seemed to be a couple of sizes too small. It was very hot and the men had marched a long way. They slumped under the weight of their packs and the curiously sensitive black faces were glistening with sweat.

As they went past a tall, very young negro turned and caught my eye. But the look he gave me was not in the least the kind of look you might expect. Not hostile, not contemptuous, not sullen, not even inquisitive. It was the shy, wide-eyed negro look, which actually is a look of profound respect. I saw how it was. This wretched boy, who is a French citizen and has therefore been dragged from the forest to scrub floors and catch syphilis in garrison towns, actually has feelings of reverence before a white skin. He has been taught that the white race are his masters, and he still believes it.

But there is one thought which every white man (and in this connection it doesn't matter twopence if he calls himself a Socialist) thinks when he sees a black army marching past. "How much longer can we go on kidding these people? How long before they turn their guns in the other direction?"

It was curious, really. Every white man there had this thought stowed somewhere or other in his mind. I had it, so had the other onlookers, so had the officers on their sweating chargers and the white N.C.O.'s marching in the ranks. It was a kind of secret which we all knew and were too clever to tell; only the negroes didn't know it. And really it was almost like watching a flock of cattle to see the long column, a mile or two miles of armed men, flowing peacefully up the road, while the great white birds drifted over them in the opposite direction, glittering like scraps of paper.

My Country Right or Left[1]

Folios of New Writing, No. 2, Autumn 1940

Contrary to popular belief, the past was not more eventful than the present. If it seems so it is because when you look backward things that happened years apart are telescoped together, and because very few of your memories come to you genuinely virgin. It is largely because of the books, films and reminiscences that have come between that the war of 1914–18 is now supposed to have had some tremendous, epic quality that the present one lacks.

But if you were alive during that war, and if you disentangle your real memories from their later accretions, you find that it was not usually the big events that stirred you at the time. I don't believe that the battle of the Marne, for instance, had for the general public the melodramatic quality that it was afterwards given. I do not even remember hearing the phrase "battle of the Marne" till years later. It was merely that the Germans were 22 miles from Paris—and certainly that was terrifying enough, after the Belgian atrocity stories—and then for some reason they had turned back. I was eleven when the war started. If I honestly sort out my memories and disregard what I have learned since, I must admit that nothing in the whole war moved me so deeply as the loss of the *Titanic* had done a few years earlier. This comparatively petty disaster shocked the whole world, and the shock has not quite died away even yet. I remember the terrible, detailed accounts read out at the breakfast table (in those days it was a common habit to read the newspaper aloud), and I remember that in all the long list of horrors the one that most impressed me was that at the last the *Titanic* suddenly up-ended and sank bow-foremost, so that the people clinging to the stern were lifted no less than three hundred feet into the air before they plunged into the abyss. It gave me a sinking sensation in the belly which I can still all but feel. Nothing in the war ever gave me quite that sensation.

Of the outbreak of war I have three vivid memories which, being petty and irrelevant, are uninfluenced by anything that has come later. One is of the cartoon of the "German Emperor" (I believe the hated name "Kaiser" was not popularized till a little later) that appeared in the last days of July. People were mildly shocked by this guying of royalty ("But he's such a handsome man, really!"), although we were on the edge of war. Another is of the time when the Army commandeered all the horses in our little country town, and a cabman burst into tears in the market-place when his horse, which had worked for him for years, was taken away from him. And another is of a mob of young men at the railway station, scrambling for the evening papers that had just arrived on the London train. And I remember the pile of pea-green papers (some of them were still green in those days), the high collars, the tightish trousers and the bowler hats, far better than I can remember the names of the terrific battles that were already raging on the French frontier.

Of the middle years of the war, I remember chiefly the square shoulders, bulging calves and jingling spurs of the artillerymen, whose uniform I much preferred to that of the infantry. As for the final period, if you ask me to say truthfully what is my chief memory, I must answer simply—margarine. It is an instance of the horrible selfishness of children that by 1917 the war had almost ceased to affect us, except through our stomachs. In the school library a huge map of the western front was pinned on an easel, with a red silk thread running across on a zig-zag of drawing-pins. Occasionally the thread moved half an inch this way or that, each movement meaning a pyramid of corpses. I paid no attention. I was at school among boys who were above the average level of intelligence, and yet I do not remember that a single major event of the time appeared to us in its true significance. The Russian Revolution, for instance, made no impression, except on the few whose parents happened to have money invested in Russia. Among the very young the pacifist reaction had set in long before the war ended. To be as slack as you dared on O.T.C. parades, and to take no interest in the war, was considered a mark of enlightenment. The young officers who had come back, hardened by their terrible experience and disgusted by the attitude of the younger generation to whom this experience meant just nothing, used to lecture us for our softness. Of course they could produce no argument that we were capable of understanding. They could only bark at you that war was "a good thing," it "made you tough," "kept you fit," etc., etc. We merely sniggered at them. Ours was the one-eyed pacifism that is peculiar to sheltered countries with strong navies. For years after the war, to have any knowledge of or interest in military matters, even to know which end of a gun the bullet comes out of, was suspect in "enlightened" circles. 1914–18 was written off as a meaningless slaughter, and even the men who had been slaughtered were held to be in some way to blame. I have often laughed to think of that recruiting poster, "What did you do in the Great War, daddy?" (a child is asking this question of its shame-stricken father), and of all the men who must have been lured into the Army by just that poster and afterwards despised by their children for not being Conscientious Objectors.

But the dead men had their revenge after all. As the war fell back into the past, my particular generation, those who had been "just too young," became conscious of the vastness of the experience they had missed. You felt yourself a little less than a man, because you had missed it. I spent the years 1922–7 mostly among men a little older than myself who had been through the war. They talked about it unceasingly, with horror, of course, but also with a steadily-growing nostalgia. You can see this nostalgia perfectly clearly in the English war-books. Besides, the pacifist reaction was only a phase, and even the "just too young" had all been trained for war. Most of the English middle class are trained for war from the cradle onwards, not technically but morally. The earliest political slogan I can remember is "We want eight (eight dreadnoughts) and we won't wait."[2] At seven years old I was a member of the Navy League and wore a sailor suit with "H.M.S. *Invincible*" on my cap. Even before my public-school O.T.C. I had been in a private-school cadet corps. On and off, I have been toting a rifle ever since I was ten, in preparation not only for war but for a particular kind of war, a war in which the guns rise to a frantic orgasm of sound, and at the appointed moment you clamber out of the trench, breaking your nails on the sandbags, and stumble across mud and wire into the machine-gun barrage. I am convinced that part of the reason for the fascination that the Spanish civil war had for people of about my age was that it was so like the Great War. At certain moments Franco was able to scrape together enough aeroplanes to raise the war to a modern level, and these were the turning-points. But for the rest it was a bad copy of 1914–18, a positional war of trenches, artillery, raids, snipers, mud, barbed wire, lice and stagnation. In early 1937 the bit of the Aragon front that I was on must have been very like a quiet sector in France in 1915. It was only the artillery that was lacking. Even on the rare occasions when all the guns in Huesca and outside it were firing simultaneously, there were only enough of them to make a fitful unimpressive noise like the ending of a thunderstorm. The shells from Franco's six-inch guns crashed loudly enough, but there were never more than a dozen of them at a time. I know that what I felt when I first heard artillery fired "in anger," as they say, was at least partly disappointment. It was so different from the tremendous, unbroken roar that my senses had been waiting for for twenty years.

I don't quite know in what year I first knew for certain that the present war was coming. After 1936, of course, the thing was obvious to anyone except an idiot. For several years the coming war was a nightmare to me, and at times I even made speeches and wrote pamphlets against it. But the night before the Russo-German pact was announced I dreamed that the war had started. It was one of those dreams which, whatever Freudian inner meaning they may have, do sometimes reveal to you the real state of your feelings. It taught me two things, first, that I should be simply relieved when the long-dreaded war started, secondly, that I was patriotic at heart, would not sabotage or act against my own side, would support the war, would fight in it if possible. I came downstairs to find the newspaper announcing Ribbentrop's flight to Moscow.[3] So war was coming, and the Government, even the Chamberlain Government, was assured of my loyalty. Needless to say this loyalty was and remains merely a gesture. As with almost everyone I know, the Government has flatly refused to employ me in any capacity whatever, even as a clerk or a private soldier. But that does not alter one's feelings. Besides, they will be forced to make use of us sooner or later.

If I had to defend my reasons for supporting the war, I believe I could do so. There is no real alternative between resisting Hitler and surrendering to him, and from a Socialist point of view I should say that it is better to resist; in any case I can see no argument for surrender that does not make nonsense of the Republican resistance in Spain, the Chinese resistance to Japan, etc., etc. But I don't pretend that that is the emotional basis of my actions. What I knew in my dream that night was that the long drilling in patriotism which the middle classes go through had done its work, and that once England was in a serious jam it would be impossible for me to sabotage. But let no one mistake the meaning of this. Patriotism has nothing to do with conservatism. It is devotion to something that is changing but is felt to be mystically the same, like the devotion of the ex-White Bolshevik to Russia. To be loyal both to Chamberlain's England and to the England of tomorrow might seem an impossibility, if one did not know it to be an everyday phenomenon. Only revolution can save England, that has been obvious for years, but now the revolution has started, and it may proceed quite quickly if only we can keep Hitler out. Within two years, maybe a year, if only we can hang on, we shall see changes that will surprise the idiots who have no foresight. I dare say the London gutters will have to run with blood. All right, let them, if it is necessary. But when the red militias are billeted in the Ritz I shall still feel that the England I was taught to love so long ago and for such different reasons is somehow persisting.

I grew up in an atmosphere tinged with militarism, and afterwards I spent five boring years within the sound of bugles. To this day it gives me a faint feeling of sacrilege not to stand to attention during "God save the King." That is childish, of course, but I would sooner have had that kind of upbringing than be like the left-wing intellectuals who are so "enlightened" that they cannot understand the most ordinary emotions. It is exactly the people whose hearts have *never* leapt at the sight of a Union Jack who will flinch from revolution when the moment comes. Let anyone compare the poem John Cornford wrote not long before he was killed ("Before the Storming of Huesca") with Sir Henry Newbolt's "There's a breathless hush in the Close tonight." Put aside the technical differences, which are merely a matter of period, and it will be seen that the emotional content of the two poems is almost exactly the same. The young Communist who died heroically in the International Brigade was public school to the core. He had changed his allegiance but not his emotions. What does that prove? Merely the possibility of building a Socialist on the bones of a Blimp, the power of one kind of loyalty to transmute itself into another, the spiritual need for patriotism and the military virtues, for which, however little the boiled rabbits of the Left may like them, no substitute has yet been found.

War-time Diary

May 28 to December 29, 1940

28.5.40: This is the first day on which newspaper posters are definitely discontinued . . . Half of the front page of the early *Star*[1] devoted to news of the Belgian surrender, the other half to news to the effect that the Belgians are holding out and the King is with them. This is presumably due to paper shortage. Nevertheless of the early *Star*'s eight pages, six are devoted to racing.

For days past there has been no real news and little possibility of inferring what is really happening. The seeming possibilities were: *i.* That the French were really about to counterattack from the south. *ii.* That they hoped to do so but that the German bombers were making it impossible to concentrate an army. *iii.* That the forces in the north were confident of being able to hold on and it was thought better not to counterattack till the German attack had spent itself, or *iv.* that the position in the north was in reality hopeless and the forces there could only fight their way south, capitulate, be destroyed entirely or escape by sea, probably losing very heavily in the process. Now only the fourth alternative seems possible. The French communiqués speak of stabilising the line along the Somme and Aisne, as though the forces cut off in the north did not exist. Horrible though it is, I hope the B.E.F.[2] is cut to pieces sooner than capitulate.

People talk a little more of the war, but very little. As always hitherto, it is impossible to overhear any comments on it in pubs, etc. Last night, E.[3] and I went to the pub to hear the 9 o'c news.

The barmaid was not going to have turned it on if we had not asked her, and to all appearances nobody listened.

29.5.40: One has to gather any major news nowadays by means of hints and allusions. The chief sensation last night was that the 9 o'c news was preceded by a cheer-up talk (quite good) by Duff-Cooper,[4] to sugar the pill, and that Churchill said in his speech that he would report again on the situation some time at the beginning of next week, and that the House must prepare itself for "dark and heavy tidings." This presumably means that they are going to attempt a withdrawal, but whether the "dark tidings" means enormous casualties, a surrender of part of the B.E.F., or what, nobody knows. Heard the news between acts at a more or less highbrow play at the Torch Theatre. The audience listened a good deal more attentively than would have been the case in a pub.

E. says the people in the Censorship Department where she works lump all "red" papers together and look on the *Tribune*[5] as being in exactly the same class as the *Daily Worker*.[6] Recently when the *Daily Worker* and *Action*[7] were prohibited from export, one of her fellow-workers asked her, "Do you know this paper, the *Daily Worker* and *Action*?"

Current rumours: That Beaverbrook[8] since his appointment has got 2,000 extra aeroplanes into the air by cutting through bottle-necks. That the air raids, possibly on London, are due to begin in 2 days' time. That Hitler's plan for invading England is to use thousands of speed-boats which can ride over the mine-fields. That there is a terrible shortage of rifles (this from several sources). That the morale of the ordinary German infantry of the line is pitiably low. That at the time of the Norway business the War office were so ill-informed as not even to know that the Norwegian nights are short, and imagined that troops which had to disembark in broad daylight would have the cover of darkness.

30.5.40: The B.E.F. are falling back on Dunkirk. Impossible not only to guess how many may get away, but how many are there. Last night a talk on the radio by a colonel who had come back from Belgium, which unfortunately I did not hear, but which from E.'s account of it contained interpolations put in by the broadcaster himself to let the public know the army had been let down (a) by the French (not counterattacking), and (b) by the military authorities at home, by equipping them badly. No word anywhere in the press of recriminations against the French, and Duff-Cooper's broadcast of two nights ago especially warned against this . . . Today's map looks as if the French contingent in Belgium are sacrificing themselves to let the B.E.F. get away.

Borkenau[9] says England is now definitely in the first stage of revolution. Commenting on this, Connolly[10] related that recently a ship was coming away from northern France with refugees on board and a few ordinary passengers. The refugees were mostly children who were in a terrible state after having been machine-gunned etc., etc. Among the passengers was Lady ————,[11] who tried to push herself to the head of the queue to get on the boat, and when ordered back said indignantly, "Do you know who I am?" The steward answered, "I don't care who you are, you bloody bitch. You can take your turn in the queue." Interesting if true.

Still no evidences of any interest in the war. Yet the by-elections, responses to appeals for men, etc., show what people's feelings are. It is seemingly quite impossible for them to grasp that they are in danger, although there is good reason to think that the invasion of England may be attempted within a few days, and all the papers are saying this. They will grasp nothing until the bombs are dropping. Connolly says they will then panic, but I don't think so.

31.5.40: Last night to see Denis Ogden's play *The Peaceful Inn.* The most fearful tripe. The interesting point was that though the play was cast in 1940, it contained no reference direct or indirect to the war.

Struck by the fewness of the men who even now have been called up. As a rule, looking round the street, it is impossible to see a uniform . . . Barbed wire entanglements are being put up at many strategic points, eg. beside the Charles I statue in Trafalgar Square . . . Have heard on so many sides of the shortage of rifles that I believe it must be true.

1.6.40: Last night to Waterloo and Victoria to see whether I could get any news of [Eric].[12] Quite impossible, of course. The men who have been repatriated have orders not to speak to civilians and are in any case removed from the railway stations as promptly as possible. Actually I saw very few British soldiers, ie. from the B.E.F., but great numbers of Belgian or French refugees, a few Belgian or French soldiers, and some sailors, including a few naval men. The refugees seemed mostly middling people of the shop-keeper-clerk type, and were in quite good trim, with a certain amount of personal belongings. One family had a parrot in a huge cage. One refugee woman was crying, or nearly so, but most seemed only bewildered by the crowds and the general strangeness. A considerable crowd was watching at Victoria and had to be held back by the police to let the refugees and others get to the street. The refugees were greeted in silence but all sailors of any description enthusiastically cheered. A naval officer in a uniform that had been in the water and parts of a soldier's equipment hurried towards a bus, smiling and touching his tin hat to either side as the women shouted at him and clapped him on the shoulder.

Saw a company of Marines marching through the station to entrain for Chatham. Was amazed by their splendid physique and bearing, the tremendous stamp of boots and the superb carriage of the officers, all taking me back to 1914, when all soldiers seemed like giants to me.

This morning's papers claim variously four-fifths and three-quarters of the B.E.F. already removed. Photos, probably selected or faked, show the men in good trim with their equipment fairly intact.

2.6.40: Impossible to tell how many men of the B.E.F. have really been repatriated, but statements appearing in various papers suggest that it is about 150,000 and that the number that originally advanced into Belgium was about 300,000. No indication as to how many French troops were with them. There are hints in several papers that it may be intended to hang onto Dunkirk instead of evacuating it completely. This would seem quite impossible without tying down a great number of aeroplanes to that one spot. But if 150,000 have really been removed, it will presumably be possible to remove large numbers more. Italy's entry into the war is now predicted at any time after June 4th, presumably with some kind of peace offer to give it a pretext. . . . . . General expectation that some attempt will now be made to invade England, if only as a diversion while Germany and Italy endeavour to polish off France. . . . The possibility of a landing in Ireland is evidently believed in by many people including de Valera.[13] This idea has barely been mentioned until the last few days, although it was an obvious one from the start.

The usual Sunday crowds drifting to and fro, perambulators, cycling clubs, people exercising dogs, knots of young men loitering at street corners, with not an indication in any face or in anything that one can overhear that these people grasp that they are likely to be invaded within a few weeks, though today all the Sunday papers are telling them so. The response to renewed appeals for evacuation of children from London has been very poor. Evidently the reasoning is, "The air raids didn't happen last time, so they won't happen this time." Yet these people will behave bravely enough when the time comes, if only they are told what to do.

Rough analysis of advertisements in today's issue of the *People:*[14]—

Paper consists of 12 pages—84 columns. Of this, just about 26½ columns (over ¼) is advertisements. These are divided up as follows:

Food and drink: 5¼ columns.

Patent medicines: 9 and a third.

Tobacco: 1.

Gambling: 2 and a third.

Clothes: 1½.

Miscellaneous: 6¾.

Of 9 food and drink adverts., 6 are for unnecessary luxuries. Of 29 adverts. for medicines, 19 are for things which are either fraudulent (baldness cured etc.), more or less deleterious (Kruschen Salts, Bile Beans etc.), or of the blackmail type ("Your child's stomach needs magnesia"). Benefit of doubt has been allowed in the case of a few medicines. Of 14 miscellaneous adverts., 4 are for soap, 1 for cosmetics, 1 for a holiday resort and 2 are government advertisements, including a large one for national savings. Only 3 adverts. in all classes are cashing in on the war.

3.6.40: From a letter from Lady Oxford[15] to the *Daily Telegraph,* on the subject of war economies:

"Since most London houses are deserted there is little entertaining . . . in any case, most people have to part with their cooks and live in hotels."

Apparently nothing will ever teach these people that the other 99% of the population exist.

6.6.40: Both Borkenau and I considered that Hitler was likely to make his next attack on France, not England, and as it turns out we were right. Borkenau considers that the Dunkirk business has proved once for all that aeroplanes cannot defeat warships if the latter have planes of their own. The figures given out were 6 destroyers and about 25 boats of other kinds lost in the evacuation of nearly 350,000 men. The number of men evacuated is presumably truthful, and even if one doubled the number of ships lost[16] it would not be a great loss for such a large undertaking, considering that the circumstances were about as favourable to the aeroplanes as they could well be.

Borkenau thinks Hitler's plan is to knock out France and demand the French fleet as part of the peace terms. After that the invasion of England with sea-borne troops might be feasible.

Huge advert. on the side of a bus: "FIRST AID IN WARTIME. FOR HEALTH, STRENGTH AND FORTITUDE. WRIGLEY'S CHEWING GUM."

7.6.40: Although newspaper posters are now suppressed,[17] one fairly frequently sees the paper-sellers displaying a poster. It appears that old ones are resuscitated and used, and ones with captions like "R.A.F. raids on Germany" or "Enormous German losses" can be used at almost all times.

8.6.40: In the middle of a fearful battle in which, I suppose, thousands of men are being killed every day, one has the impression that there is no news. The evening papers are the same as the morning ones, the morning ones are the same as those of the night before, and the radio repeats what is in the papers. As to truthfulness of news, however, there is probably more suppression than downright lying. Borkenau considers that the effect of the radio has been to make war comparatively truthful, and that the only large-scale lying hitherto has been the German claims of British ships sunk. These have certainly been fantastic. Recently one of the evening papers which had made a note of the German announcements pointed out that in about 10 days the Germans claimed to have sunk 25 capital ships, ie. 10 more than we ever possessed.

Stephen Spender said to me recently, "Don't you feel that any time during the past ten years you have been able to foretell events better than, say, the Cabinet?" I had to agree to this. Partly it is a question of not being blinded by class interests etc., eg. anyone not financially interested could see at a glance the strategic danger to England of letting Germany and Italy dominate Spain, whereas many rightwingers, even professional soldiers, simply could not grasp this most obvious fact. But where I feel that people like us understand the situation better than so-called experts is not in any power to foretell specific events, but in the power to grasp what *kind* of world we are living in. At any rate I have known since about 1931 (Spender says he has known since 1929) that the future must be catastrophic. I could not say exactly what wars and revolutions would happen, but they never surprised me when they came. Since 1934 I have known war between England and Germany was coming, and since 1936 I have known it with complete certainty. I could feel it in my belly, and the chatter of the pacifists on the one hand, and the Popular Front people who pretended to fear that Britain was preparing for war against Russia on the other, never deceived me. Similarly such horrors as the Russian purges never surprised me, because I had always felt that—not *exactly* that, but something *like* that—was implicit in Bolshevik rule. I could feel it in their literature.

. . . . Who would have believed seven years ago that Winston Churchill had any kind of political future before him? A year ago Cripps[18] was the naughty boy of the Labour Party, who expelled him and refused even to hear his defence. On the other hand, from the Conservative point of view he was a dangerous Red. Now he is ambassador in Moscow, the Beaverbrook press having led the cry for his appointment. Impossible to say yet whether he is the right man. If the Russians are disposed to come round to our side, he probably is, but if they are still hostile, it would have been better to send a man who does not admire the Russian régime.

10.6.40: Have just heard, though it is not in the papers, that Italy has declared war. . . . The allied troops are withdrawing from Norway, the reason given being that they can be used elsewhere and Narvik after its capture was rendered useless to the Germans. But in fact Narvik will not be necessary to them till the winter, it wouldn't have been much use anyway when Norway had ceased to be neutral, and I shouldn't have thought the allies had enough troops in Norway to make much difference. The real reason is probably so as not to have to waste warships.

This afternoon I remembered very vividly that incident with the taxi-driver in Paris in 1936, and was going to have written something about it in this diary. But now I feel so saddened that I can't write it. Everything is disintegrating. It makes me writhe to be writing book-reviews etc. at such a time, and even angers me that such time-wasting should still be permitted. The interview at the War Office on Saturday *may* come to something, if I am clever at faking my way past the doctor. If once in the army, I know by the analogy of the Spanish war that I shall cease to care about public events. At present I feel as I felt in 1936 when the Fascists were closing in on Madrid, only far worse. But I will write about the taxi driver some time.[19]

12.6.40: E. and I last night walked through Soho to see whether the damage to Italian shops etc. was as reported. It seemed to have been exaggerated in the newspapers, but we did see, I think,

3 shops which had had their windows smashed. The majority had hurriedly labelled themselves "British." Gennari's, the Italian grocer's, was plastered all over with printed placards saying "This establishment is entirely British." The Spaghetti House, a shop specialising in Italian foodstuffs, had renamed itself "British Food Shop." Another shop proclaimed itself Swiss, and even a French restaurant had labelled itself British. The interesting thing is that all these placards must evidently have been printed beforehand and kept in readiness.

. . . . Disgusting though these attacks on harmless Italian shopkeepers are, they are an interesting phenomenon, because English people, ie. people of a kind who would be likely to loot shops, don't as a rule take a spontaneous interest in foreign politics. I don't think there was anything of this kind during the Abyssinian war, and the Spanish war simply did not touch the mass of the people. Nor was there any popular move against the Germans resident in England until the last month or two. The low-down cold-blooded meanness of Mussolini's declaration of war at that moment must have made an impression even on people who as rule barely read the newspapers.

13.6.40: Yesterday to a group conference of the L.D.V.,[20] held in the Committee Room at Lord's. . . . Last time I was at Lord's must have been at the Eton-Harrow match in 1921. At that time I should have felt that to go into the Pavilion, not being a member of the M.C.C.,[21] was on a par with pissing on the altar, and years later would have had some vague idea that it was a legal offence for which you could be prosecuted.

I notice that one of the posters recruiting for the Pioneers, of a foot treading on a swastika with the legend "Step on it," is cribbed from a Government poster of the Spanish war, ie. cribbed as to the idea. Of course it is vulgarised and made comic, but its appearance at any rate shows that the Government are beginning to be willing to learn.

The Communist candidate in the Bow[22] by-election got about 500 votes. This is a new depth-record, though the Blackshirts have often got less (in one case about 150). The more remarkable because Bow was Lansbury's seat[23] and might be expected to contain a lot of pacifists. The whole poll was very low, however.

14.6.40: The Germans are definitely in Paris, one day ahead of schedule. It can be taken as a certainty that Hitler will go to Versailles. Why don't they mine it and blow it up while he is there? Spanish troops have occupied Tangier, obviously with a view to letting the Italians use it as a base. To conquer Spanish Morocco from French Morocco would probably be easy at this date, and to do so, ditto the other Spanish colonies, and set up Negrin[24] or someone of his kind as an alternative government, would be a severe blow at Franco. But even the present British government would never think of doing such a thing. One has almost lost the power of imagining that the Allied governments can ever take the initiative.

Always, as I walk through the Underground stations, sickened by the advertisements, the silly staring faces and strident colours, the general frantic struggle to induce people to waste labour and material by consuming useless luxuries or harmful drugs. How much rubbish this war will sweep away, if only we can hang on throughout the summer. War is simply a reversal of civilised life, its motto is "Evil be thou my good,"[25] and so much of the good of modern life is actually evil that it is questionable whether on balance war does harm.

15.6.40: It has just occurred to me to wonder whether the fall of Paris means the end of the Albatross Library, as I suppose it does.[26] If so, I am £30 to the bad. It seems incredible that people still attach any importance to long-term contracts, stocks and shares, insurance policies etc. in such times as these. The sensible thing to do now would be to borrow money right and left and buy solid goods. A short while back E. made enquiries about the hire-purchase terms for sewing machines and found they had agreements stretching over two and a half years.

P.W.[27] related that Unity Mitford,[28] besides having tried to shoot herself while in Germany, is going to have a baby. Whereupon a little man with a creased face, whose name I forget, exclaimed, "The Fuehrer wouldn't do such a thing!"

16.6.40: This morning's papers make it reasonably clear that at any rate until after the presidential election, the U.S.A. will not do anything, ie. will not declare war, which in fact is what matters. For if the U.S.A. is not actually in the war there will never be sufficient control of either business or labour to speed up production of armaments. In the last war this was the case even when the U.S.A. was a belligerent.

It is impossible even yet to decide what to do in the case of German conquest of England. The one thing I will not do is to clear out, at any rate not further than Ireland, supposing that to be feasible. If the fleet is intact and it appears that the war is to be continued from America and the Dominions, then one must remain alive if possible, if necessary in the concentration camp. If the U.S.A. is going to submit to conquest as well, there is nothing for it but to die fighting, but one must above all die *fighting* and have the satisfaction of killing somebody else first.

Talking yesterday to M.,[29] one of the Jewish members of my L.D.V. section, I said that if and when the present crisis passed there would be a revolt in the Conservative party against Churchill and an attempt to force wages down again, etc. He said that in that case there would be revolution, "or at least he hoped so." M. is a manufacturer and I imagine fairly well off.

17.6.40: The French have surrendered. This could be foreseen from last night's broadcast and in fact should have been foreseeable when they failed to defend Paris, the one place where it might have been possible to stop the German tanks. Strategically all turns on the French fleet, of which there is no news yet. . . .

Considerable excitement today over the French surrender, and people everywhere to be heard discussing it. Usual line, "Thank God we've got a navy." A Scottish private, with medals of the last war, partly drunk, making a patriotic speech in a carriage in the Underground, which the other passengers seemed rather to like. Such a rush on evening papers that I had to make four attempts before getting one.

Nowadays, when I write a review, I sit down at the typewriter and type it straight out. Till recently, indeed till six months ago, I never did this and would have said that I could not do it. Virtually all that I wrote was written at least twice, and my books as a whole three times — individual passages as many as five or ten times. It is not really that I have gained in facility, merely that I have ceased to care, so long as the work will pass inspection and bring in a little money. It is a deterioration directly due to the war.

Considerable throng at Canada House, where I went to make enquiries, as G.[30] contemplates sending her child to Canada. Apart from mothers, they are not allowing anyone between 16 and 60 to leave, evidently fearing a panic rush.

20.6.40: Went to the office of the *[New Statesman]*[31] to see what line they are taking about home defence. C.,[32] who is now in reality the big noise there, was rather against the "arm the people" line and said that its dangers outweighed its possible advantages.

If a German invading force finds civilians armed it may commit such barbarities as will cow the people altogether and make everyone anxious to surrender. He said it was dangerous to count on ordinary people being courageous and instanced the case of some riot in Glasgow when a tank was driven round the town and everyone fled in the most cowardly way. The circumstances were different, however, because the people in that case were unarmed and, as always in internal strife, conscious of fighting with ropes round their necks. . . . C. said that he thought Churchill, though a good man up to a point, was incapable of doing the necessary thing and turning this into a revolutionary war, and for that reason shielded Chamberlain and Co. and hesitated to bring the whole nation into the struggle. I don't of course think Churchill sees it in quite the same colours as we do, but I don't think he would jib at any step (eg. equalisation of incomes, independence for India) which he thought necessary for winning the war. Of course it's possible that today's secret session *may* achieve enough to get Chamberlain and Co. out for good. I asked C. what hope he thought there was of this, and he said none at all. But I remember that the day the British began to evacuate Namsos[33] I asked Bevan and Strauss,[34] who had just come from the House, what hope there was of this business unseating Chamberlain, and they also said none at all. Yet a week or so later the new government was formed.[35]

The belief in direct treachery in the higher command is now widespread, enough so to be dangerous. . . . Personally I believe that such conscious treachery as exists is only in the pro-Fascist element of the aristocracy and perhaps in the Army command. Of course the unconscious sabotage and stupidity which have got us into this situation, eg. the idiotic handling of Italy and Spain, is a different matter. R. H.[36] says that private soldiers back from Dunkirk whom he has spoken to all complain of the conduct of their officers, saying that the latter cleared off in cars and left them in the soup, etc., etc. This sort of thing is always said after a defeat and may or may not be true. One could verify it by studying the lists of casualties, if and when they are published in full. But it is not altogether bad that that sort of thing should be said, provided it doesn't lead to sudden panic, because of the absolute need for getting the whole thing onto a new class basis. In the new armies middle-class people are bound to predominate as officers, they did so even, for instance, in the Spanish militias, but it is a question of unblimping. Ditto with the L.D.V. Under the stress of emergency we shall unblimp if we have time, but time is all.[37]

A thought that occurred to me yesterday: how is it that England, with one of the smallest armies in the world, has so many retired colonels?

I notice that all the "left" intellectuals I meet believe that Hitler if he gets here will take the trouble to shoot people like ourselves and will have very extensive lists of undesirables. C.[38] says there is a move on foot to get our police records (no doubt we all have them) at Scotland Yard destroyed. Some hope! The police are the very people who would go over to Hitler once they were certain he had won. Well, if only we can hold out for a few months, in a year's time we shall see red militia billeted in the Ritz,[39] and it would not particularly surprise me to see Churchill or Lloyd George at the head of them.

Thinking always of my island in the Hebrides, which I suppose I shall never possess nor even see. Compton Mackenzie says even now most of the islands are uninhabited (there are 500 of them, only 10 per cent inhabited at normal times), and most have water and a little cultivable land, and goats will live on them. According to R.H., a woman who rented an island in the Hebrides in order to avoid air raids was the first air raid casualty of the war, the R.A.F. dropping a bomb there by mistake. Good if true.

The first air raid of any consequence on Great Britain the night before last. Fourteen killed, seven German aeroplanes claimed shot down. The papers have photos of three wrecked German planes, so possibly the claim is true.

21.6.40: No real news. I see from yesterday's paper that Chiappe[40] has been elected president of the Paris Municipal Council, presumably under German pressure. So much for the claim that Hitler is the friend of the working classes, enemy of plutocracy, etc.

Yesterday the first drill of our platoon of the L.D.V. They were really admirable, only 3 or 4 in the whole lot (about 60 men) who were not old soldiers. Some officers who were there and had, I think, come to scoff were quite impressed.

22.6.40: No real news yet of the German terms to France. They are said to be "so complicated" as to need long discussion. I suppose one may assume that what is really happening is that the Germans on the one side and Pétain[41] and Co. on the other are trying to hammer out a formula that will induce the French commanders in the colonies and the navy to surrender. Hitler has in reality no power over these except through the French government. . . . I think we have all been rather hasty in assuming that Hitler will now invade England, indeed it has been so generally expected that one might almost infer from this that he wouldn't do it. . . . . . If I were him I should march across Spain, seize Gibraltar and then clean up North Africa and Egypt. If the British have a fluid force of say ¼ million men, the proper course would be to transfer it to French Morocco, then suddenly seize Spanish Morocco and hoist the Republican flag. The other Spanish colonies could be mopped up without much trouble. Alas, no hope of any such thing happening.

The Communists are apparently swinging back to an anti-Nazi position. This morning picked up a leaflet denouncing the "betrayal" of France by Pétain and Co., although till a week or two ago these people were almost openly pro-German.

24.6.40: The German armistice terms are much as expected.... What is interesting about the whole thing is the extent to which the traditional pattern of loyalties and honour is breaking down. Pétain, ironically enough, is the originator (at Verdun) of the phrase "ils ne passeront pas," so long an anti-Fascist slogan. Twenty years ago any Frenchman who would have signed such an armistice would have had to be either an extreme leftwinger or an extreme pacifist, and even then there would have been misgivings. Now the people who are virtually changing sides in the middle of the war are the professional patriots. To Pétain, Laval,[42] Flandin[43] and Co. the whole war must have seemed like a lunatic internecine struggle at the moment when your real enemy is waiting to slosh you......
It is therefore practically certain that high-up influences in England are preparing for a similar sell-out, and while eg. ———— is at ———— there is no certainty that they won't succeed even without the invasion of England. The one good thing about the whole business is that the bottom is being knocked out of Hitler's pretence of being the poor man's friend. The people actually willing to do a deal with him are bankers, generals, bishops, kings, big industrialists, etc., etc........ Hitler is the leader of a tremendous counterattack of the capitalist class, which is forming itself into a vast corporation, losing its privileges to some extent in doing so, but still retaining its power over the working class. When it comes to resisting such an attack as this, anyone who is *of* the capitalist class must be treacherous or half-treacherous, and will swallow the most fearful indignities rather than put up a real fight.... Whichever way one looks, whether it is at the wider strategic

aspects or the most petty details of local defence, one sees that any real struggle means revolution. Churchill evidently can't see or won't accept this, so he will have to go. But whether he goes in time to save England from conquest depends on how quickly the people at large can grasp the essentials. What I fear is that they will never move until it is too late.

Strategically, all turns upon hanging on until the winter. . . . By that time, with huge armies of occupation everywhere, food almost certainly running short and the difficulty of forcing the conquered populations to work, Hitler must be in an awkward position. It will be interesting to see whether he rehabilitates the suppressed French Communist party and tries to use it against the working class in northern France as he has used Pétain against the Blimp class.

If the invasion happens and fails, all is well, and we shall have a definitely leftwing government and a conscious movement against the governing class. I think, though, people are in error in imagining that Russia would be more friendly towards us if we had a revolutionary government. After Spain, I cannot help feeling that Russia, i.e. Stalin, must be hostile to any country that is genuinely undergoing revolution. They would be moving in opposite directions. A revolution starts off with wide diffusion of the ideas of liberty, equality, etc. Then comes the growth of an oligarchy which is as much interested in holding onto its privileges as any other governing class. Such an oligarchy must necessarily be hostile to revolutions elsewhere, which inevitably re-awaken the ideas of liberty and equality. This morning's *News-Chronicle* announces that saluting of superior ranks has been re-instituted in the Red Army. A revolutionary army would *start* by abolishing saluting, and this tiny point is symptomatic of the whole situation. Not that saluting and such things are not probably necessary.

Orders to the L.D.V. that *all* revolvers are to be handed over to the police, as they are needed for the army. Clinging to useless weapons like revolvers, when the Germans have submachine guns, is typical of the British army, but I believe the real reason for the order is to prevent weapons getting into "the wrong" hands.

Both E. and G.[44] insistent that I should go to Canada if the worst comes to the worst, in order to stay alive and keep up propaganda. I will go if I have some function, e.g., if the government were transferred to Canada and I had some kind of job, but not as a refugee, nor as an expatriate journalist squealing from a safe distance. There are too many of these exiled "anti-fascists" already. Better to die if necessary, and maybe even as propaganda one's death might achieve more than going abroad and living more or less unwanted on other people's charity. Not that I want to die; I have so much to live for, in spite of poor health and having no children.

Another government leaflet this morning, on treatment of air-raid casualties. The leaflets are getting much better in tone and language, and the broadcasts are also better, especially Duff-Cooper's, which in fact are ideal for anyone down to the £5-a-week level. But there is still nothing in really demotic speech, nothing that will move the poorer working class or even be quite certainly intelligible. Most educated people simply don't realise how little impression abstract words make on the average man. When Acland was sending round his asinine "Manifesto of Plain Men" (written by himself and signed on the dotted line by "plain men" whom he selected) he told me he had the first draft vetted by the Mass Observers, who tried it on working men, and found that the most fantastic misunderstandings arose. . . . . . The first sign that things are really happening in England will be the disappearance of that horrible plummy voice from the radio. Watching in public bars, I have noticed that working men only pay attention to the broadcasts when some bit of demotic speech creeps in. E. however claims, with some truth I think, that uneducated people are often moved by a speech in solemn language which they don't actually understand but feel to be impressive. E.g. Mrs. A.[45] is impressed by Churchill's speeches, though not understanding them word for word.

25.6.40: Last night an air raid warning about 1 a.m. It was a false alarm as regards London, but evidently there was a real raid somewhere. We got up and dressed, but did not go to the shelter. This is what everyone did, i.e. got up and then simply stood about talking, which seems very foolish. But it seems natural to get up when one hears the siren, and then in the absence of gunfire or other excitement one is ashamed to go to the shelter.

I saw in one of yesterday's papers that gas masks are being issued in America, though people have to pay for them. Gas masks are probably useless to the civilian population in England and almost certainly so in America. The issue of them is simply a symbol of national solidarity, the first step towards wearing a uniform. . . . . As soon as war started the carrying or not carrying of a gas mask assumed social and political implications. In the first few days people like myself who refused to carry one were stared at and it was generally assumed that the non-carriers were "left." Then the habit wore off, and the assumption was that a person who carried a gas mask was of the ultra-cautious type, the suburban rate-payer type. With the bad news the habit has revived and I should think 20 per cent now carry them. But you are still a little stared at if you carry one without being in uniform. Until the big raids have happened and it is grasped that the Germans don't, in fact, use gas, the extent to which masks are carried will probably be a pretty good index of the impression the war news is making on the public.

Went this afternoon to the recruiting office to put my name down for the Home Service Battalions. Have to go again on Friday to be medically examined, but as it is for men from 30 to 50 I suppose the standards are low. The man who took my name, etc., was the usual imbecile, an old soldier with medals of the last war, who could barely write. In writing capital letters he more than once actually wrote them upside down.

27.6.40: It appears that the night before last, during the air-raid alarm, many people all over London were woken by the All Clear signal, took that for the warning and went to the shelters and stayed there till morning, waiting for the All Clear. This after ten months of war and God knows how many explanations of the air-raid precautions.

The fact that the government hasn't this time had to do a recruiting campaign has had a deadening effect on propaganda. . . . A striking thing is the absence of any propaganda posters of a general kind, dealing with the struggle against Fascism, etc. If only someone would show the M.O.I.[46] the posters used in the Spanish war, even the Franco ones for that matter. But how can these people possibly rouse the nation *against Fascism* when they themselves are subjectively pro-Fascist and were buttering up Mussolini till almost the moment when Italy entered the war? Butler,[47] answering questions about the Spanish occupation of Tangier, says H.M. Government has "accepted the word" of the Spanish government that the Spaniards are only doing so in order to preserve Tangier's neutrality—this after Falangist demonstrations in Madrid to celebrate the "conquest" of Tangier. . . . This morning's papers publish a "denial" that Hoare[48] in Madrid is asking questions about an armistice. In other words he *is* doing so. Only question—can we get rid of these people in the next few weeks, before it is too late?

The unconscious treacherousness of the British ruling class in what is in effect a class war is too obvious to be worth mentioning. The difficult question is how much *deliberate* treachery exists. . . . . L.M.,[49] who knows or at least has met all these people, says that with individual exceptions like Churchill the entire British aristocracy is utterly corrupt and lacking in the most ordinary patriotism, caring in fact for nothing except preserving their own standards of life. He says that they are also intensely class-conscious and recognise clearly the community of their interests with those of rich people elsewhere. The idea that Mussolini might fall has always been a nightmare to them, he says. Up to date L.M's predictions about the war, made the day it began, have been very correct. He said nothing would happen all the winter, Italy would be treated with great respect and then suddenly come in against us, and the German aim would be to force on England a puppet government through which Hitler could rule Britain without the mass of the public grasping what was happening. . . . . . . The only point where L.M. proved wrong is that like myself he assumed Russia would continue to collaborate with Germany, which now looks as if it may not happen. But then the Russians probably did not expect France to collapse so suddenly. If they can bring it off, Pétain and Co. are working towards the same kind of doublecross against Russia as Russia previously worked against England. It was interesting that at the time of the Russo-German pact nearly everyone assumed that the pact was all to Russia's advantage and that Stalin had in some way "stopped" Hitler, though one had only to look at the map in order to see that this was not so. . . . . In western Europe Communism and left extremism generally are now almost entirely a form of masturbation. People who are in fact without power over events console themselves by pretending that they are in some way controlling events. From the Communist point of view, nothing matters so long as they can persuade themselves that Russia is on top. It now seems doubtful whether the Russians gained much more from the pact than a breathing-space, though they did this much better than we did at Munich. Perhaps England and the U.S.S.R. will be forced into alliance after all, an interesting instance of real interests overriding the most hearty ideological hatred.

The *New Leader*[50] is now talking about the "betrayal" by Pétain and Co. and the "workers' struggle" against Hitler. Presumably they would be in favour of a "workers" resistance if Hitler invaded England. And what will the workers fight with? With weapons. Yet the I.L.P. clamour simultaneously for sabotage in the arms factories. These people live almost entirely in a masturbation fantasy, conditioned by the fact that nothing they say or do will ever influence events, not even the turning-out of a single shell.

28.6.40: Horribly depressed by the way things are turning out. Went this morning for my medical board and was turned down, my grade being C., in which they aren't at present taking any men in any corps. . . . . . What is appalling is the unimaginativeness of a system which can find *no* use for a man who is below the average level of fitness but at least is not an invalid. An army needs an immense amount of clerical work, most of which is done by people who are perfectly healthy and only half-literate. . . . One could forgive the government for failing to employ the intelligentsia, who on the whole are politically unreliable, if they were making any attempt to mobilise the man-power of the nation and change people over from the luxury trades to productive work. This simply isn't happening, as one can see by looking down any street.

The Russians entered Bessarabia to-day. Practically no interest aroused, and the few remarks I could overhear were mildly approving or at least not hostile. Cf. the intense popular anger over the invasion of Finland. I don't think the difference is due to a perception that Finland and Rumania are different propositions. It is probably because of our own desperate straits and the notion that this move may embarrass Hitler—as I believe it must, though evidently sanctioned by him.

29.6.40: The British government has recognised de Gaulle,[51] but apparently in some equivocal manner, i.e. it has not stated that it will not recognise the Pétain government.

One very hopeful thing is that the press is on our side and retains its independence. . . . . But contained in this is the difficulty that the "freedom" of the press really means that it depends on vested interests and largely (through its advertisements) on the luxury trades. Newspapers which would resist direct treachery can't take a strong line about cutting down luxuries when they live by advertising chocolates and silk stockings.

30.6.40: This afternoon a parade in Regent's Park of the L.D.V. of the whole "zone," i.e. 12 platoons of theoretically about 60 men each (actually a little under strength at present). Predominantly old soldiers and, allowing for the dreadful appearance that men drilling in mufti always present, not a bad lot. Perhaps 25 per cent are working class. If that percentage exists in the Regent's Park area, it must be much higher in some others. What I do not yet know is whether there has been any tendency to avoid raising L.D.V. contingents in very poor districts where the whole direction would have to be in working-class hands. At present the whole organisation is in an anomalous and confused state which has many different possibilities. Already people are spontaneously forming

local defence squads and hand-grenades are probably being man-
ufactured by amateurs. The higher-ups are no doubt thoroughly
frightened by these tendencies. . . . The general inspecting the parade was the usual senile imbecile, actually decrepit, and made one
of the most uninspiring speeches I ever heard. The men, however,
very ready to be inspired. Loud cheering at the news that rifles
have arrived at last.

Yesterday the news of Balbo's[52] death was on the posters as
C.[53] and the M.'s[54] and I walked down the street. C. and I thoroughly pleased, C. relating how Balbo and his friends had taken
the chief of the Senussi up in an aeroplane and thrown him out,
and even the M.'s (all but pure pacifists) were not ill-pleased, I
think. E. also delighted. Later in the evening (I spent the night at
Crooms Hill[55]) we found a mouse which had slipped down into
the sink and could not get up the sides. We went to great pains to
make a sort of staircase of boxes of soap flakes, etc., by which it
could climb out, but by this time it was so terrified that it fled
under the lead strip at the edge of the sink and would not move,
even when we left it alone for half an hour or so. In the end E.
gently took it out with her fingers and let it go. This sort of thing
does not matter. . . . . but when I remember how the Thetis[56] disaster upset me, actually to the point of interfering with my appetite, I do think it a dreadful effect of war that one is actually
pleased to hear of an enemy submarine going to the bottom.

1.7.40: Newspapers now reduced to 6 pages, i.e., 3 sheets. Print reduced in size. Rough analysis of to-day's *News-Chronicle:* 6 pages =
48 columns. Of these (excluding small adverts. besides headlines
on front page) 15 columns or nearly one third are adverts. About
1½ columns of this are taken up in notices of situations vacant,
etc., but the greater part of the ad.s are for more or less useless
consumption goods. The financial columns also overlap with the

advertisements, some of the reports of directors' meetings, etc., probably being paid for by the companies themselves.

To-day's *Express* consists of 6 pages = 42 columns, of which 12 are taken up in advertisements.

Rumours in all to-day's papers that Balbo was actually bumped off by his own side, as in the case of General von Fritsch.[57] Nowadays when any eminent person is killed in battle this suggestion inevitably arises. Cases in the Spanish war were Durutti and General Mola.[58] The rumour about Balbo is based on a statement by the R.A.F. that they know nothing about the air-fight in which Balbo is alleged to have been killed. If this is a lie, as it well may be, it is one of the first really good strokes the British propaganda has brought off.

3.7.40: Everywhere a feeling of something near despair among thinking people because of the failure of the government to act and the continuance of dead minds and pro-Fascists in positions of command. Growing recognition that the only thing that would certainly right the situation is an unsuccessful invasion; and coupled with this a growing fear that Hitler won't after all attempt the invasion but will go for Africa and the Near East.

5.7.40: The almost complete lack of British casualties in the action against the French warships at Oran[59] makes it pretty clear that the French seamen must have refused to serve the guns, or at any rate did so without much enthusiasm. . . . In spite of the to-do in the papers about "French fleet out of action," etc., etc., it appears from the list of ships actually given that about half the French navy is not accounted for, and no doubt more than half the submarines. But how many have actually fallen into German or Italian hands, and how many are still on the oceans, there is nothing in the papers to show. . . . . . The frightful outburst of fury by the German radio (if rightly reported, actually calling on the English people to hang Churchill in Trafalgar Square) shows how right it was to make this move.

10.7.40: They have disabled the French battleship Richelieu, which was in Dakar harbour.[60] But no move to seize any of the French West African ports, which no doubt are not strongly held. . . . . According to Vernon Bartlett,[61] the Germans are going to make a peace offer along the lines I foresaw earlier, i.e. England to keep out of Europe but retain the Empire, and the Churchill government to go out and be replaced by one acceptable to Hitler. The presumption is that a faction anxious to agree to this exists in England, and no doubt a shadow cabinet has been formed. It seems almost incredible that anyone should imagine that the mass of the people would tolerate such an arrangement, unless they had been fought to a standstill first. . . . . The Duke of Windsor[62] has been shipped off as Governor of the Bahamas, virtually a sentence of exile. . . . . . The book Gollancz has brought out, *Guilty Men,* the usual "indictment" of the Munich crowd, is selling like hot cakes. According to *Time,* the American Communists are working hand in glove with the local Nazis to prevent American arms getting to England. One can't be sure how much local freedom of action the various Communists have. Till very recently it appeared that they had none. Of late however they have sometimes pursued contradictory policies in different countries. It is possible that they are allowed to abandon the "line" when strict clinging to it would mean extinction.

16.7.40: No real news for some days, except the British government's semi-surrender to Japan, i.e. the agreement to stop sending war supplies along the Burma road for a stated period. This however is not so definite that it could not be revoked by a subsequent

government. F.[63] thinks it is the British government's last effort
(i.e. the last effort of those with investments in Hong Kong, etc.)
to appease Japan, after which they will be driven into definitely
supporting China. It may be so. But what a way to do things—
never to perform a decent action until you are kicked into it and
the rest of the world has ceased to believe that your motives can
possibly be honest.

W.[64] says that the London "left" intelligentsia are now completely defeatist, look on the situation as hopeless and all but wish
for surrender. How easy it ought to have been to foresee, under
their Popular Front bawlings, that they would collapse when the
real show began.

22.7.40: No real news for days past. The principal event of the
moment is the pan-American conference, now just beginning, and
the Russian absorption of the Baltic states, which must be directed
against Germany. Cripps's wife and daughters are going to Moscow,
so evidently he expects a long stay there. Spain is said to be im-
porting oil in large quantities, obviously for German use, and we
are not stopping it. Much hooey in the *News-Chronicle* this morning about Franco desiring to keep out of war, trying to counter
German influence, etc., etc. . . . . . It will be just as I said. Franco
will play up his pretence of being pro-British, this will be used as
a reason for handling Spain gently and allowing imports in any
quantity, and ultimately Franco will come in on the German side.

25.7.40: No news, really. . . . . . Various people who have sent their
children to Canada are already regretting it.[65] . . . . . Casualties, i.e.
fatal ones, from air-raids for last month were given out as about
340. If true, this is substantially less than the number of road
deaths in the same period. . . . The L.D.V, now said to be 1,300,000
strong, is stopping recruiting and is to be renamed the Home

Guard. There are rumours also that those acting as N.C.O's are to be replaced by men from the regular army. This seems to indicate either that the authorities are beginning to take the L.D.V. seriously as a fighting force, or that they are afraid of it.

There are now rumours that Lloyd George[66] is the potential Pétain of England. . . . . . The Italian press makes the same claim and says that L.G's silence proves it true. It is of course fairly easy to imagine L.G. playing this part out of sheer spite and jealousy because he has not been given a job, but much less easy to imagine him collaborating with the Tory clique who would in fact be in favour of such a course.

Constantly, as I walk down the street, I find myself looking up at the windows to see which of them would make good machine-gun nests. D.[67] says it is the same with him.[68]

28.7.40: This evening I saw a heron flying over Baker Street. But this is not so improbable as the thing I saw a week or two ago, i.e., a kestrel killing a sparrow in the middle of Lord's cricket ground. I suppose it is possible that the war, i.e. the diminution of traffic, tends to increase bird life in inner London.

The little man whose name I always forget used to know Joyce,[69] of the split-off Fascist party, commonly credited with being Lord Haw-Haw. He says that Joyce hated Mosley[70] passionately and talked about him in the most unprintable language. Mosley being Hitler's chief supporter in England, it is interesting that he should employ Joyce and not one of Mosley's men. This bears out what Borkenau said, that Hitler does not want a too-strong Fascist party to exist in England. Evidently the motive is always to split, and even to split the splitters. The German press is attacking the Pétain government, with what motive is not absolutely certain, and so also are elements of the French press under German control. Doriot[71] is of course to the fore here. It was a shock to me when the *Sunday Times* also stated that the Germans in Paris are making use of Bergery.[72] But I accept this with caution, knowing how these small dissident Left parties are habitually lied about by the Right and the official Left alike.

8.8.40: The Italian attack on Egypt, or rather on British Somaliland, has begun. No real news yet, but the papers hint that Somaliland can't be held with the troops we have there. The important point is Perim, loss of which would practically close the Red Sea.

H. G. Wells knows Churchill well and says that he is a good man, not mercenary and not even a careerist. He has always lived "like a Russian commissar," "requisitions" his motor cars, etc., but cares nothing about money. But [H. G. Wells] says Churchill has a certain power of shutting his eyes to facts and has the weakness of never wanting to let down a personal friend, which accounts for the non-sacking of various people. [Wells] has already made a considerable row about the persecution of refugees. He considers that the centre of all the sabotage is the War Office. He believes that the jailing of anti-Fascist refugees is a perfectly conscious piece of sabotage based on the knowledge that some of these people are in touch with underground movements in Europe and might at some moment be able to bring about a "Bolshevik" revolution, which from the point of view of the governing class is much worse than defeat. He says that Lord Swinton[73] is the man most to blame. I asked him did he think it was a conscious action on Lord [Swinton]'s part, this being always the hardest thing to decide. He said he believed Lord [Swinton] knows perfectly well what he is doing.

To-night to a lecture with lantern slides by an officer who had been in the Dunkirk campaign. Very bad lecture. He said the Bel-

gians fought well and it was not true that they surrendered without warning (actually they gave three days' warning), but spoke
badly of the French. He had one photograph of a regiment of
Zouaves in full flight after looting houses, one man being dead
drunk on the pavement.

9.8.40: The money situation is becoming completely unbearable. . . . . . . Wrote a long letter to the Income Tax people pointing out that the war had practically put an end to my livelihood
while at the same time the government refused to give me any
kind of job. The fact which is really relevant to a writer's position,
the impossibility of writing books with this nightmare going on,
would have no weight officially. . . . Towards the government I
feel no scruples and would dodge paying the tax if I could. Yet I
would give my life for England readily enough, if I thought it necessary. No one is patriotic about taxes.

No real news for days past. Only air battles, in which, if the reports are true, the British always score heavily. I wish I could talk
to some R.A.F. officer and get some kind of idea whether these reports are truthful.[74]

16.8.40: Things are evidently going badly in Somaliland, which is
the flanking operation in the attack on Egypt. Enormous air battles
over the Channel, with, if the reports are anywhere near the truth,
stupendous German losses. E.g. about 145 were reported shot
down yesterday. . . . . . The people in Inner London could do with
one real raid to teach them how to behave. At present everyone's
behaviour is foolish in the extreme, everything except transport
being held up but no precautions taken. For the first 15 seconds
there is great alarm, blowing of whistles and shouts to children
to go indoors, then people begin to congregate on the streets and

gaze expectantly at the sky. In the daytime people are apparently ashamed to go into the shelters till they hear the bombs.

On Tuesday and Wednesday had two glorious days at Wallington. No newspapers and no mention of the war. They were cutting the oats and we took Marx[75] out both days to help course the rabbits, at which Marx showed unexpected speed. The whole thing took me straight back to my childhood, perhaps the last bit of that kind of life that I shall ever have.

19.8.40: A feature of the air raids is the extreme credulity of almost everyone about damage done to distant places. George M.[76] arrived recently from Newcastle, which is generally believed here to have been seriously smashed about, and told us that the damage there was nothing to signify. On the other hand he arrived expecting to find London knocked to pieces and his first question on arrival was "whether we had had a very bad time." It is easy to see how people as far away as America can believe that London is in flames, England starving, etc., etc. And at the same time all this raises the presumption that our own raids on western Germany are much less damaging than is reported.

20.8.40: The papers are putting as good a face as possible upon the withdrawal from Somaliland, which is nevertheless a serious defeat, the first loss of British territory for centuries . . . It's a pity that the papers (at any rate the *News-Chronicle,* the only one I have seen to-day) are so resolute in treating the news as good. This might have been made the start of another agitation which would have got some more of the duds out of the government.

Complaints among the Home Guards, now that air raids are getting commoner, because sentries have no tin hats. Explanation from Gen. Macnamara, who tells us that the regular army is still short of 300,000 tin hats— this after nearly a year of war.

22.8.40: The Beaverbrook press, compared with the headlines I saw on other papers, seems to be playing down the suggestion that Trotsky's murder was carried out by the G.P.U.[77] In fact today's *Evening Standard,* with several separate items about Trotsky, didn't mention this suggestion. No doubt they still have their eye on Russia and want to placate the Russians at all costs, in spite of Low's cartoons.[78] But under this there may lie a much subtler manoeuvre. The men responsible for the *Standard's* present pro-Russian policy are no doubt shrewd enough to know that a Popular Front "line" is not really the way to secure a Russian alliance. But they also know that the mass of leftish opinion in England still takes it for granted that a full anti-fascist policy is the way to line up Russia on our side. To crack up Russia is therefore a way of pushing public opinion leftward. It is curious that I always attribute these devious motives to other people, being anything but cunning myself and finding it hard to use indirect methods even when I see the need for them.

To-day in Portman Square saw a four-wheeler cab, in quite good trim, with a good horse and a cabman quite of the pre-1914 type.

23.8.40: This morning an air-raid warning about 3 a.m. Got up, looked at the time, then felt unable to do anything and promptly went to sleep again. They are talking of rearranging the alarm system, and they will have to do so if they are to prevent every alarm from costing thousands of pounds in wasted time, lost sleep, etc. The fact that at present the alarm sounds all over a wide area when the German planes are only operating in one part of it, means not only that people are unnecessarily woken up or taken away from work, but that an impression is spread that an air-raid alarm will *always* be false, which is obviously dangerous.

Have got my Home Guard uniform, after 2½ months.

Last night to a lecture by General ———,[79] who is in command of about a quarter of a million men. He said he had been 41 years in the army. Was through the Flanders campaign, and no doubt limogé[80] for incompetence. Dilating on the Home Guard being a static defensive force, he said contemptuously and in a rather marked way that he saw no use in our practising taking cover, "crawling about on our stomachs," etc., etc., evidently as a hit at the Osterley Park training school. Our job, he said, was to die at our posts. Was also great on bayonet practice, and hinted that regular army ranks, saluting, etc., were to be introduced shortly. . . . . These wretched old blimps, so obviously silly and senile, and so degenerate in everything except physical courage, are merely pathetic in themselves, and one would feel rather sorry for them if they were not hanging round our necks like millstones. The attitude of the rank and file at these would-be pep-talks— so anxious to be enthusiastic, so ready to cheer and laugh at the jokes, and yet all the time half feeling that there is something wrong—always strikes me as pathetic. The time has almost arrived when one will only have to jump up on the platform and tell them how they are being wasted and how the war is being lost, and by whom, for them to rise up and shovel the blimps into the dustbin. When I watch them listening to one of these asinine talks, I always remember that passage in Samuel Butler's Notebook about a young calf he once saw eating dung.[81] It could not quite make up its mind whether it liked the stuff or not, and all it needed was some experienced cow to give it a prod with her horn, after which it would have remembered for life that dung is not good to eat.

It occurred to me yesterday, how will the Russian state get on without Trotsky? Or the Communists elsewhere? Probably they will be forced to invent a substitute.

26.8.40: (Greenwich). The raid which occurred on the 24th was the first real raid on London so far as I am concerned, i.e. the first in which I could hear the bombs. We were watching at the front door when the East India docks were hit. No mention of the docks being hit in Sunday's papers, so evidently they do conceal it when important objectives are hit. . . . . It was a loudish bang but not alarming and gave no impression of making the earth tremble, so evidently these are not very large bombs that they are dropping. I remember the two big bombs that dropped near Huesca when I was in the hospital at Monflorite. The first, quite 4 kilometres away, made a terrific roar that shook the houses and sent us all fleeing out of our beds in alarm. Perhaps that was a 2000 lb. bomb[82] and the ones at present being dropped are 500 lb. ones.

They will have to do something very soon about localising alarms. At present millions of people are kept awake or kept away from work every time an aeroplane appears over any part of London.

29.8.40: Air-raid alarms during the last 3 nights have totalled about 16–18 hours for the three nights. . . . . It is perfectly clear that these night raids are intended chiefly as a nuisance, and as long as it is taken for granted that at the sound of the siren everyone must dive for the shelter, Hitler only needs to send his planes over half-a-dozen at a time to hold up work and rob people of sleep to an indefinite extent. However, this idea is already wearing off. . . . For the first time in 20 years I have overheard bus conductors losing their tempers and being rude to passengers. E.g. the other night, a voice out of the darkness: "'Oo's conducting this bus, lady, me or you?" It took me straight back to the end of the last war.

. . . . . . E. and I have paid the minimum of attention to raids and I was honestly under the impression that they did not worry me at all except because of the disorganisation, etc., that they cause. This morning, however, putting in a couple of hours' sleep as I always do when returning from guard duty, I had a very disagreeable dream of a bomb dropping near me and frightening me out of my wits. Cf. the dream I used to have towards the end of our time in Spain, of being on a grass bank with no cover and mortar shells dropping round me.

31.8.40: Air-raid warnings, of which there are now half a dozen or thereabouts every 24 hours, becoming a great bore. Opinion spreading rapidly that one ought simply to disregard the raids except when they are known to be big-scale ones and in one's own area. Of the people strolling in Regent's Park, I should say at least half pay no attention to a raid-warning. . . . . Last night just as we were going to bed, a pretty heavy explosion. Later in the night woken up by a tremendous crash, said to be caused by a bomb in Maida Vale.[83] E. and I merely remarked on the loudness and fell asleep again. Falling asleep, with a vague impression of anti-aircraft guns firing, found myself mentally back in the Spanish war, on one of those nights when you had good straw to sleep on, dry feet, several hours rest ahead of you, and the sound of distant gunfire, which acts as a soporific provided it *is* distant.

1.9.40: Recently bought a forage cap. . . . . It seems that forage caps over size 7 are a great rarity. Evidently they expect all soldiers to have small heads. This tallies with the remark made by some higher-up to R.R.[84] in Paris when he tried to join the army— "Good God, you don't suppose we want intelligent men in the front line, do you?" All the Home Guard uniforms are made with 20-inch necks. . . . . Shops everywhere are beginning to cash in on the Home Guard, khaki shirts, etc., being displayed at fantastic prices with notices "suitable for the Home Guard." Just as in

Barcelona, in the early days when it was fashionable to be in the militia.

3.9.40: Yesterday talking with Mrs. C.,[85] who had recently come back from Cardiff. Raids there have been almost continuous, and finally it was decided that work in the docks must continue, raids or no raids. Almost immediately afterwards a German plane managed to drop a bomb straight into the hold of a ship, and according to Mrs. C. the remains of seven men working there "had to be brought up in pails." Immediately there was a dock strike, after which they had to go back to the practice of taking cover. This is the sort of thing that does not get into the papers. It is now stated on all sides that the casualties in the most recent raids, e.g. at Ramsgate, have been officially minimised, which greatly incenses the locals, who do not like to read about "negligible damage" when 100 people have been killed, etc., etc. Shall be interested to see the figures for casualties for this month, i.e. August. I should say that up to about 2000 a month they would tell the truth, but would cover it up for figures over that.[86]

Michael[87] estimates that in his clothing factory, evidently a small individually-owned affair, time lost in air-raids cost £50 last week.

7.9.40: Air-raid alarms now frequent enough, and lasting long enough, for people habitually to forget whether the alarm is on at the moment, or whether the All Clear has sounded. Noise of bombs and gunfire, except when very close (which probably means within two miles) now accepted as a normal background to sleep or conversation. I have still not heard a bomb go off with the sort of bang that makes you feel you are personally involved.

In Churchill's speech, number killed in air-raids during August given as 1075. Even if truthful, probably a large understatement as it includes only civilian casualties. . . . . The secretiveness officially practised about raids is extraordinary. To-day's papers report that a bomb fell in a square "in central London." Impossible to find out which square it was, though thousands of people must know.

10.9.40: Can't write much of the insanities of the last few days. It is not so much that the bombing is worrying in itself as that the disorganisation of traffic, frequent difficulty of telephoning, shutting of shops whenever there is a raid on, etc., etc., combined with the necessity of getting on with one's ordinary work, wear one out and turn life into a constant scramble to catch up lost time. Herewith a few notes on bombs, etc.:—

I have seen no bomb crater deeper than about 12 feet. One opposite the house at Greenwich was only (interrupted by air raid: continued 11.9.40) about the size of those made in Spain by 15 c.m. shells. In general the noises are formidable but not absolutely shattering like those of the huge bombs I saw dropped at Huesca.[88] Putting "screaming" bombs aside, I have frequently heard the whistle of a bomb—to hear which one must I assume be within at most a mile of it—and then a not overwhelmingly loud explosion. On the whole I conclude that they are using small bombs. Those which did most of the damage in the Old Kent Road[89] had a curiously limited effect. Often a small house would be reduced to a pile of bricks and the house next door to it barely chipped. Ditto with the incendiary bombs, which will sometimes burn the inner part of a house completely out while leaving the front almost intact.

The delayed-action bombs are a great nuisance, but they appear to be successful in locating most of them and getting all the neighbouring people out until the bomb shall have exploded. All over South London, little groups of disconsolate-looking people wandering about with suitcases and bundles, either people who have been rendered homeless or, in more cases, who have been turned out by the authorities because of an unexploded bomb.

Notable bits of damage so far: Tremendous fires in the docks on 7 and 8.9.40, Cheapside on 9.9.40. Bank of England just chipped (bomb crater about 15 feet from wall). Naval college at Greenwich also chipped. Much damage in Holborn. Bomb in Marylebone goods yard.[90] Cinema at Madame Tussauds[91] destroyed. Several other large fires, many gas mains and electric cables burst, much diversion of road traffic, London Bridge and Westminister Bridge being out of use for several days, and enough damage to railway lines to slow down rail traffic for a day or two. Power station somewhere in South London hit, stopping trams for about half a day. Said to be very heavy damage in Woolwich,[92] and, to judge by the column of flame and smoke, one or more of the big oil drums in the estuary of the Thames was hit on 7.9.40. Deliveries of milk and letters delayed to some extent, newspapers mostly coming out a few hours late, all theatres (except the Criterion,[93] which is underground) closed at 10.9.40, and I think all cinemas as well.

Most of last night in the public shelter, having been driven there by recurrent whistle and crash of bombs not very far away at intervals of about a quarter of an hour. Frightful discomfort owing to overcrowding, though the place was well-appointed, with electric light and fans. People, mostly elderly working class, grousing bitterly about the hardness of the seats and the longness of the night, but no defeatist talk. . . . . . People are now to be seen every night about dusk queuing up at the doors of the Shelters with their bedding. Those who come in first grab places on the floor and probably pass a reasonably good night. Day raids apart, the raiding hours are pretty regularly 8 p.m. to 4.30 a.m., i.e. dusk to just before dawn.

I should think 3 months of continuous raids at the same intensity as the last 4 nights would break down everyone's morale. But it is doubtful whether anyone could keep up the attack on such a scale for 3 months, especially when he is suffering much the same himself.

12.9.40: As soon as the air-raids began seriously it was noticeable that people were much readier than before to talk to strangers in the street. . . . . This morning met a youth of about 20, in dirty overalls, perhaps a garage hand. Very embittered and defeatist about the war, and horrified by the destruction he had seen in South London. He said that Churchill had visited the bombed area near the Elephant[94] and at a spot where 20 out of 22 houses had been destroyed, remarked that it was "not so bad." The youth: "I'd have wrung his bloody neck if he'd said it to me." He was pessimistic about the war, considered Hitler was sure to win and would reduce London to much the same state as Warsaw. He spoke bitterly about the people rendered homeless in South London and eagerly took up my point when I said the empty houses in the West End should be requisitioned for them. He considered that all wars were fought for the profit of the rich, but agreed with me that this one would probably end in revolution. With all this he was not unpatriotic. Part of his grouch was that he had tried to join the Air Force 4 times in the last 6 months, and always been put off.

To-night and last night they have been trying the new device of keeping up a continuous A.A. barrage, apparently firing blind or merely by sound, though I suppose there is some kind of sound-detector which estimates the height at which they must make the shells burst. . . . . . The noise is tremendous and almost continuous, but I don't mind it, feeling it to be on my side. Spent last night at S's place[95] with a battery firing in the square at short intervals throughout the night. Slept through it easily enough, no bombs being audible in that place.

The havoc in the East End and South London is terrible, by

all accounts. . . . . . . Churchill's speech last night referred very seriously to danger of imminent invasion. If invasion is actually attempted and this is not a feint, the idea is presumably either to knock out our air bases along the South Coast, after which the ground defences can be well bombed, at the same time causing all possible confusion in London and its southward communications, *or* to draw as much as possible of our defensive forces south before delivering the attack on Scotland or possibly Ireland.

Meanwhile our platoon of Home Guards, after 3½ months, have about 1 rifle for 6 men, no other weapons except incendiary bombs, and perhaps 1 uniform for 4 men. After all, they have stood out against letting the rifles be taken home by individual men.[96] They are all parked in one place, where a bomb may destroy the whole lot of them any night.

14.9.40: On the first night of the barrage,[97] which was the heaviest, they are said to have fired 500,000 shells, i.e. at an average cost of £5 per shell, £2½ millions worth. But well worth it, for the effect on morale.

15.9.40: This morning, for the first time, saw an aeroplane shot down. It fell slowly out of the clouds, nose foremost, just like a snipe that has been shot high overhead. Terrific jubilation among the people watching, punctuated every now and then by the question, "Are you sure it's a German?" So puzzling are the directions given, and so many the types of aeroplane, that no one even knows which are German planes and which are our own. My only test is that if a bomber is seen over London it must be a German, whereas a fighter is likelier to be ours.

17.9.40: Heavy bombing in this area last night till about 11 p.m. . . . . . . I was talking in the hallway of this house to two young men and a girl who was with them. Psychological attitude of all 3 was interesting. They were quite openly and unashamedly frightened, talking about how their knees were knocking together, etc., and yet at the same time excited and interested, dodging out of doors between bombs to see what was happening and pick up shrapnel splinters. Afterwards in Mrs. C's little reinforced room downstairs, with Mrs. C. and her daughter, the maid, and three young girls who are also lodgers here. All the women, except the maid, screaming in unison, clasping each other and hiding their faces, every time a bomb went past, but betweenwhiles quite happy and normal, with animated conversation proceeding. The dog subdued and obviously frightened, knowing something to be wrong. Marx is also like this during raids, i.e. subdued and uneasy. Some dogs, however, go wild and savage during a raid and have had to be shot. They allege here, and E. says the same thing about Greenwich, that all the dogs in the park now bolt for home when they hear the siren.

Yesterday when having my hair cut in the City, asked the barber if he carried on during raids. He said he did. And even if he was shaving someone? I said. Oh, yes, he carried on just the same. And one day a bomb will drop near enough to make him jump, and he will slice half somebody's face off.

Later, accosted by a man, I should think some kind of commercial traveller, with a bad type of face, while I was waiting for a bus. He began a rambling talk about how he was getting himself and his wife out of London, how his nerves were giving way and he suffered from stomach trouble, etc., etc. I don't know how much of this kind of thing there is. . . . . There has of course been a big exodus from the East End, and every night what amount to mass migrations to places where there is sufficient shelter accommodation. The practice of taking a 2d ticket and spending the night in one of the deep Tube stations, e.g. Piccadilly, is grow-

ing. . . . . . . Everyone I have talked to agrees that the empty furnished houses in the West End should be used for the homeless;
but I suppose the rich swine still have enough pull to prevent this
from happening. The other day 50 people from the East End,
headed by some of the Borough Councillors, marched into the
Savoy and demanded to use the air-raid shelter. The management
didn't succeed in ejecting them till the raid was over, when they
went voluntarily. When you see how the wealthy are *still* behaving, in what is manifestly developing into a revolutionary war, you
think of St. Petersburg in 1916.

(Evening). Almost impossible to write in this infernal racket.
(Electric lights have just gone off. Luckily I have some candles.) So
many streets in (lights on again) the quarter roped off because of
unexploded bombs, that to get home from Baker Street, say 300
yards, is like trying to find your way to the heart of a maze.

21.9.40: Have been unable for some days to buy another volume
to continue this diary because of the three or four stationers' shops
in the immediate neighbourhood, all but one are cordoned off because of unexploded bombs.

Regular features of the time: neatly swept-up piles of glass, lit-
ter of stone and splinters of flint, smell of escaping gas, knots of
sightseers waiting at the cordons.

Yesterday, at the entry to a street near here, a little crowd waiting with an A. R. P.[98] man in a black tin hat among them. A devastating roar, with a huge cloud of dust, etc. The man with the
black hat comes running towards the A. R. P. headquarters, where
another with a white hat is emerging, munching at a mouthful of
bread and butter.

The man with the black hat: "Dorset Square, sir."

The man with the white hat: "O.K." (Makes a tick in his note-book.)

Nondescript people wandering about, having been evacuated

from their houses because of delayed-action bombs. Yesterday two girls stopping me in the street, very elegant in appearance except that their faces were filthily dirty: "Please, sir, can you tell us where we are?"

Withal, huge areas of London almost normal, and everyone quite happy in the daytime, never seeming to think about the coming night, like animals which are unable to foresee the future so long as they have a bit of food and a place in the sun.

24.9.40: Oxford Street yesterday, from Oxford Circus up to the Marble Arch, completely empty of traffic, and only a few pedestrians, with the late afternoon sun shining straight down the empty roadway and glittering on innumerable fragments of broken glass. Outside John Lewis's,[99] a pile of plaster dress models, very pink and realistic, looking so like a pile of corpses that one could have mistaken them for that at a little distance. Just the same sight in Barcelona, only there it was plaster saints from desecrated churches.

Much discussion as to whether you would hear a bomb (i.e. its whistle) which was coming straight at you. All turns upon whether the bomb travels faster than sound. . . . . . . One thing I have worked out, I think satisfactorily, is that the further away from you a bomb falls, the longer the whistle you will hear. The short whizz is therefore the sound that should make you dive for cover. I think this is really the principle one goes on in dodging a shell, but there one seems to know by a kind of instinct.

The aeroplanes come back and come back, every few minutes. It is just like in an eastern country, when you keep thinking you have killed the last mosquito inside your net, and every time, as soon as you have turned the light out, another starts droning.

27.9.40: The *News-Chronicle* to-day is markedly defeatist, as well it may be after yesterday's news about Dakar.[100] But I have a feeling that the *News-Chronicle* is bound to become defeatist anyway and will be promptly to the fore when plausible peace terms come forward. These people have no definable policy and no sense of responsibility, nothing except a traditional dislike of the British ruling class, based ultimately on the Nonconformist conscience. They are only noise-makers, like the *New Statesman,* etc. All these people can be counted on to collapse when the conditions of war become intolerable.

Many bombs last night, though I think none dropped within half a mile of this house. The commotion made by the mere passage of the bomb through the air is astonishing. The whole house shakes, enough to rattle objects on the table. Of course they are dropping very large bombs now. The unexploded one in Regent's Park is said to be "the size of a pillar box." Almost every night the lights go out at least once, not suddenly flicking off as when a connection is broken, but gradually fading out, and usually coming on again in about five minutes. Why it is that the lights dip when a bomb passes close by, nobody seems to know.

15.10.40: Writing this at Wallington, having been more or less ill for about a fortnight with a poisoned arm. Not much news — i.e. only events of worldwide importance; nothing that has much affected me personally.

There are now 11 evacuee children in Wallington (12 arrived, but one ran away and had to be sent home). They come from the East End. One little girl, from Stepney, said that her grand-father had been bombed out seven times. They seem nice children and to be settling down quite well. Nevertheless there are the usual complaints against them in some quarters. E.g. of the little boy who is with Mrs. ———[101], aged seven: "He's a dirty little devil, he is. He wets his bed and dirties his breeches. I'd rub his nose in it if I had charge of him, the dirty, little devil."

Some murmurings about the number of Jews in Baldock. ————[102] declares that Jews greatly predominate among the people sheltering in the Tubes. Must try and verify this.

Potato crop very good this year, in spite of the dry weather, which is just as well.

19.10.40: The unspeakable depression of lighting the fires every morning with papers of a year ago, and getting glimpses of optimistic headlines as they go up in smoke.

21.10.40: With reference to the advertisements in the Tube stations, "Be a Man" etc. (asking able-bodied men not to shelter there but to leave the space for women and children), D.[103] says the joke going round London is that it was a mistake to print these notices in English.

Priestley,[104] whose Sunday night broadcasts were by implication Socialist propaganda, has been shoved off the air, evidently at the instance of the Conservative party. . . . . . It looks rather as though the Margesson[105] crew are now about to stage a comeback.

25.10.40: The other night examined the crowds sheltering in Chancery Lane, Oxford Circus and Baker Street stations. *Not* all Jews, but, I think, a higher proportion of Jews than one would normally see in a crowd of this size. What is bad about Jews is that they are not only conspicuous, but go out of their way to make themselves so. A fearful Jewish woman, a regular comic-paper cartoon of a Jewess, fought her way off the train at Oxford Circus, landing blows on anyone who stood in her way. It took me back to old days on the Paris Métro.

Surprised to find that D., who is distinctly Left in his views, is inclined to share the current feeling against the Jews. He says that the Jews in business circles are turning pro-Hitler, or preparing to do so. This sounds almost incredible, but according to D. they will always admire anyone who kicks them. What I do feel is that any Jew, i.e. European Jew, would prefer Hitler's kind of social system to ours, if it were not that he happens to persecute them. Ditto with almost any Central European, e.g. the refugees. They make use of England as a sanctuary, but they cannot help feeling the profoundest contempt for it. You can see this in their eyes, even when they don't say it outright. The fact is that the insular outlook and the continental outlook are completely incompatible.

According to F.,[106] it is quite true that foreigners are more frightened than English people during the raids. It is not their war, and therefore they have nothing to sustain them. I think this might also account for the fact—I am virtually sure it *is* a fact, though one mustn't mention it—that working-class people are more frightened than middle-class.

The same feeling of despair over impending events in France, Africa, Syria, Spain—the sense of foreseeing what must happen and being powerless to prevent it, and feeling with absolute certainty that a British government *cannot* act in such a way as to get its blow in first.

Air raids much milder the last few days.

16.11.40: I never thought I should live to grow blasé about the sound of gunfire, but so I have.

23.11.40: The day before yesterday lunching with H. P., editor of ————.[107] H. P. rather pessimistic about the war. Thinks there is no answer to the New Order,[108] i.e. this government is incapable of framing any answer, and people here and in America could easily be brought to accept it. I queried whether people would not for certain see any peace offer along these lines as a trap. H. P.: "Hell's bells, I could dress it up so that they'd think it was the greatest victory in the history of the world. I could make them eat it." That is true, of course. All depends on the form in which it is put to people. So long as our own newspapers don't do the dirty they will be quite indifferent to appeals from Europe. H. P., however, is certain that ————[109] and Co. are working for a sell-out. It appears that though ————[110] is not submitted for censorship, all papers are now warned not to publish interpretations of the government's policy towards Spain. A few weeks back Duff-Cooper had the press correspondents up and assured them "on his word of honour" that "things were going very well indeed in Spain." The most one can say is that Duff-Cooper's word of honour is worth more than Hoare's.

H. P. says that when France collapsed there was a Cabinet meeting to decide whether to continue the war or whether to seek terms. The vote was actually 50–50 except for one casting vote, and according to H. P. this was *Chamberlain's*. If true, I wonder whether this will ever be made public. It was poor old Chamberlain's last public act, as one might say, poor old man.

Characteristic war-time sound, in winter: the musical tinkle of raindrops on your tin hat.

28.11.40: Lunching yesterday with C.,[111] editor of *France*. . . . To my surprise he was in good spirits and had no grievances. I would have expected a French refugee to be grumbling endlessly about the food, etc. However, C. knows England well and has lived here before.

He says there is much more resistance both in occupied and unoccupied France than people here realise. The press is playing it down, no doubt because of our continued relations with Vichy. He says that at the time of the French collapse no European looked on it as conceivable that England would go on fighting, and generally speaking Americans did not either. He is evidently

somewhat of an Anglophile and considers the monarchy a great
advantage to England. According to him it has been a main fac-
tor in preventing the establishment of Fascism here. He considers
that the abdication of Edward VIII was brought about because
of Mrs. S.'s[112] known Fascist connections. . . . It is a fact that, on
the whole, anti-Fascist opinion in England was pro-Edward, but
C. is evidently repeating what was current on the continent.

C. was head of the press department during Laval's government.[113] Laval said to him in 1935 that England was now "only an
appearance" and Italy was a really strong country, so that France
must break with England and go in with Italy. On returning from
signing the Franco-Russian pact he said that Stalin was the most
powerful man in Europe. On the whole Laval's prophecies seem
to have been falsified, clever though he is.

Completely conflicting accounts, from eye witnesses, about
the damage to Coventry.[114] It seems impossible to learn the truth
about bombing at a distance. When we have a quiet night here, I
find that many people are faintly uneasy, because feeling certain
that they are getting it badly in the industrial towns. What every
one feels at the back of his mind is that we are now hardened to
it and the morale elsewhere is less reliable.

1.12.40: That bastard Chiappe[115] is cold meat. Everyone delighted,
as when Balbo[116] died. This war is at any rate killing off a few
Fascists.

8.12.40: Broadcasting the night before last. . . . . . Met there a Pole
who has only recently escaped from Poland by some underground
route he would not disclose. . . . . He said that in the siege of
Warsaw 95 per cent of the houses were damaged and about 25 per
cent demolished. All services, electricity, water, etc., broke down,
and towards the end people had no defence whatever against the

aeroplanes and, what was worse, the artillery. He described people rushing out to cut bits off a horse killed by shell-fire, then being driven back by fresh shells, then rushing out again. When Warsaw was completely cut off the people were upheld by the belief that the English were coming to help them, rumours all the while of an English army in Danzig, etc. etc. . . .

The story going round about a week back was that the report in the papers to the effect that the Italian commander in Albania had shot himself was due to a misprint.

During the bad period of the bombing, when everyone was semi-insane, not so much from the bombing itself as from broken sleep, interrupted telephone calls, the difficulty of communications, etc., etc., I found that scraps of nonsense poetry were constantly coming into my mind. They never got beyond a line or two and the tendency stopped when the bombing slacked off, but examples were:—

> An old Rumanian peasant
> Who lived at Mornington Crescent

and

> And the key doesn't fit and the bell doesn't ring,
> But we all stand up for God save the King

and

> When the Borough Surveyor has gone to roost
> On his rod, his pole or his perch.

29.12.40: From a newspaper account of a raid (not ironical): "Bombs were falling like manna."

England Your England[1]

The Lion and the Unicorn:
Socialism and the English Genius
February 19, 1941

i

As I write, highly civilized human beings are flying overhead, trying to kill me.

They do not feel any enmity against me as [an] individual, nor I against them. They are "only doing their duty," as the saying goes. Most of them, I have no doubt, are kind-hearted law-abiding men who would never dream of committing murder in private life. On the other hand, if one of them succeeds in blowing me to pieces with a well-placed bomb, he will never sleep any the worse for it. He is serving his country, which has the power to absolve him from evil.

One cannot see the modern world as it is unless one recognizes the overwhelming strength of patriotism, national loyalty. In certain circumstances it can break down, at certain levels of civilization it does not exist, but as a *positive* force there is nothing to set beside it. Christianity and international Socialism are as weak as straw in comparison with it. Hitler and Mussolini rose to power in their own countries very largely because they could grasp this fact and their opponents could not.

Also, one must admit that the divisions between nation and nation are founded on real differences of outlook. Till recently it was thought proper to pretend that all human beings are very much alike, but in fact anyone able to use his eyes knows that the average of human behaviour differs enormously from country to country. Things that could happen in one country could not happen in another. Hitler's June Purge,[2] for instance, could not have happened in England. And, as western peoples go, the English are very highly differentiated. There is a sort of backhanded admission of this in the dislike which nearly all foreigners feel for our national way of life. Few Europeans can endure living in England, and even Americans often feel more at home in Europe.

When you come back to England from any foreign country, you have immediately the sensation of breathing a different air. Even in the first few minutes dozens of small things conspire to give you this feeling. The beer is bitterer, the coins are heavier, the grass is greener, the advertisements are more blatant. The crowds in the big towns, with their mild knobby faces, their bad teeth and gentle manners, are different from a European crowd. Then the vastness of England swallows you up, and you lose for a while your feeling that the whole nation has a single identifiable character. Are there really such things as nations? Are we not 46 million individuals, all different? And the diversity of it, the chaos! The clatter of clogs in the Lancashire mill towns, the to-and-fro of the lorries on the Great North Road, the queues outside the Labour Exchanges, the rattle of pin-tables in the Soho pubs, the old maids biking to Holy Communion through the mists of the autumn mornings—all these are not only fragments, but *characteristic* fragments, of the English scene. How can one make a pattern out of this muddle?

But talk to foreigners, read foreign books or newspapers, and you are brought back to the same thought. Yes, there *is* something distinctive and recognizable in English civilization. It is a culture as individual as that of Spain. It is somehow bound up with solid breakfasts and gloomy Sundays, smoky towns and winding roads, green fields and red pillar-boxes. It has a flavour of its own. Moreover it is continuous, it stretches into the future and the past, there is something in it that persists, as in a living creature. What can

the England of 1940 have in common with the England of 1840?
But then, what have you in common with the child of five whose
photograph your mother keeps on the mantelpiece? Nothing, except that you happen to be the same person.

And above all, it is *your* civilization, it is *you*. However much
you hate it or laugh at it, you will never be happy away from it for
any length of time. The suet puddings and the red pillar-boxes
have entered into your soul. Good or evil, it is yours, you belong
to it, and this side the grave you will never get away from the marks
that it has given you.

Meanwhile England, together with the rest of the world, is
changing. And like everything else it can change only in certain directions, which up to a point can be foreseen. That is not to say
that the future is fixed, merely that certain alternatives are possible and others not. A seed may grow or not grow, but at any rate
a turnip seed never grows into a parsnip. It is therefore of the
deepest importance to try and determine what England *is*, before
guessing what part England *can play* in the huge events that are
happening.

ii

National characteristics are not easy to pin down, and when
pinned down they often turn out to be trivialities or seem to have
no connection with one another. Spaniards are cruel to animals,
Italians can do nothing without making a deafening noise, the Chinese are addicted to gambling. Obviously such things don't matter in themselves. Nevertheless, nothing is causeless, and even the
fact that Englishmen have bad teeth can tell one something about
the realities of English life.

Here are a couple of generalizations about England that would
be accepted by almost all observers. One is that the English are

not gifted artistically. They are not as musical as the Germans or Italians, painting and sculpture have never flourished in England as they have in France. Another is that, as Europeans go, the English are not intellectual. They have a horror of abstract thought, they feel no need for any philosophy or systematic "world-view." Nor is this because they are "practical," as they are so fond of claiming for themselves. One has only to look at their methods of town-planning and water-supply, their obstinate clinging to everything that is out of date and a nuisance, a spelling system that defies analysis and a system of weights and measures that is intelligible only to the compilers of arithmetic books, to see how little they care about mere efficiency. But they have a certain power of acting without taking thought. Their world-famed hypocrisy—their double-faced attitude towards the Empire, for instance — is bound up with this. Also, in moments of supreme crisis the whole nation can suddenly draw together and act upon a species of instinct, really a code of conduct which is understood by almost everyone, though never formulated. The phrase that Hitler coined for the Germans, "a sleep-walking people," would have been better applied to the English. Not that there is anything to be proud of in being a sleep-walker.

But here it is worth noticing a minor English trait which is extremely well marked though not often commented on, and that is a love of flowers. This is one of the first things that one notices when one reaches England from abroad, especially if one is coming from southern Europe. Does it not contradict the English indifference to the arts? Not really, because it is found in people who have no aesthetic feelings whatever. What it does link up with, however, is another English characteristic which is so much a part of us that we barely notice it, and that is the addiction to hobbies and spare-time occupations, the *privateness* of English life. We are a nation of flower-lovers, but also a nation of stamp-collectors, pigeon-fanciers, amateur carpenters, coupon-snippers, darts-players, crossword-puzzle fans. All the culture that is most truly native centres round things which even when they are communal are not official—the pub, the football match, the back garden, the fireside and the "nice cup of tea." The liberty of the individual is still believed in, almost as in the nineteenth century. But this has nothing to do with economic liberty, the right to exploit others for profit. It is the liberty to have a home of your own, to do what you like in your spare time, to choose your own amusements instead of having them chosen for you from above. The most hateful of all names in an English ear is Nosey Parker. It is obvious, of course, that even this purely private liberty is a lost cause. Like all other modern peoples, the English are in process of being numbered, labelled, conscripted, "co-ordinated." But the pull of their impulses is in the other direction, and the kind of regimentation that can be imposed on them will be modified in consequence. No party rallies, no Youth Movements, no coloured shirts, no Jew-baiting or "spontaneous" demonstrations. No Gestapo either, in all probability.

But in all societies the common people must live to some extent *against* the existing order. The genuinely popular culture of England is something that goes on beneath the surface, unofficially and more or less frowned on by the authorities. One thing one notices if one looks directly at the common people, especially in the big towns, is that they are not puritanical. They are inveterate gamblers, drink as much beer as their wages will permit, are devoted to bawdy jokes, and use probably the foulest language in the world. They have to satisfy these tastes in the face of astonishing, hypocritical laws (licensing laws, lottery acts, etc., etc.) which are designed to interfere with everybody but in practice allow everything to happen. Also, the common people are without definite religious belief, and have been so for centuries. The

Anglican Church never had a real hold on them, it was simply a preserve of the landed gentry, and the Nonconformist sects only influenced minorities. And yet they have retained a deep tinge of Christian feeling, while almost forgetting the name of Christ. The power-worship which is the new religion of Europe, and which has infected the English intelligentsia, has never touched the common people. They have never caught up with power politics. The "realism" which is preached in Japanese and Italian newspapers would horrify them. One can learn a good deal about the spirit of England from the comic coloured postcards that you see in the windows of cheap stationers' shops. These things are a sort of diary upon which the English people have unconsciously recorded themselves. Their old-fashioned outlook, their graded snobberies, their mixture of bawdiness and hypocrisy, their extreme gentleness, their deeply moral attitude to life, are all mirrored there.

The gentleness of the English civilization is perhaps its most marked characteristic. You notice it the instant you set foot on English soil. It is a land where the bus conductors are good-tempered and the policemen carry no revolvers. In no country inhabited by white men is it easier to shove people off the pavement. And with this goes something that is always written off by European observers as "decadence" or hypocrisy, the English hatred of war and militarism. It is rooted deep in history, and it is strong in the lower-middle class as well as the working class. Successive wars have shaken it but not destroyed it. Well within living memory it was common for "the redcoats" to be booed at in the street and for the landlords of respectable public-houses to refuse to allow soldiers on the premises. In peace-time, even when there are two million unemployed, it is difficult to fill the ranks of the tiny standing army, which is officered by the county gentry and a specialized stratum of the middle class, and manned by farm labourers and slum proletarians. The mass of the people are without military knowledge or tradition, and their attitude towards war is invariably defensive. No politician could rise to power by promising them conquests or military "glory," no Hymn of Hate has ever made any appeal to them. In the last war the songs which the soldiers made up and sang of their own accord were not vengeful but humorous and mock-defeatist.* The only enemy they ever named was the sergeant-major.

In England all the boasting and flag-wagging, the "Rule Britannia" stuff, is done by small minorities. The patriotism of the common people is not vocal or even conscious. They do not retain among their historical memories the name of a single military victory. English literature, like other literatures, is full of battle-poems, but it is worth noticing that the ones that have won for themselves a kind of popularity are always a tale of disasters and retreats. There is no popular poem about Trafalgar or Waterloo, for instance.[3] Sir John Moore's army at Corunna, fighting a desperate rear-guard action before escaping overseas (just like Dunkirk!) has more appeal than a brilliant victory.[4] The most stirring battle-poem in English is about a brigade of cavalry which charged in the wrong direction. And of the last war, the four names which have really engraved themselves on the popular memory are Mons, Ypres, Gallipoli and Passchendaele, every time a disaster. The names of the great battles that finally broke the German armies are simply unknown to the general public.

The reason why the English anti-militarism disgusts foreign observers is that it ignores the existence of the British Empire. It

---

*For example:

> I don't want to join the bloody Army,
> I don't want to go unto the war;
> I want no more to roam,
> I'd rather stay at home
> Living on the earnings of a whore.

But it was not in that spirit that they fought [Orwell's footnote].

looks like sheer hypocrisy. After all, the English have absorbed a quarter of the earth and held on to it by means of a huge navy. How dare they then turn round and say that war is wicked?

It is quite true that the English are hypocritical about their Empire. In the working class this hypocrisy takes the form of not knowing that the Empire exists. But their dislike of standing armies is a perfectly sound instinct. A navy employs comparatively few people, and it is an external weapon which cannot affect home politics directly. Military dictatorships exist everywhere, but there is no such thing as a naval dictatorship. What English people of nearly all classes loathe from the bottom of their hearts is the swaggering officer type, the jingle of spurs and the crash of boots. Decades before Hitler was ever heard of, the word "Prussian" had much the same significance in England as "Nazi" has to-day. So deep does this feeling go that for a hundred years past the officers of the British army, in peace-time, have always worn civilian clothes when off duty.

One rapid but fairly sure guide to the social atmosphere of a country is the parade-step of its army. A military parade is really a kind of ritual dance, something like a ballet, expressing a certain philosophy of life. The goose-step, for instance, is one of the most horrible sights in the world, far more terrifying than a dive-bomber. It is simply an affirmation of naked power; contained in it, quite consciously and intentionally, is the vision of a boot crashing down on a face. Its ugliness is part of its essence, for what it is saying is "Yes, I *am* ugly, and you daren't laugh at me," like the bully who makes faces at his victim. Why is the goose-step not used in England? There are, heaven knows, plenty of army officers who would be only too glad to introduce some such thing. It is not used because the people in the street would laugh. Beyond a certain point, military display is only possible in countries where the common people dare not laugh at the army. The Italians adopted the goose-step at about the time when Italy passed definitely under German control, and, as one would expect, they do it less well than the Germans. The Vichy government, if it survives, is bound to introduce a stiffer parade-ground discipline into what is left of the French army. In the British army the drill is rigid and complicated, full of memories of the eighteenth century, but without definite swagger; the march is merely a formalized walk. It belongs to a society which is ruled by the sword, no doubt, but a sword which must never be taken out of the scabbard.

And yet the gentleness of English civilization is mixed up with barbarities and anachronisms. Our criminal law is as out of date as the muskets in the Tower. Over against the Nazi Storm Trooper you have got to set that typically English figure, the hanging judge, some gouty old bully with his mind rooted in the nineteenth century, handing out savage sentences. In England people are still hanged by the neck and flogged with the cat o' nine tails. Both of these punishments are obscene as well as cruel, but there has never been any genuinely popular outcry against them. People accept them (and Dartmoor, and Borstal) almost as they accept the weather. They are part of "the law," which is assumed to be unalterable.

Here one comes upon an all-important English trait: the respect for constitutionalism and legality, the belief in "the law" as something above the State and above the individual, something which is cruel and stupid, of course, but at any rate *incorruptible*.

It is not that anyone imagines the law to be just. Everyone knows that there is one law for the rich and another for the poor. But no one accepts the implications of this, everyone takes it for granted that the law, such as it is, will be respected, and feels a sense of outrage when it is not. Remarks like "They can't run me in; I haven't done anything wrong," or "They can't do that; it's against the law," are part of the atmosphere of England. The

professed enemies of society have this feeling as strongly as anyone else. One sees it in prison-books like Wilfred Macartney's
Walls Have Mouths or Jim Phelan's *Jail Journey,* in the solemn idio-
cies that take place at the trials of Conscientious Objectors, in letters to the papers from eminent Marxist professors, pointing out
that this or that is a "miscarriage of British justice." Everyone believes in his heart that the law can be, ought to be, and, on the
whole, will be impartially administered. The totalitarian idea that
there is no such thing as law, there is only power, has never taken
root. Even the intelligentsia have only accepted it in theory.

An illusion can become a half-truth, a mask can alter the expression of a face. The familiar arguments to the effect that·de-
mocracy is "just the same as" or "just as bad as" totalitarianism
never take account of this fact. All such arguments boil down to
saying that half a loaf is the same as no bread. In England such
concepts as justice, liberty and objective truth are still believed in.
They may be illusions, but they are very powerful illusions. The
belief in them influences conduct, national life is different because
of them. In proof of which, look about you. Where are the rub-
ber truncheons, where is the castor oil? The sword is still in the
scabbard, and while it stays there corruption cannot go beyond a
certain point. The English electoral system, for instance, is an all-
but open fraud. In a dozen obvious ways it is gerrymandered in
the interest of the moneyed class. But until some deep change has
occurred in the public mind, it cannot become *completely* corrupt.
You do not arrive at the polling booth to find men with revolvers
telling you which way to vote, nor are the votes miscounted, nor
is there any direct bribery. Even hypocrisy is a powerful safeguard.
The hanging judge, that evil old man in scarlet robe and horsehair
wig, whom nothing short of dynamite will ever teach what century
he is living in, but who will at any rate interpret the law according
to the books and will in no circumstances take a money bribe, is

one of the symbolic figures of England. He is a symbol of the strange mixture of reality and illusion, democracy and privilege, humbug and decency, the subtle network of compromises, by which the nation keeps itself in its familiar shape.

iii

I have spoken all the while of "the nation," "England," "Britain," as though 45 million souls could somehow be treated as a unit. But is not England notoriously two nations, the rich and the poor? Dare one pretend that there is anything in common between people with £100,000 a year and people with £1 a week? And even Welsh and Scottish readers are likely to have been offended because I have used the word "England" oftener than "Britain," as though the whole population dwelt in London and the Home Counties and neither north nor west possessed a culture of its own.

One gets a better view of this question if one considers the minor point first. It is quite true that the so-called races of Britain feel themselves to be very different from one another. A Scotsman, for instance, does not thank you if you call him an Englishman. You can see the hesitation we feel on this point by the fact that we call our islands by no less than six different names, England, Britain, Great Britain, the British Isles, the United Kingdom and, in very exalted moments, Albion. Even the differences between north and south England loom large in our own eyes. But somehow these differences fade away the moment that any two Britons are confronted by a European. It is very rare to meet a foreigner, other than an American, who can distinguish between English and Scots or even English and Irish. To a Frenchman, the Breton and the Auvergnat seem very different beings, and the accent of Marseilles is a stock joke in Paris. Yet we speak of "France" and "the French," recognizing France as an entity, a single civilization, which in fact it is. So also with ourselves. Looked at from the outside, even the cockney and the Yorkshireman have a strong family resemblance.

And even the distinction between rich and poor dwindles somewhat when one regards the nation from the outside. There is no question about the inequality of wealth in England. It is grosser than in any European country, and you have only to look down the nearest street to see it. Economically, England is certainly two nations, if not three or four. But at the same time the vast majority of the people *feel* themselves to be a single nation and are conscious of resembling one another more than they resemble foreigners. Patriotism is usually stronger than class-hatred, and always stronger than any kind of internationalism. Except for a brief moment in 1920 (the "Hands off Russia" movement) the British working class have never thought or acted internationally. For two and a half years they watched their comrades in Spain slowly strangled, and never aided them by even a single strike.* But when their own country (the country of Lord Nuffield[5] and Mr. Montagu Norman[6]) was in danger, their attitude was very different. At the moment when it seemed likely that England might be invaded, Anthony Eden[7] appealed over the radio for Local Defence Volunteers. He got a quarter of a million men in the first twenty-four hours, and another million in the subsequent month. One has only to compare these figures with, for instance, the number of Conscientious Objectors to see how vast is the strength of traditional loyalties compared with new ones.

In England patriotism takes different forms in different classes, but it runs like a connecting thread through nearly all of

*It is true that they aided them to a certain extent with money. Still, the sums raised for the various aid-Spain funds would not equal five per cent of the turnover of the Football Pools during the same period [Orwell's footnote].

them. Only the Europeanized intelligentsia are really immune to
it. As a positive emotion it is stronger in the middle class than in
the upper class—the cheap public schools, for instance, are more
given to patriotic demonstrations than the expensive ones—but
the number of definitely treacherous rich men, the Laval-Quisling[8]
type, is probably very small. In the working class patriotism is profound, but it is unconscious. The working man's heart does not
leap when he sees a Union Jack. But the famous "insularity" and
"xenophobia" of the English is far stronger in the working class
than in the bourgeoisie. In all countries the poor are more national
than the rich, but the English working class are outstanding in
their abhorrence of foreign habits. Even when they are obliged to
live abroad for years they refuse either to accustom themselves to
foreign food or to learn foreign languages. Nearly every Englishman of working-class origin considers it effeminate to pronounce
a foreign word correctly. During the war of 1914–18 the English
working class were in contact with foreigners to an extent that is
rarely possible. The sole result was that they brought back a hatred
of all Europeans, except the Germans, whose courage they admired. In four years on French soil they did not even acquire a lik-
ing for wine. The insularity of the English, their refusal to take
foreigners seriously, is a folly that has to be paid for very heavily
from time to time. But it plays its part in the English *mystique,* and
the intellectuals who have tried to break it down have generally
done more harm than good. At bottom it is the same quality in the
English character that repels the tourist and keeps out the invader.

Here one comes back to two English characteristics that I
pointed out, seemingly rather at random, at the beginning of the
last chapter. One is the lack of artistic ability. This is perhaps another way of saying that the English are outside the European culture. For there is one art in which they have shown plenty of talent,
namely literature. But this is also the only art that cannot cross

frontiers. Literature, especially poetry, and lyric poetry most of all, is a kind of family joke, with little or no value outside its own language-group. Except for Shakespeare, the best English poets are barely known in Europe, even as names. The only poets who are widely read are Byron, who is admired for the wrong reasons, and Oscar Wilde, who is pitied as a victim of English hypocrisy. And linked up with this, though not very obviously, is the lack of philosophical faculty, the absence in nearly all Englishmen of any need for an ordered system of thought or even for the use of logic.

Up to a point, the sense of national unity is a substitute for a "world-view." Just because patriotism is all but universal and not even the rich are uninfluenced by it, there can come moments when the whole nation suddenly swings together and does the same thing, like a herd of cattle facing a wolf. There was such a moment, unmistakably, at the time of the disaster in France. After eight months of vaguely wondering what the war was about, the people suddenly knew what they had got to do: first, to get the army away from Dunkirk, and secondly to prevent invasion. It was like the awakening of a giant. Quick! Danger! The Philistines be upon thee, Samson! And then the swift unanimous action—and then, alas, the prompt relapse into sleep. In a divided nation that would have been exactly the moment for a big peace movement to arise. But does this mean that the instinct of the English will always tell them to do the right thing? Not at all, merely that it will tell them to do the same thing. In the 1931 General Election, for instance, we all did the wrong thing in perfect unison. We were as single-minded as the Gadarene swine. But I honestly doubt whether we can say that we were shoved down the slope against our will.

It follows that British democracy is less of a fraud than it sometimes appears. A foreign observer sees only the huge inequality of wealth, the unfair electoral system, the governing-class control over the Press, the radio and education, and concludes that democracy is simply a polite name for dictatorship. But this ignores the considerable agreement that does unfortunately exist between the leaders and the led. However much one may hate to admit it, it is almost certain that between 1931 and 1940 the National Government represented the will of the mass of the people. It tolerated slums, unemployment and a cowardly foreign policy. Yes, but so did public opinion. It was a stagnant period, and its natural leaders were mediocrities.

In spite of the campaigns of a few thousand left-wingers, it is fairly certain that the bulk of the English people were behind Chamberlain's foreign policy. More, it is fairly certain that the same struggle was going on in Chamberlain's mind as in the minds of ordinary people. His opponents professed to see in him a dark and wily schemer, plotting to sell England to Hitler, but it is far likelier that he was merely a stupid old man doing his best according to his very dim lights. It is difficult otherwise to explain the contradictions of his policy, his failure to grasp any of the courses that were open to him. Like the mass of the people, he did not want to pay the price either of peace or of war. And public opinion was behind him all the while, in policies that were completely incompatible with one another. It was behind him when he went to Munich, when he tried to come to an understanding with Russia, when he gave the guarantee to Poland, when he honoured it, and when he prosecuted the war half-heartedly. Only when the results of his policy became apparent did it turn against him; which is to say that it turned against its own lethargy of the past seven years. Thereupon the people picked a leader nearer to their mood, Churchill, who was at any rate able to grasp that wars are not won without fighting. Later, perhaps, they will pick another leader who can grasp that only Socialist nations can fight effectively.

Do I mean by all this that England is a genuine democracy? No, not even a reader of the *Daily Telegraph*[9] could quite swallow that.

England is the most class-ridden country under the sun. It is a land of snobbery and privilege, ruled largely by the old and silly. But in any calculation about it one has got to take into account its emotional unity, the tendency of nearly all its inhabitants to feel alike and act together in moments of supreme crisis. It is the only great country in Europe that is not obliged to drive hundreds of thousands of its nationals into exile or the concentration camp. At this moment, after a year of war, newspapers and pamphlets abusing the Government, praising the enemy and clamouring for surrender are being sold on the streets, almost without interference. And this is less from a respect for freedom of speech than from a simple perception that these things don't matter. It is safe to let a paper like *Peace News* be sold, because it is certain that ninety-five per cent of the population will never want to read it. The nation is bound together by an invisible chain. At any normal time the ruling class will rob, mismanage, sabotage, lead us into the muck; but let popular opinion really make itself heard, let them get a tug from below that they cannot avoid feeling, and it is difficult for them not to respond. The left-wing writers who denounce the whole of the ruling class as "pro-Fascist" are grossly over-simplifying. Even among the inner clique of politicians who brought us to our present pass, it is doubtful whether there were any *conscious* traitors. The corruption that happens in England is seldom of that kind. Nearly always it is more in the nature of self-deception, of the right hand not knowing what the left hand doeth. And being unconscious, it is limited. One sees this at its most obvious in the English press. Is the English press honest or dishonest? At normal times it is deeply dishonest. All the papers that matter live off their advertisements, and the advertisers exercise an indirect censorship over news. Yet I do not suppose there is one paper in England that can be straightforwardly bribed with hard cash. In the France of the Third Republic all but a very few of the newspapers could notoriously be bought over the counter like so many pounds of cheese. Public life in England has never been *openly* scandalous. It has not reached the pitch of disintegration at which humbug can be dropped.

England is not the jewelled isle of Shakespeare's much-quoted passage, nor is it the inferno depicted by Dr. Goebbels. More than either it resembles a family, a rather stuffy Victorian family, with not many black sheep in it but with all its cupboards bursting with skeletons. It has rich relations who have to be kow-towed to and poor relations who are horribly sat upon, and there is a deep conspiracy of silence about the source of the family income. It is a family in which the young are generally thwarted and most of the power is in the hands of irresponsible uncles and bedridden aunts. Still, it is a family. It has its private language and its common memories, and at the approach of an enemy it closes its ranks. A family with the wrong members in control—that, perhaps, is as near as one can come to describing England in a phrase.

iv

Probably the battle of Waterloo *was* won on the playing-fields of Eton, but the opening battles of all subsequent wars have been lost there. One of the dominant facts in English life during the past three-quarters of a century has been the decay of ability in the ruling class.

In the years between 1920 and 1940 it was happening with the speed of a chemical reaction. Yet at the moment of writing it is still possible to speak of a ruling class. Like the knife which has had two new blades and three new handles, the upper fringe of English society is still almost what it was in the mid-nineteenth century. After 1832 the old landowning aristocracy steadily lost power, but instead of disappearing or becoming a fossil they simply intermarried with the merchants, manufacturers and financiers who had replaced them, and soon turned them into accurate copies of themselves. The wealthy ship-owner or cotton-miller set up for himself an alibi as a country gentleman, while his sons learned the right mannerisms at public schools which had been designed for just that purpose. England was ruled by an aristocracy constantly recruited from parvenus. And considering what energy the self-made men possessed, and considering that they were buying their way into a class which at any rate had a tradition of public service, one might have expected that able rulers could be produced in some such way.

And yet somehow the ruling class decayed, lost its ability, its daring, finally even its ruthlessness, until a time came when stuffed shirts like Eden or Halifax[10] could stand out as men of exceptional talent. As for Baldwin,[11] one could not even dignify him with the name of stuffed shirt. He was simply a hole in the air. The mishandling of England's domestic problems during the nineteen-twenties had been bad enough, but British foreign policy between 1931 and 1939 is one of the wonders of the world. Why? What had happened? What was it that at every decisive moment made every British statesman do the wrong thing with so unerring an instinct?

The underlying fact was that the whole position of the monied class had long ceased to be justifiable. There they sat, at the centre of a vast empire and a world-wide financial network, drawing interest and profits and spending them—on what? It was fair to say that life within the British Empire was in many ways better than life outside it. Still, the Empire was undeveloped, India slept in the Middle Ages, the Dominions lay empty, with foreigners jealously barred out, and even England was full of slums and unemployment. Only half a million people, the people in the country houses, definitely benefited from the existing system. Moreover, the tendency of small businesses to merge together into large ones robbed more and more of the monied class of their function and turned them into mere *owners,* their work being done for them by salaried managers and technicians. For long past there had been in England an entirely functionless class, living on money that was invested they hardly knew where, the "idle rich," the people whose photographs you can look at in the *Tatler* and the *Bystander,*[12] always supposing that you want to. The existence of these people was by any standard unjustifiable. They were simply parasites, less useful to society than his fleas are to a dog.

By 1920 there were many people who were aware of all this. By 1930 millions were aware of it. But the British ruling class obviously could not admit to themselves that their usefulness was at an end. Had they done that they would have had to abdicate. For it was not possible for them to turn themselves into mere bandits, like the American millionaires, consciously clinging to unjust privileges and beating down opposition by bribery and tear-gas bombs. After all, they belonged to a class with a certain tradition, they had been to public schools where the duty of dying for your country, if necessary, is laid down as the first and greatest of the Commandments. They had to *feel* themselves true patriots, even while they plundered their countrymen. Clearly there was only one escape for them—into stupidity. They could keep society in its existing shape only by being *unable* to grasp that any improvement was possible. Difficult though this was, they achieved it, largely by fixing their eyes on the past and refusing to notice the changes that were going on round them.

There is much in England that this explains. It explains the decay of country life, due to the keeping-up of a sham feudalism which drives the more spirited workers off the land. It explains the immobility of the public schools, which have barely altered since the 'eighties of the last century. It explains the military incompetence which has again and again startled the world. Since the 'fifties every war in which England has engaged has started off with a series of disasters, after which the situation has been saved by people comparatively low in the social scale. The higher commanders, drawn from the aristocracy, could never prepare for modern war, because in order to do so they would have had to admit to themselves that the world was changing. They have always clung to obsolete methods and weapons, because they inevitably saw each war as a repetition of the last. Before the Boer War they prepared for the Zulu War, before 1914 for the Boer War, and before the present war for 1914. Even at this moment hundreds of thousands of men in England are being trained with the bayonet, a weapon entirely useless except for opening tins. It is worth noticing that the navy and, latterly, the Air Force, have always been more efficient than the regular army. But the navy is only partially, and the Air Force hardly at all, within the ruling-class orbit.

It must be admitted that so long as things were peaceful the methods of the British ruling class served them well enough. Their own people manifestly tolerated them. However unjustly England might be organized, it was at any rate not torn by class warfare or haunted by secret police. The Empire was peaceful as no area of comparable size has ever been. Throughout its vast extent, nearly a quarter of the earth, there were fewer armed men than would be found necessary by a minor Balkan state. As people to live under, and looking at them merely from a liberal, *negative* standpoint, the British ruling class had their points. They were preferable to the truly modern men, the Nazis and Fascists. But it had long been obvious that they would be helpless against any serious attack from the outside.

They could not struggle against Nazism or Fascism, because they could not understand them. Neither could they have struggled against Communism, if Communism had been a serious force in western Europe. To understand Fascism they would have had to study the theory of Socialism, which would have forced them to realize that the economic system by which they lived was unjust, inefficient and out of date. But it was exactly this fact that they had trained themselves never to face. They dealt with Fascism as the cavalry generals of 1914 dealt with the machine gun—by ignoring it. After years of aggression and massacres, they had grasped only one fact, that Hitler and Mussolini were hostile to Communism. Therefore, it was argued, they *must* be friendly to the British dividend-drawer. Hence the truly frightening spectacle of Conservative M.P.s wildly cheering the news that British ships, bringing food to the Spanish Republican government, had been bombed by Italian aeroplanes. Even when they had begun to grasp that Fascism was dangerous, its essentially revolutionary nature, the huge military effort it was capable of making, the sort of tactics it would use, were quite beyond their comprehension. At the time of the Spanish civil war, anyone with as much political knowledge as can be acquired from a sixpenny pamphlet on Socialism knew that if Franco won, the result would be strategically disastrous for England; and yet generals and admirals who had given their lives to the study of war were unable to grasp this fact. This vein of political ignorance runs right through English official life, through Cabinet ministers, ambassadors, consuls, judges, magistrates, policemen. The policeman who arrests the "Red" does not understand the theories the "Red" is preaching; if he did, his own position as bodyguard of the monied class might seem less pleasant to him. There is reason to think that even military espionage is hopelessly hampered by ignorance of the new economic doctrines and the ramifications of the underground parties.

The British ruling class were not altogether wrong in thinking that Fascism was on their side. It is a fact that any rich man, unless he is a Jew, has less to fear from Fascism than from either Communism or democratic Socialism. One ought never to forget this, for nearly the whole of German and Italian propaganda is designed to cover it up. The natural instinct of men like Simon, Hoare, Chamberlain,[13] etc., was to come to an agreement with Hitler. But—and here the peculiar feature of English life that I have spoken of, the deep sense of national solidarity, comes in—they could only do so by breaking up the Empire and selling their own people into semi-slavery. A truly corrupt class would have done this without hesitation, as in France. But things had not gone that distance in England. Politicians who would make cringing speeches about "the duty of loyalty to our conquerors" are hardly to be found in English public life. Tossed to and fro between their incomes and their principles, it was impossible that men like Chamberlain should do anything but make the worst of both worlds.

One thing that has always shown that the English ruling class are *morally* fairly sound, is that in time of war they are ready enough to get themselves killed. Several dukes, earls and what-not were killed in the recent campaign in Flanders. That could not happen if these people were the cynical scoundrels that they are sometimes declared to be. It is important not to misunderstand their motives, or one cannot predict their actions. What is to be expected of them is not treachery or physical cowardice, but stupidity, unconscious sabotage, an infallible instinct for doing the wrong thing. They are not wicked, or not altogether wicked; they are merely unteachable. Only when their money and power are gone will the younger among them begin to grasp what century they are living in.

v

The stagnation of the Empire in the between-war years affected everyone in England, but it had an especially direct effect upon two important subsections of the middle class. One was the military and imperialist middle class, generally nicknamed the Blimps, and the other the left-wing intelligentsia. These two seemingly hostile types, symbolic opposites—the halfpay colonel with his bull neck and diminutive brain, like a dinosaur, the highbrow with his domed forehead and stalk-like neck—are mentally linked together and constantly interact upon one another; in any case they are born to a considerable extent into the same families.

Thirty years ago the Blimp class was already losing its vitality. The middle-class families celebrated by Kipling, the prolific lowbrow families whose sons officered the army and navy and swarmed over all the waste places of the earth from the Yukon to the Irrawaddy, were dwindling before 1914. The thing that had killed them was the telegraph. In a narrowing world, more and more governed from Whitehall, there was every year less room for individual initiative. Men like Clive, Nelson, Nicholson,[14] Gordon would find no place for themselves in the modern British Empire. By 1920 nearly every inch of the colonial empire was in the grip of Whitehall. Well-meaning, over-civilized men, in dark suits and black felt hats, with neatly-rolled umbrellas crooked over the left forearm, were imposing their constipated view of life on Malaya and Nigeria, Mombasa and Mandalay. The one-time empire-builders were reduced to the status of clerks, buried deeper and deeper under mounds of paper and red tape. In the early 'twenties one could see, all over the Empire, the older officials, who had known more spacious days, writhing impotently under the changes that were happening. From that time onwards it has been next door to impossible to induce young men of spirit to take any part in imperial administration. And what was true of the official world was true also of the commercial. The great monopoly companies swallowed up hosts of petty traders. Instead of going out to trade adventurously in the Indies one went to an office stool in Bombay or Singapore. And life in Bombay or Singapore was actually duller and safer than life in London. Imperialist sentiment remained strong in the middle class, chiefly owing to family tradition, but the job of administering the Empire had ceased to appeal. Few able men went east of Suez if there was any way of avoiding it.

But the general weakening of imperialism, and to some extent of the whole British morale, that took place during the nineteen-thirties, was partly the work of the left-wing intelligentsia, itself a kind of growth that had sprouted from the stagnation of the Empire.

It should be noted that there is now no intelligentsia that is not in some sense "Left." Perhaps the last right-wing intellectual was T. E. Lawrence.[15] Since about 1930 everyone describable as an "intellectual" has lived in a state of chronic discontent with the existing order. Necessarily so, because society as it was constituted had no room for him. In an Empire that was simply stagnant, neither being developed nor falling to pieces, and in an England ruled by people whose chief asset was their stupidity, to be "clever" was to be suspect. If you had the kind of brain that could understand the poems of T. S. Eliot or the theories of Karl Marx, the higher-ups would see to it that you were kept out of any important job. The intellectuals could find a function for themselves only in the literary reviews and the left-wing political parties.

The mentality of the English left-wing intelligentsia can be studied in half a dozen weekly and monthly papers. The immediately striking thing about all these papers is their generally negative, querulous attitude, their complete lack at all times of any constructive suggestion. There is little in them except the irresponsible carping of people who have never been and never expect to be in a position of power. Another marked characteristic is the emotional shallowness of people who live in a world of ideas and have little contact with physical reality. Many intellectuals of the Left were flabbily pacifist up to 1935, shrieked for war against Germany in the years 1935–9, and then promptly cooled off when the war started. It is broadly though not precisely true that the people who were most "anti-Fascist" during the Spanish civil war are most defeatist now. And underlying this is the really important fact about so many of the English intelligentsia—their severance from the common culture of the country.

In intention, at any rate, the English intelligentsia are Europeanized. They take their cookery from Paris and their opinions from Moscow. In the general patriotism of the country they form a sort of island of dissident thought. England is perhaps the only great country whose intellectuals are ashamed of their own nationality. In left-wing circles it is always felt that there is something slightly disgraceful in being an Englishman and that it is a duty to snigger at every English institution, from horse-racing to suet puddings. It is a strange fact, but it is unquestionably true, that almost any English intellectual would feel more ashamed of standing to attention during "God save the King" than of stealing from a poor box. All through the critical years many left-wingers were chipping away at English morale, trying to spread an outlook that was sometimes squashily pacifist, sometimes violently pro-Russian, but always anti-British. It is questionable how much effect this had, but it certainly had some. If the English people suffered for several years a real weakening of morale, so that the Fascist nations judged that they were "decadent" and that it was safe to plunge into war, the intellectual sabotage from the Left was partly responsible. Both the *New Statesman* and the *News-Chronicle* cried out against the Munich settlement, but even they had done something to make it possible. Ten years of systematic Blimp-baiting affected even the Blimps themselves and made it harder than it had been before to get intelligent young men to enter the armed forces. Given the stagnation of the Empire the military middle class must have decayed in any case, but the spread of a shallow Leftism hastened the process.

It is clear that the special position of the English intellectuals during the past ten years, as purely *negative* creatures, mere anti-Blimps, was a by-product of ruling-class stupidity. Society could not use them, and they had not got it in them to see that devotion to one's country implies "for better, for worse." Both Blimps and highbrows took for granted, as though it were a law of nature, the divorce between patriotism and intelligence. If you were a patriot you read *Blackwood's Magazine* and publicly thanked God that you were "not brainy." If you were an intellectual you sniggered at the Union Jack and regarded physical courage as barbarous. It is obvious that this preposterous convention cannot continue. The Bloomsbury highbrow, with his mechanical snigger, is as out of date as the cavalry colonel. A modern nation cannot afford either of them. Patriotism and intelligence will have to come together again. It is the fact that we are fighting a war, and a very peculiar kind of war, that may make this possible.

vi

One of the most important developments in England during the past twenty years has been the upward and downward extension of the middle class. It has happened on such a scale as to make the old classification of society into capitalists, proletarians and petit-bourgeois (small property-owners) almost obsolete.

England is a country in which property and financial power are concentrated in very few hands. Few people in modern England *own* anything at all, except clothes, furniture and possibly a house. The peasantry have long since disappeared, the independent shopkeeper is being destroyed, the small business-man is diminishing in numbers. But at the same time modern industry is so complicated that it cannot get along without great numbers of managers, salesmen, engineers, chemists and technicians of all kinds, drawing fairly large salaries. And these in turn call into being a professional class of doctors, lawyers, teachers, artists, etc., etc. The tendency of advanced capitalism has therefore been to enlarge the middle class and not to wipe it out as it once seemed likely to do.

But much more important than this is the spread of middle-class ideas and habits among the working class. The British working class are now better off in almost all ways than they were thirty years ago. This is partly due to the efforts of the Trade Unions, but partly to the mere advance of physical science. It is not always realized that within rather narrow limits the standard of life of a country can rise without a corresponding rise in real-wages. Up to a point, civilization can lift itself up by its boot-tags. However unjustly society is organized, certain technical advances are bound to benefit the whole community, because certain kinds of goods are necessarily held in common. A millionaire cannot, for example, light the streets for himself while darkening them for other people. Nearly all citizens of civilized countries now enjoy the use of good roads, germ-free water, police protection, free libraries and probably free education of a kind. Public education in England has been meanly starved of money, but it has nevertheless improved, largely owing to the devoted efforts of the teachers, and the habit of reading has become enormously more widespread. To an increasing extent the rich and the poor read the same books, and they also see the same films and listen to the same radio programmes. And the differences in their way of life have been diminished by the mass-production of cheap clothes and improvements in housing. So far as outward appearance goes, the clothes of rich and poor, especially in the case of women, differ far less than they did thirty or even fifteen years ago. As to housing, England still has slums which are a blot on civilization, but much building has been done during the past ten years, largely by the local authorities. The modern Council house, with its bathroom and electric light, is smaller than the stockbroker's villa, but it is recognizably the same kind of house, which the farm labourer's cottage is not. A person who has grown up in a Council housing estate is likely to be—indeed, visibly *is*—more middle class in outlook than a person who has grown up in a slum.

The effect of all this is a general softening of manners. It is enhanced by the fact that modern industrial methods tend always to demand less muscular effort and therefore to leave people with more energy when their day's work is done. Many workers in the light industries are less truly manual labourers than is a doctor or a grocer. In tastes, habits, manners and outlook the working class and the middle class are drawing together. The unjust distinctions remain, but the real differences diminish. The old-style "proletarian"—collarless, unshaven and with muscles warped by heavy labour—still exists, but he is constantly decreasing in numbers; he only predominates in the heavy-industry areas of the north of England.

After 1918 there began to appear something that had never existed in England before: people of indeterminate social class. In 1910 every human being in these islands could be "placed" in an instant by his clothes, manners and accent. That is no longer the case. Above all, it is not the case in the new townships that have developed as a result of cheap motor cars and the southward shift of industry. The place to look for the germs of the future England is in the light-industry areas and along the arterial roads. In Slough, Dagenham, Barnet, Letchworth, Hayes—everywhere, indeed, on the outskirts of great towns—the old pattern is gradually changing into something new. In those vast new wildernesses of glass and brick the sharp distinctions of the older kind of town, with its slums and mansions, or of the country, with its manor-houses and squalid cottages, no longer exist. There are wide gradations of income, but it is the same kind of life that is being lived at different levels, in labour-saving flats or Council houses, along the concrete roads and in the naked democracy of the swimming-pools. It is a rather restless, cultureless life, centring round tinned food, *Picture Post*,[16] the radio and the internal combustion engine. It is a civilization in which children grow up with an intimate knowledge of magnetoes and in complete ignorance of the Bible. To that civilization belong the people who are most at home in and most definitely *of* the modern world, the technicians and the higher-paid skilled workers, the airmen and their mechanics, the radio experts, film producers, popular journalists and industrial chemists. They are the indeterminate stratum at which the older class distinctions are beginning to break down.

This war, unless we are defeated, will wipe out most of the existing class privileges. There are every day fewer people who wish them to continue. Nor need we fear that as the pattern changes life in England will lose its peculiar flavour. The new red cities of Greater London are crude enough, but these things are only the rash that accompanies a change. In whatever shape England emerges from the war, it will be deeply tinged with the characteristics that I have spoken of earlier. The intellectuals who hope

to see it Russianized or Germanized will be disappointed. The
gentleness, the hypocrisy, the thoughtlessness, the reverence for
law and the hatred of uniforms will remain, along with the suet
puddings and the misty skies. It needs some very great disaster,
such as prolonged subjugation by a foreign enemy, to destroy a
national culture. The Stock Exchange will be pulled down, the
horse plough will give way to the tractor, the country houses will
be turned into children's holiday camps, the Eton and Harrow
match will be forgotten, but England will still be England, an everlasting animal stretching into the future and the past, and, like all
living things, having the power to change out of recognition and
yet remain the same.

Dear Doktor Goebbels—Your British Friends Are Feeding Fine!

Daily Express, July 23, 1941

The disappearing raspberry, the invisible egg, and the onions which can be smelled but not seen, are phenomena we are all familiar with. Only because of the deadly harm they are capable of doing to morale are these stale conjuring tricks worth mentioning.

When an article is controlled in price it promptly disappears from the market. Now fruit, fish, eggs, and most vegetables cannot be kept for an indefinite time.

If they suddenly disappear it is a safe bet that they are being sold on the Q.T. at an illegal price, and, in fact, any one with moneyed acquaintances knows very well that they *are* being sold.

Eggs, for instance, are available in large quantities at 4d. each; I am informed that they always figure in the bill as "tinned peas."

Petrol, also, seems easy enough to get if you can pay about twice the proper price for it.

And apart from downright law-breaking, you have only to put your nose inside any smart hotel or restaurant to see the most obvious evasion of the spirit of the food regulations.

The "one dish" rule, for instance, is habitually broken, but the infringement does not count, because the extra dish of meat or fish is renamed hors-d'oeuvres.

In any event the fact that food eaten in restaurants is unrationed favours the man with a large income and abundant spare time. It would be easy for anyone with more than £2,000 a year to live without ever using his ration book.

But does this kind of thing really matter? And if so, why and how does it matter?

It *doesn't* matter because of the extra material consumed. And since this fact is the favourite get-out of selfish people who buy under-the-counter raspberries and use up petrol in going to the races, it is necessary to admit it, and then put it in its place.

The actual wastage of material by the wealthy is negligible because the wealthy consist of very few people.

It is the common people, who are and must be the big consumers of all the commodities, who matter.

If you took away all the extra meat, fish and sugar that find their way into the smart hotels, and divided them among the general population, no appreciable difference would be made.

For that matter, if you taxed all large incomes out of existence, it still would not make much difference to the taxes the rest of us would have to pay.

The common people receive most of the national income, just as they eat most of the food and wear out most of the clothes, because they constitute the enormous majority.

The raspberries now disappearing down favoured throats in Harrogate and Torquay do not have much direct effect on the Battle of the Atlantic.

Therefore, it is argued, what does it matter if there is a certain amount of minor unfairness? Since the food situation as a whole is hardly affected, why shouldn't half a million fortunate people have as good a time as circumstances permit?

This argument is a complete fallacy, because it leaves out of account the effect of envy on morale, on the "we-are-all-in-it-together" feeling which is absolutely necessary in time of war.

There is no way of making war without lowering the general standard of living. The essential act of war is to divert labour from consumption goods to armaments, which means that the common people must eat less, work longer hours, put up with fewer amusements.

And why should they do so — at any rate, how can you expect them to do so — when they have before their eyes a small minority who are suffering no privations whatever?

So long as it is known that the rarer kinds of food are habitually bootlegged, how can you ask people to cut down their milk consumption and be enthusiastic about oatmeal and potatoes?

"War Socialism" can have an important moral effect even when it is of no importance statistically. The few shiploads of oranges that reached England recently are an example.

I wonder how many of those oranges got to the children in the back streets of London. If they had been shared out equally it would only have been a question of one or two oranges apiece for the whole population.

In terms of vitamins it would have made no difference whatever; but it would have given a meaning to the current talk about "equality of sacrifice."

Experience shows that human beings can put up with nearly anything so long as they feel that they are being fairly treated.

The Spanish Republicans put up with hardships which we as yet have hardly dreamed of. For the last year of the civil war the Republican Army was fighting almost without cigarettes: the soldiers put up with it because it was the same for all of them, general and private alike.

And we can do the same, if necessary.

If we are honest we must admit that, air raids apart, the civil population has not had to suffer much hardship — nothing compared with what we went through in 1918, for instance.

It is later, in the moment of crisis, when it may be necessary suddenly to impose the most drastic restrictions of every kind, that our national solidarity will be tested.

If we guard against that moment now, crack down on the Black Market, catch half a dozen food-hogs and petrol-wanglers and give them stiff enough sentences to frighten others of the same kind, prohibit the more blatant kinds of luxury, and, in general, prove that equality of sacrifice is not merely a phrase, we shall be all right.

But at present—and you can test this statement by having a look round the grill-room of any smart hotel, should you succeed in getting past the commissionaires—Dr. Goebbels's endless gibes about "British plutocracy" are hardly needed.

A few score thousand of idle and selfish people are doing his work for him unpaid.

Looking Back on the Spanish War

———

[1942?]

i

First of all the physical memories, the sounds, the smells and the surfaces of things.

It is curious that more vividly than anything that came afterwards in the Spanish War I remember the week of so-called training that we received before being sent to the front—the huge cavalry barracks in Barcelona with its draughty stables and cobbled yards, the icy cold of the pump where one washed, the filthy meals made tolerable by pannikins of wine, the trousered militiawomen chopping firewood, and the roll-call in the early mornings where my prosaic English name made a sort of comic interlude among the resounding Spanish ones, Manuel Gonzalez, Pedro Aguilar, Ramon Fenellosa, Roque Ballaster, Jaime Domenech, Sebastian Viltron, Ramon Nuvo Bosch. I name those particular men because I remember the faces of all of them. Except for two who were mere riff-raff and have doubtless become good Falangists by this time, it is probable that all of them are dead. Two of them I know to be dead. The eldest would have been about twenty-five, the youngest sixteen.

One of the essential experiences of war is never to be able to escape from disgusting smells of human origin. Latrines are an overworked subject in war literature, and I would not mention them if it were not that the latrine in our barracks did its necessary bit towards puncturing my own illusions about the Spanish Civil War.

The Latin type of latrine, at which you have to squat, is bad enough at its best, but these were made of some kind of polished stone so slippery that it was all you could do to keep on your feet. In addition they were always blocked. Now I have plenty of other disgusting things in my memory, but I believe it was these latrines that first brought home to me the thought, so often to recur: "Here we are, soldiers of a revolutionary army, defending Democracy against Fascism, fighting a war which is *about* something, and the detail of our lives is just as sordid and degrading as it could be in prison, let alone in a bourgeois army." Many other things reinforced this impression later; for instance, the boredom and animal hunger of trench life, the squalid intrigues over scraps of food, the mean, nagging quarrels which people exhausted by lack of sleep indulge in.

The essential horror of army life (whoever has been a soldier will know what I mean by the essential horror of army life) is barely affected by the nature of the war you happen to be fighting in. Discipline, for instance, is ultimately the same in all armies. Orders have to be obeyed and enforced by punishment if necessary, the relationship of officer and man has to be the relationship of superior and inferior. The picture of war set forth in books like *All Quiet on the Western Front* is substantially true. Bullets hurt, corpses stink, men under fire are often so frightened that they wet their trousers. It is true that the social background from which an army springs will colour its training, tactics and general efficiency, and also that the consciousness of being in the right can bolster up morale, though this affects the civilian population more than the troops. (People forget that a soldier anywhere near the front line is usually too hungry, or frightened, or cold, or, above all, too tired to bother about the political origins of the war.) But the laws of nature are not suspended for a "red" army any more than for a "white" one. A louse is a louse and a bomb is a bomb, even though the cause you are fighting for happens to be just.

Why is it worth while to point out anything so obvious? Because the bulk of the British and American intelligentsia were manifestly unaware of it then, and are now. Our memories are short nowadays, but look back a bit, dig out the files of *New Masses* or the *Daily Worker,* and just have a look at the romantic war-mongering muck that our left-wingers were spilling at that time. All the stale old phrases! And the unimaginative callousness of it! The sang-froid with which London faced the bombing of Madrid! Here I am not bothering about the counter-propagandists of the Right, the Lunns, Garvins *et hoc genus*; they go without saying. But here were the very people who for twenty years had hooted and jeered at the "glory" of war, at atrocity stories, at patriotism, even at physical courage, coming out with stuff that with the alteration of a few names would have fitted into the *Daily Mail* of 1918. If there was one thing that the British intelligentsia were committed to, it was the debunking version of war, the theory that war is all corpses and latrines and never leads to any good result. Well, the same people who in 1933 sniggered pityingly if you said that in certain circumstances you would fight for your country, in 1937 were denouncing you as a Trotsky-Fascist if you suggested that the stories in *New Masses* about freshly wounded men clamouring to get back into the fighting might be exaggerated. And the Left intelligentsia made their swing-over from "War is hell" to "War is glorious" not only with no sense of incongruity but almost without any intervening stage. Later the bulk of them were to make other transitions equally violent. There must be a quite large number of people, a sort of central core of the intelligentsia, who approved the "King and Country" declaration in 1935, shouted for a "firm line" against Germany in 1937, supported the People's Convention in 1940, and are demanding a Second Front now.[1]

As far as the mass of the people go, the extraordinary swings of opinion which occur nowadays, the emotions which can be turned on and off like a tap, are the result of newspaper and radio hypnosis. In the intelligentsia I should say they result rather from money and mere physical safety. At a given moment they may be "pro-war" or "anti-war," but in either case they have no realistic picture of war in their minds. When they enthused over the Spanish War they knew, of course, that people were being killed and that to be killed is unpleasant, but they did feel that for a soldier in the Spanish Republican Army the experience of war was somehow not degrading. Somehow the latrines stank less, discipline was less irksome. You have only to glance at the *New Statesman* to see that they believed that; exactly similar blah is being written about the Red army at this moment. We have become too civilised to grasp the obvious. For the truth is very simple. To survive you often have to fight, and to fight you have to dirty yourself. War is evil, and it is often the lesser evil. Those who take the sword perish by the sword, and those who don't take the sword perish by smelly diseases. The fact that such a platitude is worth writing down shows what the years of *rentier* capitalism have done to us.

ii

In connection with what I have just said, a footnote on atrocities.

I have little direct evidence about the atrocities in the Spanish Civil War. I know that some were committed by the Republicans, and far more (they are still continuing) by the Fascists. But what impressed me then, and has impressed me ever since, is that atrocities are believed in or disbelieved in solely on grounds of political predilection. Everyone believes in the atrocities of the enemy and disbelieves in those of his own side, without ever bothering to examine the evidence. Recently I drew up a table of atrocities during the period between 1918 and the present, there was never a year when atrocities were not occurring somewhere or other, and there was hardly a single case when the Left and the Right believed in the same stories simultaneously. And stranger yet, at any moment the situation can suddenly reverse itself and yesterday's proved-to-the-hilt atrocity story can become a ridiculous lie, merely because the political landscape has changed.

In the present war we are in the curious situation that our "atrocity campaign" was done largely before the war started, and done mostly by the Left, the people who normally pride themselves on their incredulity. In the same period the Right, the atrocity-mongers of 1914–18, were gazing at Nazi Germany and flatly refusing to see any evil in it. Then as soon as war broke out it was the pro-Nazis of yesterday who were repeating horror-stories, while the anti-Nazis suddenly found themselves doubting whether the Gestapo really existed. Nor was this solely the result of the Russo-German Pact. It was partly because before the war the Left had wrongly believed that Britain and Germany would never fight and were therefore able to be anti-German and anti-British simultaneously; partly also because official war-propaganda, with its disgusting hypocrisy and self-righteousness, always tends to make thinking people sympathise with the enemy. Part of the price we paid for the systematic lying of 1914–18 was the exaggerated pro-German reaction which followed. During the years 1918–33 you were hooted at in left-wing circles if you suggested that Germany bore even a fraction of responsibility for the war. In all the denunciations of Versailles I listened to during those years I don't think I ever once heard the question, "What would have happened if Germany had won?" even mentioned, let alone discussed. So also with atrocities. The truth, it is felt, becomes untruth when your enemy utters it. Recently I noticed that the very people who swallowed any and every horror story about the Japanese in Nanking in 1937 refused to believe exactly the same stories about Hong Kong in 1942. There was even a tendency to feel that the

Nanking atrocities had become, as it were, retrospectively untrue because the British Government now drew attention to them.

But unfortunately the truth about atrocities is far worse than that they are lied about and made into propaganda. The truth is that they happen. The fact often adduced as a reason for scepticism—that the same horror stories come up in war after war—merely makes it rather more likely that these stories are true. Evidently they are widespread fantasies, and war provides an opportunity of putting them into practice. Also, although it has ceased to be fashionable to say so, there is little question that what one may roughly call the "whites" commit far more and worse atrocities than the "reds." There is not the slightest doubt, for instance, about the behaviour of the Japanese in China. Nor is there much doubt about the long tale of Fascist outrages during the last ten years in Europe. The volume of testimony is enormous, and a respectable proportion of it comes from the German press and radio. These things really happened, that is the thing to keep one's eye on. They happened even though Lord Halifax said they happened. The raping and butchering in Chinese cities, the tortures in the cellars of the Gestapo, the elderly Jewish professors flung into cesspools, the machine-gunning of refugees along the Spanish roads—they all happened, and they did not happen any the less because the *Daily Telegraph* has suddenly found out about them when it is five years too late.

iii

Two memories, the first not proving anything in particular, the second, I think, giving one a certain insight into the atmosphere of a revolutionary period.

Early one morning another man and I had gone out to snipe at the Fascists in the trenches outside Huesca. Their line and ours here lay three hundred yards apart, at which range our aged rifles would not shoot accurately, but by sneaking out to a spot about a hundred yards from the Fascist trench you might, if you were lucky, get a shot at someone through a gap in the parapet. Unfortunately the ground between was a flat beetfield with no cover except a few ditches, and it was necessary to go out while it was still dark and return soon after dawn, before the light became too good. This time no Fascists appeared, and we stayed too long and were caught by the dawn. We were in a ditch, but behind us were two hundred yards of flat ground with hardly enough cover for a rabbit. We were still trying to nerve ourselves to make a dash for it when there was an uproar and a blowing of whistles in the Fascist trench. Some of our aeroplanes were coming over. At this moment a man, presumably carrying a message to an officer, jumped out of the trench and ran along the top of the parapet in full view. He was half-dressed and was holding up his trousers with both hands as he ran. I refrained from shooting at him. It is true that I am a poor shot and unlikely to hit a running man at a hundred yards, and also that I was thinking chiefly about getting back to our trench while the Fascists had their attention fixed on the aeroplanes. Still, I did not shoot partly because of that detail about the trousers. I had come here to shoot at "Fascists"; but a man who is holding up his trousers isn't a "Fascist," he is visibly a fellow creature, similar to yourself, and you don't feel like shooting at him.

What does this incident demonstrate? Nothing very much, because it is the kind of thing that happens all the time in all wars. The other is different. I don't suppose that in telling it I can make it moving to you who read it, but I ask you to believe that it is moving to me, as an incident characteristic of the moral atmosphere of a particular moment in time.

One of the recruits who joined us while I was at the barracks was a wild-looking boy from the back streets of Barcelona. He was ragged and barefooted. He was also extremely dark (Arab blood, I dare say), and made gestures you do not usually see a European make; one in particular—the arm outstretched, the palm vertical—was a gesture characteristic of Indians. One day a bundle of cigars, which you could still buy dirt cheap at that time, was stolen out of my bunk. Rather foolishly I reported this to the officer, and one of the scallywags I have already mentioned promptly came forward and said quite untruly that twenty-five pesetas had been stolen from his bunk. For some reason the officer instantly decided that the brown-faced boy must be the thief. They were very hard on stealing in the militia, and in theory people could be shot for it. The wretched boy allowed himself to be led off to the guardroom to be searched. What most struck me was that he barely attempted to protest his innocence. In the fatalism of his attitude you could see the desperate poverty in which he had been bred. The officer ordered him to take his clothes off. With a humility which was horrible to me he stripped himself naked, and his clothes were searched. Of course neither the cigars nor the money were there; in fact he had not stolen them. What was most painful of all was that he seemed no less ashamed after his innocence had been established. That night I took him to the pictures and gave him brandy and chocolate. But that too was horrible— I mean the attempt to wipe out an injury with money. For a few minutes I had half believed him to be a thief, and that could not be wiped out.

Well, a few weeks later, at the front, I had trouble with one of the men in my section. By this time I was a "*cabo*," or corporal, in command of twelve men. It was static warfare, horribly cold, and the chief job was getting sentries to stay awake and at their posts. One day a man suddenly refused to go to a certain post, which he said, quite truly, was exposed to enemy fire. He was a feeble creature, and I seized hold of him and began to drag him towards his post. This roused the feelings of the others against me, for Spaniards, I think, resent being touched more than we do. Instantly I was surrounded by a ring of shouting men: "Fascist! Fascist! Let that man go! This isn't a bourgeois army. Fascist!" etc., etc. As best I could in my bad Spanish I shouted back that orders had got to be obeyed, and the row developed into one of those enormous arguments by means of which discipline is gradually hammered out in revolutionary armies. Some said I was right, others said I was wrong. But the point is that the one who took my side the most warmly of all was the brown-faced boy. As soon as he saw what was happening he sprang into the ring and began passionately defending me. With his strange, wild, Indian gesture he kept exclaiming, "He's the best corporal we've got!" (¡No hay cabo como el!) Later on he applied for leave to exchange into my section.

Why is this incident touching to me? Because in any normal circumstances it would have been impossible for good feelings ever to be re-established between this boy and myself. The implied accusation of theft would not have been made any better, probably somewhat worse, by my efforts to make amends. One of the effects of safe and civilised life is an immense oversensitiveness which makes all the primary emotions seem somewhat disgusting. Generosity is as painful as meanness, gratitude as hateful as ingratitude. But in Spain in 1936 we were not living in a normal time. It was a time when generous feelings and gestures were easier than they ordinarily are. I could relate a dozen similar incidents, not really communicable but bound up in my own mind with the special atmosphere of the time, the shabby clothes and the gay-coloured revolutionary posters, the universal use of the word "comrade," the anti-Fascist ballads printed on flimsy paper and sold for a penny, the phrases like "international proletarian solidarity," pathetically repeated by ignorant men who believed them to mean something. Could you feel friendly towards

somebody, and stick up for him in a quarrel, after you had been ig-
nominiously searched in his presence for property you were supposed to have stolen from him? No, you couldn't; but you might
if you had both been through some emotionally widening experience. That is one of the by-products of revolution, though in this
case it was only the beginnings of a revolution, and obviously fore-
doomed to failure.

iv

The struggle for power between the Spanish Republican parties is
an unhappy, far-off thing which I have no wish to revive at this
date. I only mention it in order to say: believe nothing, or next to
nothing, of what you read about internal affairs on the Government side. It is all, from whatever source, party propaganda—
that is to say, lies. The broad truth about the war is simple enough.
The Spanish bourgeoisie saw their chance of crushing the labour
movement, and took it, aided by the Nazis and by the forces of reaction all over the world. It is doubtful whether more than that
will ever be established.

I remember saying once to Arthur Koestler, "History stopped
in 1936," at which he nodded in immediate understanding. We
were both thinking of totalitarianism in general, but more particularly of the Spanish Civil War. Early in life I had noticed that no
event is ever correctly reported in a newspaper, but in Spain, for
the first time, I saw newspaper reports which did not bear any relation to the facts, not even the relationship which is implied in
an ordinary lie. I saw great battles reported where there had been
no fighting, and complete silence where hundreds of men had
been killed. I saw troops who had fought bravely denounced as
cowards and traitors, and others who had never seen a shot fired
hailed as the heroes of imaginary victories; and I saw newspapers

in London retailing these lies and eager intellectuals building emotional superstructures over events that had never happened. I saw,
in fact, history being written not in terms of what happened but
of what ought to have happened according to various "party
lines." Yet in a way, horrible as all this was, it was unimportant. It
concerned secondary issues—namely, the struggle for power between the Comintern and the Spanish left-wing parties, and the efforts of the Russian Government to prevent revolution in Spain.
But the broad picture of the war which the Spanish Government
presented to the world was not untruthful. The main issues were
what it said they were. But as for the Fascists and their backers,
how could they come even as near to the truth as that? How could
they possibly mention their real aims? Their version of the war
was pure fantasy, and in the circumstances it could not have been
otherwise.

The only propaganda line open to the Nazis and Fascists was
to represent themselves as Christian patriots saving Spain from a
Russian dictatorship. This involved pretending that life in Government Spain was just one long massacre (vide the Catholic Herald
or the Daily Mail—but these were child's play compared with the
continental Fascist press), and it involved immensely exaggerating
the scale of Russian intervention. Out of the huge pyramid of lies
which the Catholic and reactionary press all over the world built
up, let me take just one point—the presence in Spain of a Russian
army. Devout Franco partisans all believed in this; estimates of its
strength went as high as half a million. Now, there was no Russian
army in Spain. There may have been a handful of airmen and other
technicians, a few hundred at the most, but an army there was not.
Some thousands of foreigners who fought in Spain, not to mention
millions of Spaniards, were witnesses of this. Well, their testimony
made no impression at all upon the Franco propagandists, not one
of whom had set foot in Government Spain. Simultaneously these

people refused utterly to admit the fact of German or Italian intervention, at the same time as the German and Italian press were openly boasting about the exploits of their "legionaries." I have chosen to mention only one point, but in fact the whole of Fascist propaganda about the war was on this level.

This kind of thing is frightening to me, because it often gives me the feeling that the very concept of objective truth is fading out of the world. After all, the chances are that those lies, or at any rate similar lies, will pass into history. How will the history of the Spanish War be written? If Franco remains in power his nominees will write the history books, and (to stick to my chosen point) that Russian army which never existed will become historical fact, and schoolchildren will learn about it generations hence. But suppose Fascism is finally defeated and some kind of democratic government restored in Spain in the fairly near future; even then, how is the history of the war to be written? What kind of records will Franco have left behind him? Suppose even that the records kept on the Government side are recoverable — even so, how is a true history of the war to be written? For, as I have pointed out already, the Government also dealt extensively in lies. From the anti-Fascist angle one could write a broadly truthful history of the war, but it would be a partisan history, unreliable on every minor point. Yet, after all, *some* kind of history will be written, and after those who actually remember the war are dead, it will be universally accepted. So for all practical purposes the lie will have become truth.

I know it is the fashion to say that most of recorded history is lies anyway. I am willing to believe that history is for the most part inaccurate and biased, but what is peculiar to our own age is the abandonment of the idea that history *could* be truthfully written. In the past people deliberately lied, or they unconsciously coloured what they wrote, or they struggled after the truth, well knowing that they must make many mistakes; but in each case they believed that "the facts" existed and were more or less discoverable. And in practice there was always a considerable body of fact which would have been agreed to by almost everyone. If you look up the history of the last war in, for instance, the *Encyclopaedia Britannica,* you will find that a respectable amount of the material is drawn from German sources. A British and a German historian would disagree deeply on many things, even on fundamentals, but there would still be that body of, as it were, neutral fact on which neither would seriously challenge the other. It is just this common basis of agreement, with its implication that human beings are all one species of animal, that totalitarianism destroys. Nazi theory indeed specifically denies that such a thing as "the truth" exists. There is, for instance, no such thing as "science." There is only "German science," "Jewish science" etc. The implied objective of this line of thought is a nightmare world in which the Leader, or some ruling clique, controls not only the future but *the past.* If the Leader says of such and such an event, "It never happened"— well, it never happened. If he says that two and two are five— well, two and two are five. This prospect frightens me much more than bombs—and after our experiences of the last few years that is not a frivolous statement.

But is it perhaps childish or morbid to terrify oneself with visions of a totalitarian future? Before writing off the totalitarian world as a nightmare that can't come true, just remember that in 1925 the world of today would have seemed a nightmare that couldn't come true. Against that shifting phantasmagoric world in which black may be white tomorrow and yesterday's weather can be changed by decree, there are in reality only two safeguards. One is that however much you deny the truth, the truth goes on existing, as it were, behind your back, and you consequently can't violate it in ways that impair military efficiency. The other is that so long as some parts of the earth remain unconquered, the liberal tradition can be kept alive. Let Fascism, or possibly even a combination of several Fascisms, conquer the whole world, and those two conditions no longer exist. We in England underrate the danger of this kind of thing, because our traditions and our past security have given us a sentimental belief that it all comes right in the end and the thing you most fear never really happens. Nourished for hundreds of years on a literature in which Right invariably triumphs in the last chapter, we believe half-instinctively that evil always defeats itself in the long run. Pacifism, for instance, is founded largely on this belief. Don't resist evil, and it will somehow destroy itself. But why should it? What evidence is there that it does? And what instance is there of a modern industrialised state collapsing unless conquered from the outside by military force?

Consider for instance the re-institution of slavery. Who could have imagined twenty years ago that slavery would return to Europe? Well, slavery has been restored under our noses. The forced-labour camps all over Europe and North Africa where Poles, Russians, Jews and political prisoners of every race toil at road-making or swamp-draining for their bare rations, are simple chattel slavery. The most one can say is that the buying and selling of slaves by individuals is not yet permitted. In other ways—the breaking-up of families, for instance—the conditions are probably worse than they were on the American cotton plantations. There is no reason for thinking that this state of affairs will change while any totalitarian domination endures. We don't grasp its full implications, because in our mystical way we feel that a régime founded on slavery *must* collapse. But it is worth comparing the duration of the slave empires of antiquity with that of any modern state. Civilisations founded on slavery have lasted for such periods as four thousand years.

When I think of antiquity, the detail that frightens me is that those hundreds of millions of slaves on whose backs civilisation rested generation after generation have left behind them no record whatever. We do not even know their names. In the whole of Greek and Roman history, how many slaves' names are known to you? I can think of two, or possibly three. One is Spartacus and the other is Epictetus. Also, in the Roman room at the British Museum there is a glass jar with the maker's name inscribed on the bottom, "*Felix fecit.*" I have a vivid mental picture of poor Felix (a Gaul with red hair and a metal collar round his neck), but in fact he may not have been a slave; so there are only two slaves whose names I definitely know, and probably few people can remember more. The rest have gone down into utter silence.

V

The backbone of the resistance against Franco was the Spanish working class, especially the urban trade union members. In the long run—it is important to remember that it is only in the long run—the working class remains the most reliable enemy of Fascism, simply because the working class stands to gain most by a decent reconstruction of society. Unlike other classes or categories, it can't be permanently bribed.

To say this is not to idealise the working class. In the long struggle that has followed the Russian Revolution it is the manual workers who have been defeated, and it is impossible not to feel that it was their own fault. Time after time, in country after country, the organised working-class movements have been crushed by open, illegal violence, and their comrades abroad, linked to them in theoretical solidarity, have simply looked on and done nothing; and underneath this, secret cause of many betrayals, has lain the fact that between white and coloured workers there is not even lip-service to solidarity. Who can believe in the class-conscious international proletariat after the events of the past ten years? To the British working class the massacre of their comrades in Vienna, Berlin, Madrid, or wherever it might be, seemed less interesting and less important than yesterday's football match. Yet this does not alter the fact that the working class will go on struggling against Fascism after the others have caved in. One feature of the Nazi conquest of France was the astonishing defections among the intelligentsia, including some of the left-wing political intelligentsia. The intelligentsia are the people who squeal loudest against Fascism, and yet a respectable proportion of them collapse into defeatism when the pinch comes. They are far-sighted enough to see the odds against them, and moreover they can be bribed—for it is evident that the Nazis think it worth while to bribe intellectuals. With the working class it is the other way about. Too ignorant to see through the trick that is being played on them, they easily swallow the promises of Fascism, yet sooner or later they always take up the struggle again. They must do so, because in their own bodies they always discover that the promises of Fascism cannot be fulfilled. To win over the working class permanently, the Fascists would have to raise the general standard of living, which they are unable and probably unwilling to do. The struggle of the working class is like the growth of a plant. The plant is blind and stupid, but it knows enough to keep pushing upwards towards the light, and it will do this in the face of endless discouragements. What are the workers struggling for? Simply for the decent life which they are more and more aware is now technically possible. Their consciousness of this aim ebbs and flows. In Spain, for a while, people were acting consciously, moving towards a goal which they wanted to reach and believed they could reach. It accounted for the curiously buoyant feeling that life in Government Spain had during the early months of the war. The common people knew in their bones that the Republic was their friend and Franco was their enemy. They knew that they were in the right, because they were fighting for something which the world owed them and was able to give them.

One has to remember this to see the Spanish War in its true perspective. When one thinks of the cruelty, squalor, and futility of war—and in this particular case of the intrigues, the persecutions, the lies and the misunderstandings—there is always the temptation to say: "One side is as bad as the other. I am neutral." In practice, however, one cannot be neutral, and there is hardly such a thing as a war in which it makes no difference who wins. Nearly always one side stands more or less for progress, the other side more or less for reaction. The hatred which the Spanish Republic excited in millionaires, dukes, cardinals, play-boys, Blimps and what not would in itself be enough to show one how the land lay. In essence it was a class war. If it had been won, the cause of the common people everywhere would have been strengthened. It was lost, and the dividend-drawers all over the world rubbed their hands. That was the real issue; all else was froth on its surface.

vi

The outcome of the Spanish War was settled in London, Paris, Rome, Berlin—at any rate not in Spain. After the summer of 1937 those with eyes in their heads realised that the Government could not win the war unless there was some profound change in the international set-up, and in deciding to fight on Negrin and the others may have been partly influenced by the expectation that the world war which actually broke out in 1939 was coming in 1938. The much-publicised disunity on the Government side was not a main cause of defeat. The Government militias were hurriedly raised, ill-armed and unimaginative in their military outlook, but they would have been the same if complete political agreement had existed from the start. At the outbreak of war the average Spanish factory-worker did not even know how to fire a rifle (there had never been universal conscription in Spain), and the traditional pacifism of the Left was a great handicap. The thousands of foreigners who served in Spain made good infantry, but there were very few experts of any kind among them. The Trotskyist thesis that the war could have been won if the revolution had not been sabotaged was probably false. To nationalise factories, demolish churches, and issue revolutionary manifestos would not have made the armies more efficient. The Fascists won because they were the stronger; they had modern arms and the others hadn't. No political strategy could offset that.

The most baffling thing in the Spanish War was the behaviour of the great powers. The war was actually won for Franco by the Germans and Italians, whose motives were obvious enough. The motives of France and Britain are less easy to understand. In 1936 it was clear to everyone that if Britain would only help the Spanish Government, even to the extent of a few million pounds' worth of arms, Franco would collapse and German strategy would be severely dislocated. By that time one did not need to be a clairvoyant to foresee that war between Britain and Germany was coming; one could even foretell within a year or two when it would come. Yet in the most mean, cowardly, hypocritical way the British ruling class did all they could to hand Spain over to Franco and the Nazis. Why? Because they were pro-Fascist, was the obvious answer. Undoubtedly they were, and yet when it came to the final showdown they chose to stand up to Germany. It is still very uncertain what plan they acted on in backing Franco, and they may have had no clear plan at all. Whether the British ruling class are wicked or merely stupid is one of the most difficult questions of our time, and at certain moments a very important question. As to the Russians, their motives in the Spanish War are completely inscrutable. Did they, as the pinks believed, intervene in Spain in order to defend democracy and thwart the Nazis? Then why did they intervene on such a niggardly scale and finally leave Spain in the lurch? Or did they, as the Catholics maintained, intervene in order to foster revolution in Spain? Then why did they do all in their power to crush the Spanish revolutionary movements, defend private property and hand power to the middle class as against the working class? Or did they, as the Trotskyists suggested, intervene simply in order to *prevent* a Spanish revolution? Then why not have backed Franco? Indeed, their actions are most easily explained if one assumes that they were acting on several contradictory motives. I believe that in the future we shall come to feel that Stalin's foreign policy, instead of being so diabolically clever as it is claimed to be, has been merely opportunistic and stupid. But at any rate, the Spanish Civil War demonstrated that the Nazis knew what they were doing and their opponents did not. The war was fought at a low technical level and its major strategy was very simple. That side which had arms would win. The Nazis and the Italians gave arms to their Spanish Fascist friends, and the western democracies and the Russians didn't give arms to those who should have been their friends. So the Spanish Republic perished, having "gained what no republic missed."[2]

Whether it was right, as all left-wingers in other countries undoubtedly did, to encourage the Spaniards to go on fighting when they could not win is a question hard to answer. I myself think it was right, because I believe that it is better even from the point of view of survival to fight and be conquered than to surrender without fighting. The effects on the grand strategy of the struggle against Fascism cannot be assessed yet. The ragged, weaponless armies of the Republic held out for two and a half years, which was undoubtedly longer than their enemies expected. But whether that dislocated the Fascist time-table, or whether, on the other hand, it merely postponed the major war and gave the Nazis extra time to get their war machine into trim, is still uncertain.

vii

I never think of the Spanish War without two memories coming into my mind. One is of the hospital ward at Lérida and the rather sad voices of the wounded militiamen singing some song with a refrain that ended:

> *Una resolucion,*
> *Luchar hast' al fin!*[3]

Well, they fought to the end all right. For the last eighteen months of the war the Republican armies must have been fighting almost without cigarettes, and with precious little food. Even when I left Spain in the middle of 1937, meat and bread were scarce, tobacco a rarity, coffee and sugar almost unobtainable.

The other memory is of the Italian militiaman who shook my hand in the guardroom, the day I joined the militia. I wrote about this man at the beginning of my book on the Spanish War,[4] and do not want to repeat what I said there. When I remember—oh, how vividly!—his shabby uniform and fierce, pathetic, innocent face, the complex side-issues of the war seem to fade away and I see clearly that there was at any rate no doubt as to who was in the right. In spite of power politics and journalistic lying, the central issue of the war was the attempt of people like this to win the decent life which they knew to be their birthright. It is difficult to think of this particular man's probable end without several kinds of bitterness. Since I met him in the Lenin Barracks he was probably a Trotskyist or an Anarchist, and in the peculiar conditions of our time, when people of that sort are not killed by the Gestapo they are usually killed by the GPU. But that does not affect the long-term issues. This man's face, which I saw only for a minute or two, remains with me as a sort of visual reminder of what the war was really about. He symbolises for me the flower of the European working class, harried by the police of all countries, the people who fill the mass graves of the Spanish battlefields and are now, to the tune of several millions, rotting in forced-labour camps.

When one thinks of all the people who support or have supported Fascism, one stands amazed at their diversity. What a crew! Think of a programme which at any rate for a while could bring Hitler, Pétain, Montagu Norman, Pavelitch, William Randolph Hearst, Streicher, Buchman, Ezra Pound, Juan March, Cocteau, Thyssen, Father Coughlin, the Mufti of Jerusalem, Arnold Lunn, Antonescu, Spengler, Beverley Nichols, Lady Houston, and Marinetti all into the same boat! But the clue is really very simple. They are all people with something to lose, or people who long for a hierarchical society and dread the prospect of a world of free and equal human beings. Behind all the ballyhoo that is talked about "godless" Russia and the "materialism" of the working class lies the simple intention of those with money or privileges to cling to them. Ditto, though it contains a partial truth, with all the talk about the worthlessness of social reconstruction not accompanied by a "change of heart." The pious ones, from the Pope to the yogis of California,[5] are great on the "change of heart,"[6] much more reassuring from their point of view than a change in the economic system. Pétain attributes the fall of France to the common people's "love of pleasure." One sees this in its right perspective if one stops to wonder how much pleasure the ordinary French peasant's or workingman's life would contain compared with Pétain's own. The damned impertinence of these politicians, priests, literary men, and what not who lecture the working-class Socialist for his "materialism"! All that the workingman demands is what these others would consider the indispensable minimum without which human life cannot be lived at all. Enough to eat, freedom from the haunting terror of unemployment, the knowledge that your children will get a fair chance, a bath once a day, clean linen reasonably often, a roof that doesn't leak, and short enough working hours to leave you with a little energy when the day is done. Not one of those who preach against "materialism" would consider life livable without these things. And how easily that minimum could be attained if we chose to set our minds to it for only twenty years! To raise the standard of living of the whole world to that of Britain would not be a greater undertaking than this war we are now fighting. I don't claim, and I don't know who does, that that would solve anything in itself. It is merely that privation and brute labour have to be abolished before the real problems of humanity can be tackled. The major problem of our time is the decay of the belief in personal immortality, and it cannot be dealt with while the average human being is either drudging like an ox or shivering in fear of the secret police. How right the working classes are in their "materialism"! How right they are to realise that the real belly comes before the soul, not in the scale of values but in point of time! Understand that, and the long horror that we are enduring becomes at least intelligible. All the considerations that are likely to make one falter—the siren voices of a Pétain or of a Gandhi, the inescapable fact that in order to fight one has to degrade oneself, the equivocal moral position of Britain, with its democratic phrases and its coolie empire, the sinister development of Soviet Russia, the squalid farce of left-wing politics—all this fades away and one sees only the struggle of the gradually awakening common people against the lords of property and their hired liars and bumsuckers. The question is very simple. Shall people like that Italian soldier be allowed to live the decent, fully human life which is now technically achievable, or shan't they? Shall the common man be pushed back into the mud, or shall he not? I myself believe, perhaps on insufficient grounds, that the common man will win his fight sooner or later, but I want it to be sooner and not later — some time within the next hundred years, say, and not some time within the next ten thousand years. That was the real issue of the Spanish War, and of the present war, and perhaps of other wars yet to come.

I never saw the Italian militiaman again, nor did I ever learn his name. It can be taken as quite certain that he is dead. Nearly two years later, when the war was visibly lost, I wrote these verses in his memory:

> The Italian soldier shook my hand
> Beside the guard-room table;
> The strong hand and the subtle hand
> Whose palms are only able
>
> To meet within the sound of guns,
> But oh! what peace I knew then
> In gazing on his battered face
> Purer than any woman's!
>
> For the fly-blown words that make me spew
> Still in his ears were holy,
> And he was born knowing what I had learned
> Out of books and slowly.
>
> The treacherous guns had told their tale
> And we both had bought it,
> But my gold brick was made of gold —
> Oh! who ever would have thought it?

Good luck go with you, Italian soldier!
But luck is not for the brave;
What would the world give back to you?
Always less than you gave.

Between the shadow and the ghost,
Between the white and the red,
Between the bullet and the lie,
Where would you hide your head?

For where is Manuel Gonzalez,
And where is Pedro Aguilar,
And where is Ramon Fenellosa?
The earthworms know where they are.

Your name and your deeds were forgotten
Before your bones were dry,
And the lie that slew you is buried
Under a deeper lie;

But the thing that I saw in your face
No power can disinherit:
No bomb that ever burst
Shatters the crystal spirit.

As I Please, 1

Tribune, December 3, 1943

Scene in a tobacconist's shop. Two American soldiers sprawling across the counter, one of them just sober enough to make unwanted love to the two young women who run the shop, the other at the stage known as "fighting drunk." Enter Orwell in search of matches. The pugnacious one makes an effort and stands upright.

Soldier: "Wharrishay is, perfijious Albion. You heard that? Perfijious Albion. Never trust a Britisher. You can't trust the b——s."

Orwell: "Can't trust them with what?"

Soldier: "Wharrishay is, down with Britain. Down with the British. You wanna do anything 'bout that? Then you can —— well do it." (Sticks his face out like a tomcat on a garden wall.)

Tobacconist: "He'll knock your block off if you don't shut up."

Soldier: "Wharrishay is, down with Britain." (Subsides across the counter again. The tobacconist lifts his head delicately out of the scales.)

This kind of thing is not exceptional. Even if you steer clear of Piccadilly with its seething swarms of drunks and whores, it is difficult to go anywhere in London without having the feeling that Britain is now Occupied Territory. The general consensus of opinion seems to be that the only American soldiers with decent manners are the Negroes. On the other hand the Americans have their own justifiable complaints—in particular, they complain of the children who follow them night and day, cadging sweets.

Does this sort of thing matter? The answer is that it might matter at some moment when Anglo-American relations were in the balance, and when the still powerful forces in this country which want an understanding with Japan were able to show their faces again. At such moments popular prejudice can count for a great deal. Before the war there was no popular anti-American feeling in this country. It all dates from the arrival of the American troops, and it is made vastly worse by the tacit agreement never to discuss it in print.

Seemingly it is our fixed policy in this war not to criticise our allies, nor to answer their criticisms of us. As a result things have happened which are capable of causing the worst kind of trouble sooner or later. An example is the agreement by which American troops in this country are not liable to British courts for offences against British subjects—practically "extra-territorial rights." Not one English person in ten knows of the existence of this agreement; the newspapers barely reported it and refrained from commenting on it. Nor have people been made to realise the extent of anti-British feeling in the United States. Drawing their picture of America from films carefully edited for the British market, they have no notion of the kind of thing that Americans are brought up to believe about us. Suddenly to discover, for instance, that the average American thinks the U.S.A. had more casualties than Britain in the last war comes as a shock, and the kind of shock that can cause a violent quarrel. Even such a fundamental difficulty as the fact that an American soldier's pay is five times that of a British soldier has never been properly ventilated. No sensible person wants to whip up Anglo-American jealousy. On the contrary, it is just because one does want a good relationship between the two countries that one wants plain speaking. Our official soft-soaping policy does us no good in America, while in this country it allows dangerous resentments to fester just below the surface.

Since 1935, when pamphleteering revived, I have been a steady collector of pamphlets political, religious and what-not. To anyone who happens to come across it and has a shilling to spare I recommend *The 1946 MS.*, by Robin Maugham,[1] published by the War Facts Press. It is a good example of that small but growing school of literature, the non-party Radical school. It purports to describe the establishment in Britain of a Fascist dictatorship, starting in 1944 and headed by a successful general who is (I think) drawn from a living model.[2] I found it interesting because it gives you the average middle-class man's conception of what Fascism would be like, and more important, of the reasons why Fascism might succeed. Its appearance (along with other similar pamphlets I have in my collection) shows how far that average middle-class man has travelled since 1939, when Socialism still meant dividing the money up and what happened in Europe was none of our business.

Who wrote this?

"As we walked over the Drury Lane gratings of the cellars a most foul stench came up, and one in particular that I remember to this day. A man half dressed pushed open a broken window beneath us, just as we passed by, and there issued such a blast of corruption, made up of gases bred by filth, air breathed and rebreathed a hundred times, charged with the odours of unnameable personal uncleanness and disease, that I staggered to the gutter with a qualm which I could scarcely conquer . . . I did not know, till I came in actual contact with them, how far away the classes which lie at the bottom of great cities are from those above them; how completely they are inaccessible to motives which act upon

ordinary human beings, and how deeply they are sunk beyond ray of sun or stars, immersed in the selfishness naturally
begotten of their incessant struggle for existence and incessant warfare with society. It was an awful thought to me, ever
present on those Sundays, and haunting me at other times,
that men, women, and children were living in such brutish
degradation, and that as they died others would take their
place. Our civilisation seemed nothing but a thin film or
crust lying over a volcanic pit, and I often wondered whether
some day the pit would not break up through it and destroy
us all."[3]

You would know, at any rate, that this comes from some
nineteenth-century writer. Actually it is from a novel, *Mark Rutherford's Deliverance*. (Mark Rutherford, whose real name was Hale
White, wrote this book as a pseudo-autobiography.) Apart from
the prose, you could recognise this as coming from the nineteenth
century because of that description of the unendurable filth of the
slums. The London slums of that day *were* like that, and all honest
writers so described them. But even more characteristic is that notion of a whole block of the population being so degraded as to
be beyond contact and beyond redemption.

Almost all nineteenth-century English writers are agreed upon
this, even Dickens. A large part of the town working class, ruined
by industrialism, are simply savages. Revolution is not a thing to be
hoped for: it simply means the swamping of civilisation by the
sub-human. In this novel (it is one of the best novels in English)
Mark Rutherford describes the opening of a sort of mission or
settlement near Drury Lane. Its object was "gradually to attract
Drury Lane to come and be saved." Needless to say this was a
failure. Drury Lane not only did not want to be saved in the religious sense, it didn't even want to be civilised. All that Mark

Rutherford and his friend succeeded in doing, all that one could do, indeed, at that time, was to provide a sort of refuge for the few people of the neighbourhood who did not belong to their surroundings. The general masses were outside the pale.

Mark Rutherford was writing of the 'seventies, and in a footnote dated 1884 he remarks that "socialism, nationalisation of the land and other projects" have now made their appearance, and may perhaps give a gleam of hope. Nevertheless, he assumes that the condition of the working class will grow worse and not better as time goes on. It was natural to believe this (even Marx seems to have believed it), because it was hard at that time to foresee the enormous increase in the productivity of labour. Actually, such an improvement in the standard of living has taken place as Mark Rutherford and his contemporaries would have considered quite impossible.

The London slums are still bad enough, but they are nothing to those of the nineteenth century. Gone are the days when a single room used to be inhabited by four families, one in each corner, and when incest and infanticide were taken almost for granted. Above all, gone are the days when it seemed natural to write off a whole stratum of the population as irredeemable savages. The most snobbish Tory alive would not now write of the London working class as Mark Rutherford does. And Mark Rutherford — like Dickens, who shared his attitude — was a Radical! Progress does happen, hard though it may be to believe it, in this age of concentration camps and big beautiful bombs.

As I Please, 2

Tribune, December 10, 1943

The recently-issued special supplement to the *New Republic* entitled *The Negro: His Future in America* is worth a reading, but it raises more problems than it discusses. The facts it reveals about the present treatment of Negroes in the U.S.A. are bad enough in all conscience. In spite of the quite obvious necessities of war, Negroes are still pushed out of skilled jobs, segregated and insulted in the Army, assaulted by white policemen and discriminated against by white magistrates. In a number of the Southern States they are disenfranchised by means of a poll tax. On the other hand, those of them who have votes are so fed up with the present Administration that they are beginning to swing towards the Republican Party—that is, in effect, to give their support to Big Business. But all this is merely a single facet of the world-wide problem of colour. And what the authors of this supplement fail to point out is that that problem simply cannot be solved inside the capitalist system.

One of the big unmentionable facts of politics is the differential standard of living. An English working-man spends on cigarettes about the same sum as an Indian peasant has for his entire income. It is not easy for Socialists to admit this, or at any rate to emphasise it. If you want people to rebel against the existing system, you have got to show them that they are badly off, and it is doubtful tactics to *start* by telling an Englishman on the dole that in the eyes of an Indian coolie he would be next door to a millionaire. Almost complete silence reigns on this subject, at any rate at the European end, and it contributes to the lack of solidarity between white and coloured workers. Almost without knowing it—and perhaps without wanting to know it—the white worker exploits the coloured worker, and in revenge the coloured worker can be and is used against the white. Franco's Moors in Spain were only doing more dramatically the same thing as is done by half-starved Indians in Bombay mills or Japanese factory-girls sold into semi-slavery by their parents. As things are, Asia and Africa are simply a bottomless reserve of scab labour.

The coloured worker cannot be blamed for feeling no solidarity with his white comrades. The gap between their standard of living and his own is so vast that it makes any differences which may exist in the West seem negligible. In Asiatic eyes the European class struggle is a sham. The Socialist movement has never gained a real foothold in Asia or Africa, or even among the American Negroes: it is everywhere side-tracked by nationalism and race-hatred. Hence the spectacle of thoughtful Negroes getting ready to vote for Dewey,[1] and Indian Congressmen preferring their own capitalists to the British Labour Party. There is no solution until the living-standards of the thousand million people who are not "white" can be forced up to the same level as our own. But as this might mean temporarily *lowering* our own standards the subject is systematically avoided by Left and Right alike.

Is there anything that one can do about this, as an individual? One can at least remember that the colour problem exists. And there is one small precaution which is not much trouble, and which can perhaps do a little to mitigate the horrors of the colour war. That is to avoid using insulting nicknames. It is an astonishing thing that few journalists, even in the Left wing press, bother to find out which names are and which are not resented by members of other races. The word "native," which makes any Asiatic

boil with rage, and which has been dropped even by British officials in India these ten years past, is flung about all over the place.
"Negro" is habitually printed with a small n, a thing most Negroes
resent. One's information about these matters needs to be kept
up to date. I have just been carefully going through the proofs of
a reprinted book of mine,[2] cutting out the word "Chinaman"
wherever it occurred and substituting "Chinese." The book was
written less than a dozen years ago, but in the intervening time
"Chinaman" has become a deadly insult. Even "Mahomedan" is
now beginning to be resented: one should say "Moslem." These
things are childish, but then nationalism is childish. And after all
we ourselves do not actually like being called "Limeys" or
"Britishers."

As I Please, 3

Tribune, December 17, 1943

So many letters have arrived, attacking me for my remarks about the American soldiers in this country,[1] that I must return to the subject.

Contrary to what most of my correspondents seem to think, I was not trying to make trouble between ourselves and our Allies, nor am I consumed by hatred for the United States. I am much less anti-American than most English people are at this moment. What I say, and what I repeat, is that our policy of not criticising our Allies, and not answering their criticism of us (we don't answer the Russians either, nor even the Chinese) is a mistake, and is likely to defeat its own object in the long run. And so far as Anglo-American relations go, there are three difficulties which badly need dragging into the open and which simply don't get mentioned in the British press.

1. *Anti-American feeling in Britain.*——Before the war, anti-American feeling was a middle-class, and perhaps upper-class thing, resulting from imperialist and business jealousy and disguising itself as dislike of the American accent, etc. The working class, so far from being anti-American, were becoming rapidly Americanised in speech by means of the films and jazz songs. Now, in spite of what my correspondents may say, I can hear few good words for the Americans anywhere. This obviously results from the arrival of the American troops. It has been made worse by the fact that, for various reasons, the Mediterranean campaign

had to be represented as an American show while most of the casualties had to be suffered by the British. (See Philip Jordan's remarks in his *Tunis Diary*.[2]) I am not saying that popular English prejudices are always justified: I am saying that they exist.

2. *Anti-British feeling in America.*—We ought to face the fact that large numbers of Americans are brought up to dislike and despise us. There is a large section of the press whose main accent is anti-British, and countless other papers which attack Britain in a more sporadic way. In addition there is a systematic guying of what are supposed to be British habits and manners on the stage and in comic strips and cheap magazines. The typical Englishman is represented as a chinless ass with a title, a monocle and a habit of saying "Haw, haw." This legend is believed in by relatively responsible Americans, for example by the veteran novelist Theodore Dreiser, who remarks in a public speech that "the British are horse-riding aristocratic snobs." (Forty-six million horse-riding snobs!) It is a commonplace on the American stage that the Englishman is almost never allowed to play a favourable role, any more than the Negro is allowed to appear as anything more than a comic. Yet right up to Pearl Harbour the American movie industry had an agreement with the Japanese Government never to present a Japanese character in an unfavourable light!

I am not blaming the Americans for all this. The anti-British press has powerful business forces behind it, besides ancient quarrels in many of which Britain was in the wrong. As for popular anti-British feeling, we partly bring it on ourselves by exporting our worst specimens. But what I do want to emphasise is that these anti-British currents in the U.S.A. are very strong, and that the British press has consistently failed to draw attention to them. There has never been in England anything that one could call an anti-American press: and since the war there has been a steady refusal to answer criticism, and a careful censorship of the radio to cut out anything that the Americans might object to. As a result, many English people don't realise how they are regarded, and get a shock when they find out.

3. *Soldiers' Pay.*—It is now nearly two years since the first American troops reached this country, and I rarely see American and British soldiers together. Quite obviously the major cause of this is the difference of pay. You can't have really close and friendly relations with somebody whose income is five times your own. Financially, the whole American army is in the middle class. In the field this might not matter, but in the training period it makes it almost impossible for British and American soldiers to fraternise. If you don't want friendly relations between the British Army and the American Army, well and good. But if you do, you must either pay the British soldier ten shillings a day or make the American soldier bank the surplus of his pay in America. I don't profess to know which of these alternatives is the right one.

One way of feeling infallible is not to keep a diary. Looking back through the diary I kept in 1940 and 1941 I find that I was usually wrong when it was possible to be wrong. Yet I was not so wrong as the Military Experts. Experts of various schools were telling us in 1939 that the Maginot Line was impregnable, and that the Russo-German pact had put an end to Hitler's eastward expansion; in early 1940 they were telling us that the days of tank warfare were over; in mid 1940 they were telling us that the Germans would invade Britain forthwith; in mid 1941 that the Red Army would fold up in six weeks; in December, 1941, that Japan would collapse after 90 days; in July, 1942, that Egypt was lost—and so on, more or less indefinitely.

Where now are the men who told us those things? Still on the job, drawing fat salaries. Instead of the unsinkable battleship we have the unsinkable Military Expert.

To be politically happy these days you need to have no more memory than an animal. The people who demonstrated most loudly against Mosley's release were the leaders of the defunct People's Convention, which at the time when Mosley was interned was running a "stop the war" campaign barely distinguishable from Mosley's own. And I myself know of a ladies' knitting circle which was formed to knit comforts for the Finns, and which two years later—with no sense of incongruity—finished off various garments that had been left on its hands and sent them to the Russians. Early in 1942 a friend of mine bought some fried fish done up in a piece of newspaper of 1940. On one side was an article proving that the Red Army was no good, and on the other a write-up of that gallant sailor and well-known Anglophile, Admiral Darlan. But my favourite in this line is the *Daily Express* leader which began, a few days after the U.S.S.R. entered the war: "This paper has always worked for good relations between Britain and Soviet Russia."

Books have gone up in price like everything else, but the other day I picked up a copy of Lemprière's *Classical Dictionary*,[3] the *Who's Who* of the ancients, for only sixpence. Opening it at random, I came upon the biography of Laïs, the famous courtesan, daughter of the mistress of Alcibiades:

"She first began to sell her favours at Corinth for 10,000 drachmas, and the immense number of princes, noblemen, philosophers, orators and plebeians who courted her, bear witness to her personal charms . . . Demosthenes visited Corinth for the sake of Laïs, but informed by the courtesan that admittance to her bed was to be bought at the enormous sum of about £200 English money, the orator departed, and observed that he would not buy repentance at so dear a price . . . She ridiculed the austerity of philosophers, and the weakness of those who pretend to have gained a superiority over their passions, by observing that sages and philosophers were not above the rest of mankind, for she found them at her door as often as the rest of the Athenians."

There is more in the same vain. However, it ends on a good moral, for "the other women, jealous of her charms, assassinated her in the temple of Venus about 340 B.C." That was 2,283 years ago. I wonder how many of the present denizens of *Who's Who* will seem worth reading about in A.D. 4226?

As I Please, 16

Tribune, March 17, 1944

With no power to put my decrees into operation, but with as much authority as most of the exile "governments" now sheltering in various parts of the world, I pronounce sentence of death on the following words and expressions:—

Achilles heel, jackboot, hydra-headed, ride roughshod over, stab in the back, petty-bourgeois, stinking corpse, liquidate, iron heel, blood-stained oppressor, cynical betrayal, lackey, flunkey, mad dog, jackal, hyena, blood bath.

No doubt this list will have to be added to from time to time, but it will do to go on with. It contains a fair selection of the dead metaphors and ill-translated foreign phrases which have been current in Marxist literature for years past.

There are, of course, many other perversions of the English language besides this one. There is official English, or Stripe-trouser, the language of White Papers, Parliamentary debates (in their more decorous moments) and B.B.C. news bulletins. There are the scientists and the economists, with their instinctive preference for words like "contraindicate" and "deregionalisation." There is American slang, which for all its attractiveness probably tends to impoverish the language in the long run. And there is the general slovenliness of modern English speech with its decadent vowel sounds (throughout the London area you have to use sign language to distinguish between "threepence" and "three-half-pence") and its tendency to make verbs and nouns interchangeable. But here I am concerned only with one kind of bad English, Marxist English, or Pamphletese, which can be studied in the *Daily Worker*, the *Labour Monthly*, *Plebs*, the *New Leader*, and similar papers.

Many of the expressions used in political literature are simply euphemisms or rhetorical tricks. "Liquidate," for instance (or "eliminate"), is a polite word for "to kill," while "realism" normally means "dishonesty." But Marxist phraseology is peculiar in that it consists largely of translations. Its characteristic vocabulary comes ultimately from German or Russian phrases which have been adopted in one country after another with no attempt to find suitable equivalents. Here, for instance, is a piece of Marxist writing—it happens to be an address delivered to the Allied armies by the citizens of Pantelleria:—

The citizens of Pantelleria "pay grateful homage to the Anglo-American forces for the promptness with which they have liberated them from the evil yoke of a megalomaniac and satanic regime which, not content with having sucked like a monstrous octopus the best energies of true Italians for twenty years, is now reducing Italy to a mass of ruins and misery for one motive only—the insane personal profit of its chiefs, who, under an ill-concealed mask of hollow, so-called patriotism, hide the basest passions, and, plotting together with the German pirates, hatch the lowest egoism and blackest treatment while all the time, with revolting cynicism, they tread on the blood of thousands of Italians."

This filthy stew of words is presumably a translation from the Italian, but the point is that one would not recognize it as such. It might be a translation from any other European language, or it might come straight out of the *Daily Worker*, so truly international is this style of writing. Its characteristic is the endless use of ready-made metaphors. In the same spirit, when Italian submarines were sinking the ships that took arms to Republican Spain, the *Daily*

Worker urged the British Admiralty to "sweep the mad dogs from the seas." Clearly, people capable of using such phrases have ceased to remember that words have meanings.

A Russian friend tells me that the Russian language is richer than English in terms of abuse, so that Russian invective cannot always be accurately translated. Thus when Molotov referred to the Germans as "cannibals," he was perhaps using some word which sounded natural in Russian, but to which "cannibal" was only a rough approximation. But our local Communists have taken over, from the defunct *Inprecorr*[1] and similar sources, a whole series of these crudely-translated phrases, and from force of habit have come to think of them as actual English expressions. The Communist vocabulary of abuse (applied to Fascists or Socialists according to the "line" of the moment) includes such terms as hyena, corpse, lackey, pirate, hangman, bloodsucker, mad dog, criminal, assassin. Whether at first, second or third hand, these are all translations, and by no means the kind of word that an English person naturally uses to express disapproval. And language of this kind is used with an astonishing indifference as to its meaning. Ask a journalist what a jackboot is, and you will find that he does not know. Yet he goes on talking about jackboots. Or what is meant by "to ride roughshod"? Very few people know that either. For that matter, in my experience, very few Socialists know the meaning of the word "proletariat."

You can see a good example of Marxist language at its worst in the words "lackey" and "flunkey." Pre-revolutionary Russia was still a feudal country in which hordes of idle menservants were part of the social set-up; in that context "lackey," as a word of abuse, had a meaning. In England, the social landscape is quite different. Except at public functions, the last time I saw a foot-man in livery was in 1921. And, in fact, in ordinary speech, the word "flunkey" has been obsolete since the 'nineties, and the word "lackey" for about a century. Yet they and other equally inappropriate words are dug up for pamphleteering purposes. The result is a style of writing that bears the same relation to writing real English as doing a jigsaw puzzle bears to painting a picture. It is just a question of fitting together a number of ready-made pieces. Just talk about hydra-headed jackboots riding roughshod over blood-stained hyenas, and you are all right. For confirmation of which, see almost any pamphlet issued by the Communist Party—or by any other political party, for that matter.

Revenge Is Sour

Tribune, November 9, 1945

Whenever I read phrases like "war guilt trials," "punishment of war criminals," and so forth, there comes back into my mind the memory of something I saw in a prisoner-of-war camp in South Germany, earlier this year.

Another correspondent and myself were being shown round the camp by a little Viennese Jew who had been enlisted in the branch of the American army which deals with the interrogation of prisoners. He was an alert, fair-haired, rather good-looking youth of about twenty-five, and politically so much more knowledgeable than the average American officer that it was a pleasure to be with him. The camp was on an airfield, and, after we had been round the cages, our guide led us to a hangar where various prisoners who were in a different category from the others were being "screened."

Up at one end of the hangar about a dozen men were lying in a row on the concrete floor. These, it was explained, were S.S. officers who had been segregated from the other prisoners. Among them was a man in dingy civilian clothes who was lying with his arm across his face and apparently asleep. He had strangely and horribly deformed feet. The two of them were quite symmetrical, but they were clubbed out into an extraordinary globular shape which made them more like a horse's hoof than anything human. As we approached the group the little Jew seemed to be working himself up into a state of excitement.

"That's the real swine!" he said, and suddenly he lashed out with his heavy army boot and caught the prostrate man a fearful kick right on the bulge of one of his deformed feet.

"Get up, you swine!" he shouted as the man started out of sleep, and then repeated something of the kind in German. The prisoner scrambled to his feet and stood clumsily to attention. With the same air of working himself up into a fury—indeed he was almost dancing up and down as he spoke—the Jew told us the prisoner's history. He was a "real" Nazi: his party number indicated that he had been a member since the very early days, and he had held a post corresponding to a general in the political branch of the S.S. It could be taken as quite certain that he had had charge of concentration camps and had presided over tortures and hangings. In short, he represented everything that we had been fighting against during the past five years.

Meanwhile, I was studying his appearance. Quite apart from the scrubby, unfed, unshaven look that a newly captured man generally has, he was a disgusting specimen. But he did not look brutal or in any way frightening: merely neurotic and, in a low way, intellectual. His pale, shifty eyes were deformed by powerful spectacles. He could have been an unfrocked clergyman, an actor ruined by drink, or a spiritualist medium. I have seen very similar people in London common lodging-houses, and also in the Reading Room of the British Museum. Quite obviously he was mentally unbalanced—indeed, only doubtfully sane, though at this moment sufficiently in his right mind to be frightened of getting another kick. And yet everything that the Jew was telling me of his history could have been true, and probably was true! So the Nazi torturer of one's imagination, the monstrous figure against whom one had struggled for so many years, dwindled to this pitiful wretch, whose obvious need was not for punishment, but for some kind of psychological treatment.

Later, there were further humiliations. Another S.S. officer, a large brawny man, was ordered to strip to the waist and show the blood-group number tattooed on his under-arm; another was forced to explain to us how he had lied about being a member of the S.S. and attempted to pass himself off as an ordinary soldier of the Wehrmacht. I wondered whether the Jew was getting any real kick out of this new-found power that he was exercising. I concluded that he wasn't really enjoying it, and that he was merely—like a man in a brothel, or a boy smoking his first cigar, or a tourist traipsing round a picture gallery—*telling* himself that he was enjoying it, and behaving as he had planned to behave in the days when he was helpless.

It is absurd to blame any German or Austrian Jew for getting his own back on the Nazis. Heaven knows what scores this particular man may have had to wipe out: very likely his whole family had been murdered; and, after all, even a wanton kick to a prisoner is a very tiny thing compared with the outrages committed by the Hitler regime. But what this scene, and much else that I saw in Germany, brought home to me was that the whole idea of revenge and punishment is a childish daydream. Properly speaking, there is no such thing as revenge. Revenge is an act which you want to commit when you are powerless and because you are powerless: as soon as the sense of impotence is removed, the desire evaporates also.

Who would not have jumped for joy, in 1940, at the thought of seeing S.S. officers kicked and humiliated? But when the thing becomes possible, it is merely pathetic and disgusting. It is said that when Mussolini's corpse was exhibited in public, an old woman drew a revolver and fired five shots into it, exclaiming, "Those are for my five sons!" It is the kind of story that the newspapers make up, but it might be true. I wonder how much satisfaction she got out of those five shots, which, doubtless, she had dreamed years earlier of firing. The condition of her being able to get near enough to Mussolini to shoot at him was that he should be a corpse.

In so far as the big public in this country is responsible for the monstrous peace settlement now being forced on Germany, it is because of a failure to see in advance that punishing an enemy brings no satisfaction. We acquiesced in crimes like the expulsion of all Germans from East Prussia—crimes which in some cases we could not prevent but might at least have protested against— because the Germans had angered and frightened us, and there- fore we were certain that when they were down we should feel no pity for them. We persist in these policies, or let others persist in them on our behalf, because of a vague feeling that, having set out to punish Germany, we ought to go ahead and do it. Actually there is little acute hatred of Germany left in this country, and even less, I should expect to find, in the army of occupation. Only the mi- nority of sadists, who must have their "atrocities" from one source or another, take a keen interest in the hunting-down of war crim- inals and quislings. If you ask the average man what crime Goe- ring, Ribbentrop and the rest are to be charged with at their trial, he cannot tell you. Somehow the punishment of these monsters ceases to seem attractive when it becomes possible: indeed, once under lock and key, they almost cease to be monsters.

Unfortunately, there is often need of some concrete incident before one can discover the real state of one's feelings. Here is an- other memory from Germany. A few hours after Stuttgart was captured by the French army, a Belgian journalist and myself en- tered the town, which was still in some disorder. The Belgian had been broadcasting throughout the war for the European Service of the B.B.C., and, like nearly all Frenchmen or Belgians, he had a very much tougher attitude towards "the Boche" than an English- man or an American would have. All the main bridges into the town had been blown up, and we had to enter by a small foot-bridge which the Germans had evidently made efforts to defend. A dead German soldier was lying supine at the foot of the steps. His face was a waxy yellow. On his breast someone had laid a bunch of the lilac which was blossoming everywhere.

The Belgian averted his face as we went past. When we were well over the bridge he confided to me that this was the first time he had seen a dead man. I suppose he was thirty-five years old, and for four years he had been doing war propaganda over the radio. For several days after this, his attitude was quite different from what it had been earlier. He looked with disgust at the bomb-wrecked town and the humiliations the Germans were undergoing, and even on one occasion intervened to prevent a particularly bad bit of looting. When we left, he gave the residue of the coffee we had brought with us to the Germans on whom we were billeted. A week earlier he would probably have been scandalised at the idea of giving coffee to a "Boche." But his feelings, he told me, had undergone a change at the sight of "*ce pauvre mort*" beside the bridge: it had suddenly brought home to him the meaning of war. And yet, if we had happened to enter the town by another route, he might have been spared the experience of seeing even one corpse out of the — perhaps — twenty million that the war has produced.

The Case for the Open Fire

Evening Standard, December 8, 1945

Before long the period of hurriedly constructed prefabs will be over, and Britain will be tackling on a big scale the job of building permanent houses.

It will then be necessary to decide what kind of heating we want our houses to have, and one can be sure in advance that a small but noisy minority will want to do away with the old-fashioned coal fire.

These people — they are also the people who admire gaspipe chairs and glass-topped tables, and regard labour-saving as an end in itself—will argue that the coal fire is wasteful, dirty and inefficient. They will urge that dragging buckets of coal upstairs is a nuisance and that raking out the cinders in the morning is a grisly job, and they will add that the fogs of our cities are made thicker by the smoking of thousands of chimneys.

All of which is perfectly true, and yet comparatively unimportant if one thinks in terms of living and not merely of saving trouble.

I am not arguing that coal fires should be the sole form of heating, merely that every house or flat should have at least one open fire round which the family can sit. In our climate anything that keeps you warm is to be welcomed, and under ideal conditions every form of heating apparatus would be installed in every house.

For any kind of workroom central heating is the best arrangement. It needs no attention, and, since it warms all parts of the
room evenly, one can group the furniture according to the needs
of work.

For bedrooms, gas or electric fires are best. Even the humble
oilstove throws out a lot of heat, and has the virtue of being
portable. It is a great comfort to carry an oilstove with you into the
bathroom on a winter morning. But for a room that is to be lived
in, only a coal fire will do.

The first great virtue of a coal fire is that, just because it only
warms one end of the room, it forces people to group themselves
in a sociable way. This evening, while I write, the same pattern is
being reproduced in hundreds of thousands of British homes.

To one side of the fireplace sits Dad, reading the evening
paper. To the other side sits Mum, doing her knitting. On the
hearthrug sit the children, playing snakes and ladders. Up against
the fender, roasting himself, lies the dog. It is a comely pattern, a
good background to one's memories, and the survival of the family as an institution may be more dependent on it than we realise.

Then there is the fascination, inexhaustible to a child, of the
fire itself. A fire is never the same for two minutes together, you
can look into the red heart of the coals and see caverns or faces or
salamanders, according to your imagination: you can even, if your
parents will let you, amuse yourself by heating the poker red-hot
and bending it between the bars, or sprinkling salt on the flames
to turn them green.

A gas or electric fire, or even an anthracite stove, is a dreary
thing by comparison. The most dismal objects of all are those
phoney electric fires which are so constructed as to look like coal
fires. Is not the mere fact of imitation an admission that the real
thing is superior?

If, as I maintain, an open fire makes for sociability and has an æsthetic appeal which is particularly important to young children, it is well worth the trouble that it entails.

It is quite true that it is wasteful, messy and the cause of avoidable work: all the same things could be said with equal truth of a baby. The point is that household appliances should be judged not simply by their efficiency but by the pleasure and comfort that one gets out of them.

A vacuum cleaner is good because it saves much dreary labour with brush and pan. Gaspipe furniture is bad because it destroys the friendly look of a room without appreciably adding to one's comfort.

Our civilisation is haunted by the notion that the quickest way of doing anything is invariably the best. The agreeable warming-pan, which warms the whole bed as hot as toast before you jump into it, went out in favour of the clammy, unsatisfying hot-water bottle simply because the warming-pan is a nuisance to carry up-stairs and has to be polished daily.

Some people, obsessed by "functionalism," would make every room in the house as bare, clean and labour-saving as a prison cell. They do not reflect that houses are meant to be lived in and that you therefore need different qualities in different rooms. In the kitchen, efficiency; in the bedrooms, warmth; in the living-room, a friendly atmosphere—which in this country demands a good, prodigal coal fire for about seven months of the year.

I am not denying that coal fires have their drawbacks, especially in these days of dwindled newspapers. Many a devout Communist has been forced against all his principles to take in a capitalist paper merely because the *Daily Worker* is not large enough to light the fire with.

Also there is the slowness with which a fire gets under way in the morning. It would be a good idea, when the new houses are built, if every open fireplace were provided with what used to be called a "blower"—that is, a removable sheet of metal which can be used to create a draught. This works far better than a pair of bellows.

But even the worst fire, even a fire which smokes in your face and has to be constantly poked, is better than none.

In proof of which, imagine the dreariness of spending Christmas evening in sitting—like the family of Arnold Bennett's super-efficient hero in his novel *The Card*—round a gilded radiator!

The Sporting Spirit

Tribune, December 14, 1945

Now that the brief visit of the Dynamo football team[1] has come to an end, it is possible to say publicly what many thinking people were saying privately before the Dynamos ever arrived. That is, that sport is an unfailing cause of ill-will, and that if such a visit as this had any effect at all on Anglo-Soviet relations, it could only be to make them slightly worse than before.

Even the newspapers have been unable to conceal the fact that at least two of the four matches played led to much bad feeling. At the Arsenal match, I am told by someone who was there, a British and a Russian player came to blows and the crowd booed the referee. The Glasgow match, someone else informs me, was simply a free-for-all from the start. And then there was the controversy, typical of our nationalistic age, about the composition of the Arsenal team. Was it really an all-England team, as claimed by the Russians, or merely a league team, as claimed by the British? And did the Dynamos end their tour abruptly in order to avoid playing an all-England team? As usual, everyone answers these questions according to his political predilections. Not quite everyone, however. I noted with interest, as an instance of the vicious passions that football provokes, that the sporting correspondent of the Russophile *News Chronicle* took the anti-Russian line and maintained that Arsenal was *not* an all-England team. No doubt the controversy will continue to echo for years in the footnotes of history books. Meanwhile the result of the Dynamos' tour, in so far as it has had any result, will have been to create fresh animosity on both sides.

And how could it be otherwise? I am always amazed when I hear people saying that sport creates goodwill between the nations, and that if only the common peoples of the world could meet one another at football or cricket, they would have no inclination to meet on the battlefield. Even if one didn't know from concrete examples (the 1936 Olympic Games, for instance) that international sporting contests lead to orgies of hatred, one could deduce it from general principles.

Nearly all the sports practised nowadays are competitive. You play to win, and the game has little meaning unless you do your utmost to win. On the village green, where you pick up sides and no feeling of local patriotism is involved, it is possible to play simply for the fun and the exercise: but as soon as the question of prestige arises, as soon as you feel that you and some larger unit will be disgraced if you lose, the most savage combative instincts are aroused. Anyone who has played even in a school football match knows this. At the international level sport is frankly mimic warfare. But the significant thing is not the behaviour of the players but the attitude of the spectators: and, behind the spectators, of the nations who work themselves into furies over these absurd contests, and seriously believe — at any rate for short periods — that running, jumping and kicking a ball are tests of national virtue.

Even a leisurely game like cricket, demanding grace rather than strength, can cause much ill-will, as we saw in the controversy over body-line bowling and over the rough tactics of the Australian team that visited England in 1921. Football, a game in which everyone gets hurt and every nation has its own style of play which seems unfair to foreigners, is far worse. Worst of all is boxing. One of the most horrible sights in the world is a fight between white and coloured boxers before a mixed audience. But a boxing audience is always disgusting, and the behaviour of the women, in particular, is such that the Army, I believe, does not allow them to attend its contests. At any rate, two or three years ago, when Home Guards and regular troops were holding a boxing tournament, I was placed on guard at the door of the hall, with orders to keep the women out.

In England, the obsession with sport is bad enough, but even fiercer passions are aroused in young countries where games-playing and nationalism are both recent developments. In countries like India or Burma, it is necessary at football matches to have strong cordons of police to keep the crowd from invading the field. In Burma, I have seen the supporters of one side break through the police and disable the goalkeeper of the opposing side at a critical moment. The first big football match that was played in Spain, about fifteen years ago, led to an uncontrollable riot. As soon as strong feelings of rivalry are aroused, the notion of playing the game according to the rules always vanishes. People want to see one side on top and the other side humiliated, and they forget that victory gained through cheating or through the intervention of the crowd is meaningless. Even when the spectators don't intervene physically, they try to influence the game by cheering their own side and "rattling" opposing players with boos and insults. Serious sport has nothing to do with fair play. It is bound up with hatred, jealousy, boastfulness, disregard of all rules and sadistic pleasure in witnessing violence: in other words it is war minus the shooting.

Instead of blah-blahing about the clean, healthy rivalry of the football field and the great part played by the Olympic Games in bringing the nations together, it is more useful to inquire how and why this modern cult of sport arose. Most of the games we now play are of ancient origin, but sport does not seem to have been taken very seriously between Roman times and the Nineteenth century. Even in the English public schools the games cult did not start till the later part of the last century. Dr. Arnold, generally regarded as the founder of the modern public school, looked on games as simply a waste of time. Then, chiefly in England and the United States, games were built up into a heavily-financed activity, capable of attracting vast crowds and rousing savage passions, and the infection spread from country to country. It is the most violently combative sports, football and boxing, that have spread the widest. There cannot be much doubt that the whole thing is bound up with the rise of nationalism—that is, with the lunatic modern habit of identifying oneself with large power units and seeing everything in terms of competitive prestige. Also, organised games are more likely to flourish in urban communities where the average human being lives a sedentary or at least a confined life, and does not get much opportunity for creative labour. In a rustic community a boy or young man works off a good deal of his surplus energy by walking, swimming, snowballing, climbing trees, riding horses, and by various sports involving cruelty to animals, such as fishing, cock-fighting and ferreting for rats. In a big town one must indulge in group activities if one wants an outlet for one's physical strength or for one's sadistic impulses. Games are taken seriously in London and New York, and they were taken seriously in Rome and Byzantium: in the Middle Ages they were played, and probably played with much physical brutality, but they were not mixed up with politics nor a cause of group hatreds.

If you wanted to add to the vast fund of ill-will existing in the world at this moment, you could hardly do it better than by a series of football matches between Jews and Arabs, Germans and Czechs, Indians and British, Russians and Poles, and Italians and Jugoslavs, each match to be watched by a mixed audience of 100,000 spectators. I do not, of course, suggest that sport is one of the main causes of international rivalry; big-scale sport is itself,

I think, merely another effect of the causes that have produced nationalism. Still, you do make things worse by sending forth a team of eleven men, labelled as national champions, to do battle against some rival team, and allowing it to be felt on all sides that whichever nation is defeated will "lose face."

I hope, therefore, that we shan't follow up the visit of the Dynamos by sending a British team to the U.S.S.R. If we must do so, then let us send a second-rate team which is sure to be beaten and cannot be claimed to represent Britain as a whole. There are quite enough real causes of trouble already, and we need not add to them by encouraging young men to kick each other on the shins amid the roars of infuriated spectators.

In Defence of English Cooking

Evening Standard, December 15, 1945

We have heard a good deal of talk in recent years about the desirability of attracting foreign tourists to this country. It is well known that England's two worst faults, from a foreign visitor's point of view, are the gloom of our Sundays and the difficulty of buying a drink.

Both of those are due to fanatical minorities who will need a lot of quelling, including extensive legislation. But there is one point on which public opinion could bring about a rapid change for the better: I mean cooking.

It is commonly said, even by the English themselves, that English cooking is the worst in the world. It is supposed to be not merely incompetent, but also imitative, and I even read quite recently, in a book by a French writer, the remark: "The best English cooking is, of course, simply French cooking."

Now that is simply not true. As anyone who has lived long abroad will know, there is a whole host of delicacies which it is quite impossible to obtain outside the English-speaking countries. No doubt the list could be added to, but here are some of the things that I myself have sought for in foreign countries and failed to find.

First of all, kippers, Yorkshire pudding, Devonshire cream, muffins and crumpets. Then a list of puddings that would be interminable if I gave it in full: I will pick out for special mention Christmas pudding, treacle tart and apple dumplings. Then an almost equally long list of cakes: for instance, dark plum cake (such as you used to get at Buszard's before the war), shortbread and saffron buns. Also innumerable kinds of biscuit, which exist, of course, elsewhere, but are generally admitted to be better and crisper in England.

Then there are the various ways of cooking potatoes that are peculiar to our own country. Where else do you see potatoes roasted under the joint, which is far and away the best way of cooking them? Or the delicious potato cakes that you get in the north of England? And it is far better to cook new potatoes in the English way—that is, boiled with mint then served with a little melted butter or margarine—than to fry them, as is done in most countries.

Then there are the various sauces peculiar to England. For instance, bread sauce, horseradish sauce, mint sauce, and apple sauce, not to mention red currant jelly, which is excellent with mutton as well as with hare, and various kinds of sweet pickle, which we seem to have in greater profusion than most countries.

What else? Outside these islands I have never seen a haggis, except one that came out of a tin, nor Dublin prawns, nor Oxford marmalade, nor several other kinds of jam (marrow jam and bramble jelly, for instance), nor sausages of quite the same kind as ours.

Then there are the English cheeses. There are not many of them, but I fancy that Stilton is the best cheese of its type in the world, with Wensleydale not far behind. English apples are also outstandingly good, particularly the Cox's Orange Pippin.

And finally, I would like to put in a word for English bread. All bread is good, from the enormous Jewish loaves flavoured with caraway seeds to the Russian rye bread which is the colour of black treacle. Still, if there is anything quite as good as the soft part of the crust from an English cottage loaf (how soon shall we be seeing cottage loaves again?), I do not know of it.

No doubt some of the things I have named above *could* be obtained in continental Europe, just as it is *possible* in London to obtain vodka or bird's nest soup. But they are all native to our shores, and over huge areas they are literally unheard of.

South of, say, Brussels, I do not imagine that you would succeed in getting hold of a suet pudding. In French there is not even a word that exactly translates "suet." The French, also, never use mint in cookery, and do not use black currants except as the basis of a drink.

It will be seen that we have no cause to be ashamed of our cookery, so far as originality goes, or so far as the ingredients go. And yet, it must be admitted that there is a serious snag from the foreign visitor's point of view. This is, that you practically don't find good English cooking outside a private house. If you want, say, a good, rich slice of Yorkshire pudding, you are more likely to get it in the poorest English home than in a restaurant, which is where the visitor necessarily eats most of his meals.

It is a fact that restaurants which are distinctively English, and which also sell good food, are very hard to find. Pubs, as a rule, sell no food at all, other than potato crisps and tasteless sandwiches. The expensive restaurants and hotels almost all imitate French cookery and write their menus in French, while if you want a good cheap meal you gravitate naturally towards a Greek, Italian or Chinese restaurant.

We are not likely to succeed in attracting tourists while England is thought of as a country of bad food and unintelligible by-laws. At present one cannot do much about it, but sooner or later rationing will come to an end, and then will be the moment for our cookery to revive. It is not a law of nature that every restaurant in England should be either foreign or bad, and the first step towards an improvement will be a less long-suffering attitude in the British public itself.

A Nice Cup of Tea

Saturday Essay, *Evening Standard,* January 12, 1946

If you look up "tea" in the first cookery book that comes to hand you will probably find that it is unmentioned; or at most you will find a few lines of sketchy instructions which give no ruling on several of the most important points.

This is curious, not only because tea is one of the mainstays of civilisation in this country, as well as in Eire, Australia and New Zealand, but because the best manner of making it is the subject of violent disputes.

When I look through my own recipe for the perfect cup of tea, I find no fewer than 11 outstanding points. On perhaps two of them there would be pretty general agreement, but at least four others are acutely controversial. Here are my own 11 rules, every one of which I regard as golden:

First of all, one should use Indian or Ceylonese tea. China tea has virtues which are not to be despised nowadays—it is economical, and one can drink it without milk—but there is not much stimulation in it. One does not feel wiser, braver or more optimistic after drinking it. Anyone who uses that comforting phrase, "a nice cup of tea," invariably means Indian tea.

Secondly, tea should be made in small quantities—that is, in a teapot. Tea out of an urn is always tasteless, while Army tea, made in a cauldron, tastes of grease and whitewash. The teapot should be made of china or earthenware. Silver or Britannia-ware

pots produce inferior tea and enamel pots are worse: though curiously enough a pewter teapot (a rarity nowadays) is not so bad.

Thirdly, the pot should be warmed beforehand. This is better
done by placing it on the hob than by the usual method of swill-
ing it out with hot water.

Fourthly, the tea should be strong. For a pot holding a quart,
if you are going to fill it nearly to the brim, six heaped teaspoons
would be about right. In a time of rationing this is not an ideal
that can be realised on every day of the week, but I maintain that
one strong cup of tea is better than 20 weak ones. All true tea-
lovers not only like their tea strong, but like it a little stronger with
each year that passes—a fact which is recognized in the extra ration issued to old age pensioners.

Fifthly, the tea should be put straight into the pot. No strain-
ers, muslin bags or other devices to imprison the tea. In some
countries teapots are fitted with little dangling baskets under the
spout, to catch the stray leaves, which are supposed to be harmful. Actually one can swallow tea leaves in considerable quantities
without ill effect, and if the tea is not loose in the pot it never in-
fuses properly.

Sixthly, one should take the teapot to the kettle, and not the
other way about. The water should be actually boiling at the moment of impact, which means that one should keep it on the flame
while one pours. Some people add that one should only use water
that has been freshly brought to the boil, but I have never noticed
that this makes any difference.

Seventhly, after making the tea, one should stir it or, better,
give the pot a good shake, afterwards allowing the leaves to settle.

Eighthly, one should drink out of a breakfast cup—that is,
the cylindrical type of cup, not the flat, shallow type. The breakfast cup holds more, and with the other kind one's tea is always
half cold before one has well started on it.

Ninthly, one should pour the cream off the milk before using it for tea. Milk that is too creamy always gives tea a sickly taste.

Tenthly, one should pour tea into the cup first. This is one of the most controversial points of all; indeed in every family in Britain there are probably two schools of thought on the subject.

The milk-first school can bring forward some fairly strong arguments, but I maintain that my own argument is unanswerable. This is that, by putting the tea in first and then stirring as one pours, one can exactly regulate the amount of milk whereas one is liable to put in too much milk if one does it the other way round.

Lastly, tea—unless one is drinking it in the Russian style—should be drunk *without sugar*. I know very well that I am in a minority here. But still, how can you call yourself a true tea-lover if you destroy the flavour of your tea by putting sugar in it? It would be equally reasonable to put [in] pepper or salt.

Tea is meant to be bitter, just as beer is meant to be bitter. If you sweeten it, you are no longer tasting the tea, you are merely tasting the sugar: you could make a very similar drink by dissolving sugar in plain hot water.

Some people would answer that they don't like tea in itself, that they only drink it in order to be warmed and stimulated, and they need sugar to take the taste away. To those misguided people I would say: Try drinking tea without sugar for, say, a fortnight, and it is very unlikely that you will ever want to ruin your tea by sweetening it again.

These are not the only controversial points that arise in connection with tea-drinking, but they are sufficient to show how subtilised the whole business has become.

There is also the mysterious social etiquette surrounding the teapot (why is it considered vulgar to drink out of your saucer, for instance?) and much might be written about the subsidiary uses of tea leaves, such as telling fortunes, predicting the arrival of visitors, feeding rabbits, healing burns and sweeping the carpet.

It is worth paying attention to such details as warming the pot and using water that is really boiling, so as to make quite sure of wringing out of one's ration the 20 good, strong cups that two ounces, properly handled ought to represent.

The Moon Under Water

Saturday Essay, *Evening Standard,* February 9, 1946

My favourite public-house, the Moon Under Water, is only two minutes from a bus stop, but it is on a side-street, and drunks and rowdies never seem to find their way there, even on Saturday nights.

Its clientele, though fairly large, consists mostly of "regulars" who occupy the same chair every evening and go there for conversation as much as for the beer.

If you are asked why you favour a particular public-house, it would seem natural to put the beer first, but the thing that most appeals to me about the Moon Under Water is what people call its "atmosphere."

To begin with, its whole architecture and fittings are uncompromisingly Victorian. It has no glass-topped tables or other modern miseries, and, on the other hand, no sham roof-beams, ingle-nooks or plastic panels masquerading as oak. The grained woodwork, the ornamental mirrors behind the bar, the cast-iron fireplaces, the florid ceiling stained dark yellow by tobacco-smoke, the stuffed bull's head over the mantelpiece — everything has the solid, comfortable ugliness of the nineteenth century.

In winter there is generally a good fire burning in at least two of the bars, and the Victorian lay-out of the place gives one plenty of elbow-room. There are a public bar, a saloon bar, a ladies' bar, a bottle-and-jug for those who are too bashful to buy their supper beer publicly, and, upstairs, a dining-room.

Games are only played in the public, so that in the other bars you can walk about without constantly ducking to avoid flying darts.

In the Moon Under Water it is always quiet enough to talk. The house possesses neither a radio nor a piano, and even on Christmas Eve and such occasions the singing that happens is of a decorous kind.

The barmaids know most of their customers by name, and take a personal interest in everyone. They are all middle-aged women—two of them have their hair dyed in quite surprising shades—and they call everyone "dear," irrespective of age or sex. ("Dear," not "Ducky": pubs where the barmaid calls you "ducky" always have a disagreeable raffish atmosphere.)

Unlike most pubs, the Moon Under Water sells tobacco as well as cigarettes, and it also sells aspirins and stamps, and is obliging about letting you use the telephone.

You cannot get dinner at the Moon Under Water, but there is always the snack counter where you can get liver-sausage sandwiches, mussels (a speciality of the house), cheese, pickles and those large biscuits with caraway seeds in them which only seem to exist in public-houses.

Upstairs, six days a week, you can get a good, solid lunch—for example, a cut off the joint, two vegetables and boiled jam roll—for about three shillings.

The special pleasure of this lunch is that you can have draught stout with it. I doubt whether as many as 10 per cent of London pubs serve draught stout, but the Moon Under Water is one of them. It is a soft, creamy sort of stout, and it goes better in a pewter pot.

They are particular about their drinking vessels at the Moon Under Water, and never, for example, make the mistake of serving a pint of beer in a handleless glass. Apart from glass and pewter mugs, they have some of those pleasant strawberry-pink china ones which are now seldom seen in London. China mugs went out about 30 years ago, because most people like their drink to be transparent, but in my opinion beer tastes better out of china.

The great surprise of the Moon Under Water is its garden. You go through a narrow passage leading out of the saloon, and find yourself in a fairly large garden with plane trees, under which there are little green tables with iron chairs round them. Up at one end of the garden there are swings and a chute for the children.

On summer evenings there are family parties, and you sit under the plane trees having beer or draught cider to the tune of delighted squeals from children going down the chute. The prams with the younger children are parked near the gate.

Many as are the virtues of the Moon Under Water, I think that the garden is its best feature, because it allows whole families to go there instead of Mum having to stay at home and mind the baby while Dad goes out alone.

And though, strictly speaking, they are only allowed in the garden, the children tend to seep into the pub and even to fetch drinks for their parents. This, I believe, is against the law, but it is a law that deserves to be broken, for it is the puritanical nonsense of excluding children—and therefore, to some extent, women—from pubs that has turned these places into mere boozing-shops instead of the family gathering-places that they ought to be.

The Moon Under Water is my ideal of what a pub should be—at any rate, in the London area. (The qualities one expects of a country pub are slightly different.)

But now is the time to reveal something which the discerning and disillusioned reader will probably have guessed already. There is no such place as the Moon Under Water.

That is to say, there may well be a pub of that name, but I don't know of it, nor do I know any pub with just that combination of qualities.

I know pubs where the beer is good but you can't get meals, others where you can get meals but which are noisy and crowded, and others which are quiet but where the beer is generally sour. As for gardens, offhand I can only think of three London pubs that possess them.

But, to be fair, I do know of a few pubs that almost come up to the Moon Under Water. I have mentioned above ten qualities that the perfect pub should have and I know one pub that has eight of them. Even there, however, there is no draught stout, and no china mugs.

And if anyone knows of a pub that has draught stout, open fires, cheap meals, a garden, motherly barmaids and no radio, I should be glad to hear of it, even though its name were something as prosaic as the Red Lion or the Railway Arms.

In Front of Your Nose

Tribune, March 22, 1946

Many recent statements in the press have declared that it is almost, if not quite, impossible for us to mine as much coal as we need for home and export purposes, because of the impossibility of inducing a sufficient number of miners to remain in the pits. One set of figures which I saw last week estimated the annual "wastage" of mineworkers at 60,000 and the annual intake of new workers at 10,000. Simultaneously with this—and sometimes in the same column of the same paper—there have been statements that it would be undesirable to make use of Poles or Germans because this might lead to unemployment in the coal industry. The two utterances do not always come from the same sources, but there must certainly be many people who are capable of holding these totally contradictory ideas in their heads at a single moment.

This is merely one example of a habit of mind which is extremely widespread, and perhaps always has been. Bernard Shaw, in the preface to *Androcles and the Lion,* cites as another example the first chapter of the Gospel of Matthew, which starts off by establishing the descent of Joseph, father of Jesus, from Abraham. In the first verse, Jesus is described as "the son of David, the son of Abraham," and the genealogy is then followed up through fifteen verses: then, in the next verse but one, it is explained that as a matter of fact Jesus was *not* descended from Abraham, since he was not the son of Joseph. This, says Shaw, presents no difficulty to a religious believer, and he names as a parallel case the rioting in the

East End of London by the partisans of the Tichborne Claimant, who declared that a British working-man was being done out of his rights.[1]

Medically, I believe, this manner of thinking is called schizophrenia: at any rate, it is the power of holding simultaneously two beliefs which cancel out. Closely allied to it is the power of ignoring facts which are obvious and unalterable, and which will have to be faced sooner or later. It is especially in our political thinking that these vices flourish. Let me take a few sample subjects out of the hat. They have no organic connection with each other: they are merely cases, taken almost at random, of plain, unmistakable facts being shirked by people who in another part of their mind are aware of those facts.

Hong Kong. For years before the war everyone with knowledge of Far Eastern conditions knew that our position in Hong Kong was untenable and that we should lose it as soon as a major war started. This knowledge, however, was intolerable, and government after government continued to cling to Hong Kong instead of giving it back to the Chinese. Fresh troops were even pushed into it, with the certainty that they would be uselessly taken prisoner, a few weeks before the Japanese attack began. Then war came, and Hong Kong promptly fell—as everyone had known all along that it would do.

Conscription. For years before the war, nearly all enlightened people were in favour of standing up to Germany: the majority of them were also against having enough armaments to make such a stand effective. I know very well the arguments that are put forward in defence of this attitude; some of them are justified, but in the main they are simply forensic excuses. As late as 1939, the Labour Party voted against conscription, a step which probably played its part in bringing about the Russo-German pact and certainly had a disastrous effect on morale in France. Then came

1940, and we nearly perished for lack of a large, efficient army, which we could only have had if we had introduced conscription at least three years earlier.

The Birth Rate. Twenty or twenty-five years ago, contraception and enlightenment were held to be almost synonymous. To this day, the majority of people argue — the argument is variously expressed, but always boils down to more or less the same thing — that large families are impossible for economic reasons. At the same time, it is widely known that the birth rate is highest among the low-standard nations, and, in our own population, highest among the worst-paid groups. It is also argued that a smaller population would mean less unemployment and more comfort for everybody, while on the other hand it is well established that a dwindling and aging population is faced with calamitous and perhaps insoluble economic problems. Necessarily the figures are uncertain, but it is quite possible that in only 70 years our population will amount to about eleven millions, over half of whom will be Old Age Pensioners. Since, for complex reasons, most people don't want large families, the frightening facts can exist somewhere or other in their consciousness, simultaneously known and not known.

U.N.O. In order to have any efficacy whatever, a world organisation must be able to override big States as well as small ones. It must have power to inspect and limit armaments, which means that its officials must have access to every square inch of every country. It must also have at its disposal an armed force bigger than any other armed force and responsible only to the organisation itself. The two or three great States that really matter have never even pretended to agree to any of these conditions, and they have so arranged the constitution of U.N.O. that their own actions cannot even be discussed. In other words, U.N.O.'s usefulness as an instrument of world peace is nil. This was just as obvious before it began functioning as it is now. Yet only a few months ago millions of well-informed people believed that it was going to be a success.

There is no use in multiplying examples. The point is that we are all capable of believing things which we *know* to be untrue, and then, when we are finally proved wrong, impudently twisting the facts so as to show that we were right. Intellectually, it is possible to carry on this process for an indefinite time: the only check on it is that sooner or later a false belief bumps up against solid reality, usually on a battlefield.

When one looks at the all-prevailing schizophrenia of democratic societies, the lies that have to be told for vote-catching purposes, the silence about major issues, the distortions of the press, it is tempting to believe that in totalitarian countries there is less humbug, more facing of the facts. There, at least, the ruling groups are not dependent on popular favour and can utter the truth crudely and brutally. Goering could say "Guns before butter," while his democratic opposite numbers had to wrap the same sentiment up in hundreds of hypocritical words.

Actually, however, the avoidance of reality is much the same everywhere, and has much the same consequences. The Russian people were taught for years that they were better off than everybody else, and propaganda posters showed Russian families sitting down to abundant meals while the proletariat of other countries starved in the gutter. Meanwhile the workers in the western countries were so much better off than those of the U.S.S.R. that non-contact between Soviet citizens and outsiders had to be a guiding principle of policy. Then, as a result of the war, millions of ordinary Russians penetrated far into Europe, and when they return home the original avoidance of reality will inevitably be paid for in frictions of various kinds. The Germans and the Japanese lost the war quite largely because their rulers were unable to see facts which were plain to any dispassionate eye.

To see what is in front of one's nose needs a constant struggle. One thing that helps towards it is to keep a diary, or, at any rate, to keep some kind of record of one's opinions about important events. Otherwise, when some particularly absurd belief is exploded by events, one may simply forget that one ever held it. Political predictions are usually wrong, but even when one makes a correct one, to discover *why* one was right can be very illuminating. In general, one is only right when either wish or fear coincides with reality. If one recognises this, one cannot, of course, get rid of one's subjective feelings, but one can to some extent insulate them from one's thinking and make predictions cold-bloodedly, by the book of arithmetic. In private life most people are fairly realistic. When one is making out one's weekly budget, two and two invariably make four. Politics, on the other hand, is a sort of subatomic or non-Euclidean world where it is quite easy for the part to be greater than the whole or for two objects to be in the same place simultaneously. Hence the contradictions and absurdities I have chronicled above, all finally traceable to a secret belief that one's political opinions, unlike the weekly budget, will not have to be tested against solid reality.

Some Thoughts on the Common Toad

Tribune, April 12, 1946

Before the swallow, before the daffodil, and not much later than the snowdrop, the common toad salutes the coming of Spring after his own fashion, which is to emerge from a hole in the ground, where he has lain buried since the previous autumn, and crawl as rapidly as possible towards the nearest suitable patch of water. Something — some kind of shudder in the earth, or perhaps merely a rise of a few degrees in the temperature — has told him that it is time to wake up: though a few toads appear to sleep the clock round and miss out a year from time to time — at any rate, I have more than once dug them up, alive and apparently well, in the middle of the summer.

At this period, after his long fast, the toad has a very spiritual look, like a strict Anglo-Catholic towards the end of Lent. His movements are languid but purposeful, his body is shrunken, and by contrast his eyes look abnormally large. This allows one to notice, what one might not at another time, that a toad has about the most beautiful eye of any living creature. It is like gold, or more exactly it is like the gold-coloured semi-precious stone which one sometimes sees in signet rings, and which I think is called a chrysoberyl.

For a few days after getting into the water the toad concentrates on building up his strength by eating small insects. Presently he has swollen to his normal size again, and then he goes through a phase of intense sexiness. All he knows, at least if he is a male toad, is that he wants to get his arms round something, and if you offer him a stick, or even your finger, he will cling to it with surprising strength and take a long time to discover that it is not a female toad. Frequently one comes upon shapeless masses of ten or twenty toads rolling over and over in the water, one clinging to another without distinction of sex. By degrees, however, they sort themselves out into couples, with the male duly sitting on the female's back. You can now distinguish males from females, because the male is smaller, darker and sits on top, with his arms tightly clasped round the female's neck. After a day or two the spawn is laid in long strings which wind themselves in and out of the reeds and soon become invisible. A few more weeks, and the water is alive with masses of tiny tadpoles which rapidly grow larger, sprout hind-legs, then fore-legs, then shed their tails: and finally, about the middle of the summer, the new generation of toads, smaller than one's thumb-nail but perfect in every particular, crawl out of the water to begin the game anew.

I mention the spawning of the toads because it is one of the phenomena of Spring which most deeply appeal to me, and because the toad, unlike the skylark and the primrose, has never had much of a boost from the poets. But I am aware that many people do not like reptiles or amphibians, and I am not suggesting that in order to enjoy the Spring you have to take an interest in toads. There are also the crocus, the missel thrush, the cuckoo, the blackthorn, etc. The point is that the pleasures of Spring are available to everybody, and cost nothing. Even in the most sordid street the coming of Spring will register itself by some sign or other, if it is only a brighter blue between the chimney pots or the vivid green of an elder sprouting on a blitzed site. Indeed it is remarkable how Nature goes on existing unofficially, as it were, in the very heart of London. I have seen a kestrel flying over the Deptford gasworks, and I have heard a first-rate performance by a blackbird in the

Euston Road. There must be some hundreds of thousands, if not millions, of birds living inside the four-mile radius, and it is rather a pleasing thought that none of them pays a halfpenny of rent.

As for Spring, not even the narrow and gloomy streets round the Bank of England are quite able to exclude it. It comes seeping in everywhere, like one of those new poison gases which pass through all filters. The Spring is commonly referred to as "a miracle," and during the past five or six years this worn-out figure of speech has taken on a new lease of life. After the sort of winters we have had to endure recently, the Spring does seem miraculous, because it has become gradually harder and harder to believe that it is actually going to happen. Every February since 1940 I have found myself thinking that this time Winter is going to be permanent. But Persephone, like the toads, always rises from the dead at about the same moment. Suddenly, towards the end of March, the miracle happens and the decaying slum in which I live is transfigured. Down in the square the sooty privets have turned bright green, the leaves are thickening on the chestnut trees, the daffodils are out, the wallflowers are budding, the policeman's tunic looks positively a pleasant shade of blue, the fishmonger greets his customers with a smile, and even the sparrows are quite a different colour, having felt the balminess of the air and nerved themselves to take a bath, their first since last September.

Is it wicked to take a pleasure in Spring and other seasonal changes? To put it more precisely, is it politically reprehensible, while we are all groaning, or at any rate ought to be groaning, under the shackles of the capitalist system, to point out that life is frequently more worth living because of a blackbird's song, a yellow elm tree in October, or some other natural phenomenon which does not cost money and does not have what the editors of Left-wing newspapers call a class angle? There is no doubt that many people think so. I know by experience that a favourable reference to "Nature" in one of my articles is liable to bring me abusive letters, and though the key-word in these letters is usually "sentimental," two ideas seem to be mixed up in them. One is that any pleasure in the actual process of life encourages a sort of political quietism. People, so the thought runs, ought to be discontented, and it is our job to multiply our wants and not simply to increase our enjoyment of the things we have already. The other idea is that this is the age of machines and that to dislike the machine, or even to want to limit its domination, is backward-looking, reactionary and slightly ridiculous. This is often backed up by the statement that a love of Nature is a foible of urbanised people who have no notion what Nature is really like. Those who really have to deal with the soil, so it is argued, do not love the soil, and do not take the faintest interest in birds or flowers, except from a strictly utilitarian point of view. To love the country one must live in the town, merely taking an occasional week-end ramble at the warmer times of year.

This last idea is demonstrably false. Medieval literature, for instance, including the popular ballads, is full of an almost Georgian enthusiasm for Nature, and the art of agricultural peoples such as the Chinese and Japanese centres always round trees, birds, flowers, rivers, mountains. The other idea seems to me to be wrong in a subtler way. Certainly we ought to be discontented, we ought not simply to find out ways of making the best of a bad job, and yet if we kill all pleasure in the actual process of life, what sort of future are we preparing for ourselves? If a man cannot enjoy the return of Spring, why should he be happy in a labour-saving Utopia? What will he do with the leisure that the machine will give him? I have always suspected that if our economic and political problems are ever really solved, life will become simpler instead of more complex, and that the sort of pleasure one gets from finding the first primrose will loom larger than the sort of pleasure one gets from eating an ice to the tune of a Wurlitzer. I think that by retaining one's childhood love of such things as trees, fishes, butterflies and — to return to my first instance — toads, one makes a peaceful and decent future a little more probable, and that by preaching the doctrine that nothing is to be admired except steel and concrete, one merely makes it a little surer that human beings will have no outlet for their surplus energy except in hatred and leader-worship.

At any rate, Spring is here, even in London N.1, and they can't stop you enjoying it. This is a satisfying reflection. How many a time have I stood watching the toads mating, or a pair of hares having a boxing match in the young corn, and thought of all the important persons who would stop me enjoying this if they could. But luckily they can't. So long as you are not actually ill, hungry, frightened or immured in a prison or a holiday camp, Spring is still Spring. The atom bombs are piling up in the factories, the police are prowling through the cities, the lies are streaming from the loudspeakers, but the earth is still going round the sun, and neither the dictators nor the bureaucrats, deeply as they disapprove of the process, are able to prevent it.

A Good Word for the Vicar of Bray

Tribune, April 26, 1946

Some years ago a friend took me to the little Berkshire church of which the celebrated Vicar of Bray was once the incumbent. (Actually it is a few miles from Bray, but perhaps at that time the two livings were one.) In the churchyard, there stands a magnificent yew tree which, according to a notice at its foot, was planted by no less a person than the Vicar of Bray himself. And it struck me at the time as curious that such a man should have left such a relic behind him.

The Vicar of Bray, though he was well equipped to be a leader-writer on the *Times,* could hardly be described as an admirable character. Yet, after this lapse of time, all that is left of him is a comic song and a beautiful tree, which has rested the eyes of generation after generation and must surely have outweighed any bad effects which he produced by his political quislingism.

Thibaw, the last King of Burma, was also far from being a good man. He was a drunkard, he had five hundred wives—he seems to have kept them chiefly for show, however—and when he came to the throne his first act was to decapitate seventy or eighty of his brothers. Yet he did posterity a good turn by planting the dusty streets of Mandalay with tamarind trees which cast a pleasant shade until the Japanese incendiary bombs burned them down in 1942.

The poet, James Shirley, seems to have generalised too freely when he said that "Only the actions of the just Smell sweet and blossom in their dust." Sometimes the actions of the unjust make quite a good showing after the appropriate lapse of time. When I saw the Vicar of Bray's yew tree it reminded me of something, and afterwards I got hold of a book of selections from the writings of John Aubrey and re-read a pastoral poem which must have been written some time in the first half of the seventeenth century, and which was inspired by a certain Mrs. Overall.

Mrs. Overall was the wife of a Dean and was extensively unfaithful to him.[1] According to Aubrey she "could scarcely denie any one," and she had "the loveliest Eies that were ever seen, but wondrous wanton." The poem (the "shepherd swaine" seems to have been somebody called Sir John Selby) starts off:

> Downe lay the Shepherd Swaine
> So sober and demure
> Wishing for his wench againe
> So bonny and so pure
> With his head on hillock lowe
> And his arms akimboe
> And all was for the losse of his
> Hye nonny nonny noe. . . .
>
> Sweet she was, as kind a love
> As ever fetter'd Swaine;
> Never such a daynty one
> Shall man enjoy again.
> Sett a thousand on a rowe
> I forbid that any showe
> Ever the like of her
> Hye nonny nonny noe.

As the poem proceeds through another five[2] verses, the refrain "hye nonny nonny noe" takes on an unmistakably obscene meaning, but it ends with the exquisite stanza:

> But gone she is the prettiest lasse
> That ever trod on plaine.
> What ever hath betide of her
> Blame not the Shepherd Swaine.
> For why? She was her owne Foe.
> And gave herself the overthrowe
> By being so franke of her
> Hye nonny nonny noe.

Mrs. Overall was no more an exemplary character than the Vicar of Bray, though a more attractive one. Yet in the end all that remains of her is a poem which still gives pleasure to many people, though for some reason it never gets into the anthologies. The suffering which she presumably caused, and the misery and futility in which her own life must have ended, have been transformed into a sort of lingering fragrance like the smell of tobacco-plants on a summer evening.

But to come back to trees. The planting of a tree, especially one of the long-living hardwood trees, is a gift which you can make to posterity at almost no cost and with almost no trouble, and if the tree takes root it will far outlive the visible effect of any of your other actions, good or evil. A year or two ago I wrote a few paragraphs in *Tribune* about some sixpenny rambler roses from Woolworth's which I had planted before the war. This brought me an indignant letter from a reader who said that roses are bourgeois, but I still think that my sixpence was better spent than if it had gone on cigarettes or even on one of the excellent Fabian Research Pamphlets.

Recently, I spent a day at the cottage where I used to live, and noted with a pleased surprise — to be exact, it was a feeling of having done good unconsciously — the progress of the things I had planted nearly ten years ago. I think it is worth recording what some of them cost, just to show what you can do with a few shillings if you invest them in something that grows.

First of all there were the two ramblers from Woolworth's, and three polyantha roses, all at sixpence each. Then there were two bush roses which were part of a job lot from a nursery garden. This job lot consisted of six fruit trees, three rose bushes and two gooseberry bushes, all for ten shillings. One of the fruit trees and one of the rose bushes died, but the rest are all flourishing. The sum total is five fruit trees, seven roses and two gooseberry bushes, all for twelve and sixpence. These plants have not entailed much work, and have had nothing spent on them beyond the original amount. They never even received any manure, except what I occasionally collected in a bucket when one of the farm horses happened to have halted outside the gate.

Between them, in nine years, those seven rose bushes will have given what would add up to a hundred or a hundred and fifty months of bloom. The fruit trees, which were mere saplings when I put them in, are now just about getting in their stride. Last week one of them, a plum, was a mass of blossom, and the apples looked as if they were going to do fairly well. What had originally been the weakling of the family, a Cox's Orange Pippin — it would hardly have been included in the job lot if it had been a good plant — had grown into a sturdy tree with plenty of fruit spurs on it. I maintain that it was a public-spirited action to plant that Cox, for these trees do not fruit quickly and I did not expect to stay there long. I never had an apple off it myself, but it looks as if somebody else will have quite a lot. By their fruits ye shall know them, and the Cox's Orange Pippin is a good fruit to be known by.

Yet I did not plant it with the conscious intention of doing any-body a good turn. I just saw the job lot going cheap and stuck the things into the ground without much preparation.

A thing which I regret, and which I will try to remedy some time, is that I have never in my life planted a walnut. Nobody does plant them nowadays—when you see a walnut it is almost invari-ably an old tree. If you plant a walnut you are planting it for your grandchildren, and who cares a damn for his grandchildren? Nor does anybody plant a quince, a mulberry or a medlar. But these are garden trees which you can only be expected to plant if you have a patch of ground of your own. On the other hand, in any hedge or in any piece of waste ground you happen to be walking through, you can do something to remedy the appalling massacre of trees, especially oaks, ashes, elms and beeches, which has happened dur-ing the war years.

Even an apple tree is liable to live for about 100 years, so that the Cox I planted in 1936 may still be bearing fruit well into the twenty-first century. An oak or a beech may live for hundreds of years and be a pleasure to thousands or tens of thousands of people before it is finally sawn up into timber. I am not suggest-ing that one can discharge all one's obligations towards society by means of a private re-afforestation scheme. Still, it might not be a bad idea, every time you commit an anti-social act, to make a note of it in your diary, and then, at the appropriate season, push an acorn into the ground.

And, if even one in twenty of them came to maturity, you might do quite a lot of harm in your lifetime, and still, like the Vicar of Bray, end up as a public benefactor after all.

Why I Write

Gangrel, [No. 4, Summer] 1946

From a very early age, perhaps the age of five or six, I knew that when I grew up I should be a writer. Between the ages of about seventeen and twenty-four I tried to abandon this idea, but I did so with the consciousness that I was outraging my true nature and that sooner or later I should have to settle down and write books.

I was the middle child of three, but there was a gap of five years on either side, and I barely saw my father before I was eight. For this and other reasons I was somewhat lonely, and I soon developed disagreeable mannerisms which made me unpopular throughout my schooldays. I had the lonely child's habit of making up stories and holding conversations with imaginary persons, and I think from the very start my literary ambitions were mixed up with the feeling of being isolated and undervalued. I knew that I had a facility with words and a power of facing unpleasant facts, and I felt that this created a sort of private world in which I could get my own back for my failure in everyday life. Nevertheless the volume of serious — i.e. seriously intended — writing which I produced all through my childhood and boyhood would not amount to half a dozen pages. I wrote my first poem at the age of four or five, my mother taking it down to dictation. I cannot remember anything about it except that it was about a tiger and the tiger had "chair-like teeth"—a good enough phrase, but I fancy the poem was a plagiarism of Blake's "Tiger, Tiger." At eleven, when the war of 1914–18 broke out, I wrote a patriotic poem which was printed in the local newspaper, as was another, two years later, on the death of Kitchener. From time to time, when I was bit older, I wrote bad and usually unfinished "nature poems" in the Georgian style. I also, about twice, attempted a short story which was a ghastly failure. That was the total of the would-be serious work that I actually set down on paper during all those years.

However, throughout this time I did in a sense engage in literary activities. To begin with there was the made-to-order stuff which I produced quickly, easily and without much pleasure to myself. Apart from school work, I wrote *vers d'occasion,* semi-comic poems which I could turn out at what now seems to me astonishing speed—at fourteen I wrote a whole rhyming play, in imitation of Aristophanes, in about a week—and helped to edit school magazines, both printed and in manuscript. These magazines were the most pitiful burlesque stuff that you could imagine, and I took far less trouble with them than I now would with the cheapest journalism. But side by side with all this, for fifteen years or more, I was carrying out a literary exercise of a quite different kind: this was the making up of a continuous "story" about myself, a sort of diary existing only in the mind. I believe this is a common habit of children and adolescents. As a very small child I used to imagine that I was, say, Robin Hood and picture myself as the hero of thrilling adventures, but quite soon my "story" ceased to be narcissistic in a crude way and became more and more a mere description of what I was doing and the things I saw. For minutes at a time this kind of thing would be running through my head: "He pushed the door open and entered the room. A yellow beam of sunlight, filtering through the muslin curtains, slanted on to the table, where a matchbox, half open, lay beside the inkpot. With his right hand in his pocket he moved across to the window.

Down in the street a tortoiseshell cat was chasing a dead leaf," etc.,
etc. This habit continued till I was about twenty-five, right through
my non-literary years. Although I had to search, and did search, for
the right words, I seemed to be making this descriptive effort almost against my will, under a kind of compulsion from outside.
The "story" must, I suppose, have reflected the styles of the various writers I admired at different ages, but so far as I remember
it always had the same meticulous descriptive quality.

When I was about sixteen I suddenly discovered the joy of
mere words, i.e. the sounds and associations of words. The lines
from *Paradise Lost*—

> *So hee with difficulty and labour hard*
> *Moved on: with difficulty and labour hee,*[1]

which do not now seem to me so very wonderful, sent shivers
down my backbone; and the spelling "hee" for "he" was an added
pleasure. As for the need to describe things, I knew all about it already. So it is clear what kind of books I wanted to write, in so far
as I could be said to want to write books at that time. I wanted to
write enormous naturalistic novels with unhappy endings, full of
detailed descriptions and arresting similes, and also full of purple
passages in which words were used partly for the sake of their
sound. And in fact my first completed novel, *Burmese Days,* which
I wrote when I was thirty but projected much earlier, is rather that
kind of book.

I give all this background information because I do not think
one can assess a writer's motives without knowing something of his
early development. His subject-matter will be determined by the
age he lives in—at least this is true in tumultuous, revolutionary
ages like our own—but before he ever begins to write he will have

acquired an emotional attitude from which he will never completely escape. It is his job, no doubt, to discipline his temperament and avoid getting stuck at some immature stage, or in some perverse mood: but if he escapes from his early influences altogether, he will have killed his impulse to write. Putting aside the need to earn a living, I think there are four great motives for writing, at any rate for writing prose. They exist in different degrees in every writer, and in any one writer the proportions will vary from time to time, according to the atmosphere in which he is living. They are:

(i) Sheer egoism. Desire to seem clever, to be talked about, to be remembered after death, to get your own back on grown-ups who snubbed you in childhood, etc., etc. It is humbug to pretend that this is not a motive, and a strong one. Writers share this characteristic with scientists, artists, politicians, lawyers, soldiers, successful business men — in short, with the whole top crust of humanity. The great mass of human beings are not acutely selfish. After the age of about thirty they abandon individual ambition — in many cases, indeed, they almost abandon the sense of being individuals at all — and live chiefly for others, or are simply smothered under drudgery. But there is also the minority of gifted, wilful people who are determined to live their own lives to the end, and writers belong in this class. Serious writers, I should say, are on the whole more vain and self-centred than journalists, though less interested in money.

(ii) Aesthetic enthusiasm. Perception of beauty in the external world, or, on the other hand, in words and their right arrangement. Pleasure in the impact of one sound on another, in the firmness of good prose or the rhythm of a good story. Desire to share an experience which one feels is valuable and ought not to be missed. The aesthetic motive is very feeble in a lot of writers, but even a pamphleteer or a writer of textbooks will have pet words and phrases which appeal to him for non-utilitarian reasons; or he may feel strongly about typography, width of margins, etc. Above the level of a railway guide, no book is quite free from aesthetic considerations.

(iii) Historical impulse. Desire to see things as they are, to find out true facts and store them up for the use of posterity.

(iv) Political purpose — using the word "political" in the widest possible sense. Desire to push the world in a certain direction, to alter other people's idea of the kind of society that they should strive after. Once again, no book is genuinely free from political bias. The opinion that art should have nothing to do with politics is itself a political attitude.

It can be seen how these various impulses must war against one another, and how they must fluctuate from person to person and from time to time. By nature — taking your "nature" to be the state you have attained when you are first adult — I am a person in whom the first three motives would outweigh the fourth. In a peaceful age I might have written ornate or merely descriptive books, and might have remained almost unaware of my political loyalties. As it is I have been forced into becoming a sort of pamphleteer. First I spent five years in an unsuitable profession (the Indian Imperial Police, in Burma), and then I underwent poverty and the sense of failure. This increased my natural hatred of authority and made me for the first time fully aware of the existence of the working classes, and the job in Burma had given me some understanding of the nature of imperialism: but these experiences were not enough to give me an accurate political orientation. Then came Hitler, the Spanish civil war, etc. By the end of 1935 I had still failed to reach a firm decision. I remember the last three stanzas of a little poem that I wrote at that date, expressing my dilemma:

I am the worm who never turned,
The eunuch without a harem;
Between the priest and the commissar
I walk like Eugene Aram;

And the commissar is telling my fortune
While the radio plays,
But the priest has promised an Austin Seven,
For Duggie always pays.

I dreamed I dwelt in marble halls,
And woke to find it true;
I wasn't born for an age like this;
Was Smith? Was Jones? Were you?[2]

The Spanish war and other events in 1936–7 turned the scale and thereafter I knew where I stood. Every line of serious work that I have written since 1936 has been written, directly or indirectly, *against* totalitarianism and *for* democratic Socialism, as I understand it. It seems to me nonsense, in a period like our own, to think that one can avoid writing of such subjects. Everyone writes of them in one guise or another. It is simply a question of which side one takes and what approach one follows. And the more one is conscious of one's political bias, the more chance one has of acting politically without sacrificing one's aesthetic and intellectual integrity.

What I have most wanted to do throughout the past ten years is to make political writing into an art. My starting point is always a feeling of partisanship, a sense of injustice. When I sit down to write a book, I do not say to myself, "I am going to produce a work of art." I write it because there is some lie that I want to expose, some fact to which I want to draw attention, and my initial concern is to get a hearing. But I could not do the work of writing a book, or even a long magazine article, if it were not also an aesthetic experience. Anyone who cares to examine my work will see that even when it is downright propaganda it contains much that a full-time politician would consider irrelevant. I am not able, and I do not want, completely to abandon the world-view that I acquired in childhood. So long as I remain alive and well I shall continue to feel strongly about prose style, to love the surface of the earth, and to take a pleasure in solid objects and scraps of useless information. It is no use trying to suppress that side of myself. The job is to reconcile my ingrained likes and dislikes with the essentially public, non-individual activities that this age forces on all of us.

It is not easy. It raises problems of construction and of language, and it raises in a new way the problem of truthfulness. Let me give just one example of the cruder kind of difficulty that arises. My book about the Spanish civil war, *Homage to Catalonia,* is, of course, a frankly political book, but in the main it is written with a certain detachment and regard for form. I did try very hard in it to tell the whole truth without violating my literary instincts. But among other things it contains a long chapter, full of newspaper quotations and the like, defending the Trotskyists who were accused of plotting with Franco. Clearly such a chapter, which after a year or two would lose its interest for any ordinary reader, must ruin the book. A critic whom I respect read me a lecture about it. "Why did you put in all that stuff?" he said. "You've turned what might have been a good book into journalism." What he said was true, but I could not have done otherwise. I happened to know, what very few people in England had been allowed to know, that innocent men were being falsely accused. If I had not been angry about that I should never have written the book.

In one form or another this problem comes up again. The problem of language is subtler and would take too long to discuss. I will only say that of late years I have tried to write less picturesquely and more exactly. In any case I find that by the time you have perfected any style of writing, you have always outgrown it. *Animal Farm* was the first book in which I tried, with full consciousness of what I was doing, to fuse political purpose and artistic purpose into one whole. I have not written a novel for seven years, but I hope to write another fairly soon. It is bound to be a failure, every book is a failure, but I do know with some clarity what kind of book I want to write.

Looking back through the last page or two, I see that I have made it appear as though my motives in writing were wholly public-spirited. I don't want to leave that as the final impression. All writers are vain, selfish and lazy, and at the very bottom of their motives there lies a mystery. Writing a book is a horrible, exhausting struggle, like a long bout of some painful illness. One would never undertake such a thing if one were not driven on by some demon whom one can neither resist nor understand. For all one knows that demon is simply the same instinct that makes a baby squall for attention. And yet it is also true that one can write nothing readable unless one constantly struggles to efface one's own personality. Good prose is like a window pane. I cannot say with certainty which of my motives are the strongest, but I know which of them deserve to be followed. And looking back through my work, I see that it is invariably where I lacked a *political* purpose that I wrote lifeless books and was betrayed into purple passages, sentences without meaning, decorative adjectives and humbug generally.

How the Poor Die

Now, [n.s.] No. 6, November 1946

In the year 1929 I spent several weeks in the Hôpital X, in the fifteenth Arrondissement of Paris.[1] The clerks put me through the usual third-degree at the reception desk, and indeed I was kept answering questions for some twenty minutes before they would let me in. If you have ever had to fill up forms in a Latin country you will know the kind of questions I mean. For some days past I had been unequal to translating Reaumur into Fahrenheit, but I know that my temperature was round about 103, and by the end of the interview I had some difficulty in standing on my feet. At my back a resigned little knot of patients, carrying bundles done up in coloured handkerchiefs, waited their turn to be questioned.

After the questioning came the bath—a compulsory routine for all newcomers, apparently, just as in prison or the workhouse. My clothes were taken away from me, and after I had sat shivering for some minutes in five inches of warm water I was given a linen nightshirt and a short blue flannel dressing-gown—no slippers, they had none big enough for me, they said—and led out into the open air. This was a night in February and I was suffering from pneumonia.[2] The ward we were going to was 200 yards away and it seemed that to get to it you had to cross the hospital grounds. Someone stumbled in front of me with a lantern. The gravel path was frosty underfoot, and the wind whipped the nightshirt round my bare calves. When we got into the ward I was aware of a strange feeling of familiarity whose origin I did not succeed in pinning down till later in the night. It was a long, rather low, ill-lit room, full of murmuring voices and with three rows of beds surprisingly close together. There was a foul smell, faecal and yet sweetish. As I lay down I saw on a bed nearly opposite me a small, round-shouldered, sandy-haired man sitting half naked while a doctor and a student performed some strange operation on him. First the doctor produced from his black bag a dozen small glasses like wine glasses, then the student burned a match inside each glass to exhaust the air, then the glass was popped on to the man's back or chest and the vacuum drew up a huge yellow blister. Only after some moments did I realise what they were doing to him. It was something called cupping, a treatment which you can read about in old medical textbooks but which till then I had vaguely thought of as one of those things they do to horses.

The cold air outside had probably lowered my temperature, and I watched this barbarous remedy with detachment and even a certain amount of amusement. The next moment, however, the doctor and the student came across to my bed, hoisted me upright and without a word began applying the same set of glasses, which had not been sterilised in any way. A few feeble protests that I uttered got no more response than if I had been an animal. I was very much impressed by the impersonal way in which the two men started on me. I had never been in the public ward of a hospital before, and it was my first experience of doctors who handle you without speaking to you, or, in a human sense, taking any notice of you. They only put on six glasses in my case, but after doing so they scarified the blisters and applied the glasses again. Each glass now drew out about a dessert-spoonful of dark-coloured blood. As I lay down again, humiliated, disgusted and frightened by the thing that had been done to me, I reflected that now at least they would leave me alone. But no, not a bit of it. There was another treatment coming, the mustard poultice, seemingly a matter of routine like the hot bath. Two slatternly nurses had already got the poultice ready, and they lashed it round my chest as tight as a strait jacket while some men who were wandering about the ward in shirt and trousers began to collect round my bed with half-sympathetic grins. I learned later that watching a patient have a mustard poultice was a favourite pastime in the ward. These things are normally applied for a quarter of an hour and certainly they are funny enough if you don't happen to be the person inside. For the first five minutes the pain is severe, but you believe you can bear it. During the second five minutes this belief evaporates, but the poultice is buckled at the back and you can't get it off. This is the period the onlookers most enjoy. During the last five minutes, I noted, a sort of numbness supervenes. After the poultice had been removed a waterproof pillow packed with ice was thrust beneath my head and I was left alone. I did not sleep, and to the best of my knowledge this was the only night of my life — I mean the only night spent in bed — in which I have not slept at all, not even a minute.

During my first hour in the Hôpital X I had had a whole series of different and contradictory treatments, but this was misleading, for in general you got very little treatment at all, either good or bad, unless you were ill in some interesting and instructive way. At five in the morning the nurses came round, woke the patients and took their temperatures, but did not wash them. If you were well enough you washed yourself, otherwise you depended on the kindness of some walking patient. It was generally patients, too, who carried the bedbottles and the grim bedpan, nicknamed *la casserole*. At eight breakfast arrived, called army-fashion *la soupe*. It was soup, too, a thin vegetable soup with slimy hunks of bread floating about in it. Later in the day the tall, solemn, black-bearded doctor made his rounds, with an interne and a troop of students following at his heels, but there were about

sixty of us in the ward and it was evident that he had other wards
to attend to as well. There were many beds past which he walked
day after day, sometimes followed by imploring cries. On the other
hand if you had some disease with which the students wanted to
familiarise themselves you got plenty of attention of a kind. I myself, with an exceptionally fine specimen of a bronchial rattle,
sometimes had as many as a dozen students queuing up to listen
to my chest. It was a very queer feeling—queer, I mean, because
of their intense interest in learning their job, together with a seeming lack of any perception that the patients were human beings. It
is strange to relate, but sometimes as some young student stepped
forward to take his turn at manipulating you he would be actually
tremulous with excitement, like a boy who has at last got his hands
on some expensive piece of machinery. And then ear after ear—
ears of young men, of girls, of negroes—pressed against your
back, relays of fingers solemnly but clumsily tapping, and not from
any one of them did you get a word of conversation or a look direct in your face. As a non-paying patient, in the uniform nightshirt, you were primarily *a specimen,* a thing I did not resent but
could never quite get used to.

After some days I grew well enough to sit up and study the
surrounding patients. The stuffy room, with its narrow beds so
close together that you could easily touch your neighbour's hand,
had every sort of disease in it except, I suppose, acutely infectious
cases. My right-hand neighbour was a little red-haired cobbler with
one leg shorter than the other, who used to announce the death
of any other patient (this happened a number of times, and my
neighbour was always the first to hear of it) by whistling to me, exclaiming "Numero 43!" (or whatever it was) and flinging his arms
above his head. This man had not much wrong with him, but in
most of the other beds within my angle of vision some squalid
tragedy or some plain horror was being enacted. In the bed that

was foot to foot with mine there lay, until he died (I didn't see him die — they moved him to another bed), a little weazened man who was suffering from I do not know what disease, but something that made his whole body so intensely sensitive that any movement from side to side, sometimes even the weight of the bedclothes, would make him shout out with pain. His worst suffering was when he urinated, which he did with the greatest difficulty. A nurse would bring him the bedbottle and then for a long time stand beside his bed, whistling, as grooms are said to do with horses, until at last with an agonised shriek of *"Je pisse!"* he would get started. In the bed next to him the sandy-haired man whom I had seen being cupped used to cough up blood-streaked mucus at all hours. My left-hand neighbour was a tall, flaccid-looking young man who used periodically to have a tube inserted into his back and astonishing quantities of frothy liquid drawn off from some part of his body. In the bed beyond that a veteran of the war of 1870 was dying, a handsome old man with a white imperial, round whose bed, at all hours when visiting was allowed, four elderly female relatives dressed all in black sat exactly like crows, obviously scheming for some pitiful legacy. In the bed opposite me in the further row was an old baldheaded man with drooping moustaches and greatly swollen face and body, who was suffering from some disease that made him urinate almost incessantly. A huge glass receptacle stood always beside his bed. One day his wife and daughter came to visit him. At sight of them the old man's bloated face lit up with a smile of surprising sweetness, and as his daughter, a pretty girl of about twenty, approached the bed I saw that his hand was slowly working its way from under the bedclothes. I seemed to see in advance the gesture that was coming — the girl kneeling beside the bed, the old man's hand laid on her head in his dying blessing. But no, he merely handed her the bedbottle, which she promptly took from him and emptied into the receptacle.

About a dozen beds away from me was Numero 57—I think that was his number—a cirrhosis of the liver case. Everyone in the ward knew him by sight because he was sometimes the subject of a medical lecture. On two afternoons a week the tall, grave doctor would lecture in the ward to a party of students, and on more than one occasion old Numero 57 was wheeled on a sort of trolley into the middle of the ward, where the doctor would roll back his nightshirt, dilate with his fingers a huge flabby protuberance on the man's belly—the diseased liver, I suppose—and explain solemnly that this was a disease attributable to alcoholism, commoner in the wine-drinking countries. As usual he neither spoke to his patient nor gave him a smile, a nod or any kind of recognition. While he talked, very grave and upright, he would hold the wasted body beneath his two hands, sometimes giving it a gentle roll to and fro, in just the attitude of a woman handling a rolling-pin. Not that Numero 57 minded this kind of thing. Obviously he was an old hospital inmate, a regular exhibit at lectures, his liver long since marked down for a bottle in some pathological museum. Utterly uninterested in what was said about him, he would lie with his colourless eyes gazing at nothing, while the doctor showed him off like a piece of antique china. He was a man of about sixty, astonishingly shrunken. His face, pale as vellum, had shrunken away till it seemed no bigger than a doll's.

One morning my cobbler neighbour woke me by plucking at my pillow before the nurses arrived. "Numero 57!"—he flung his arms above his head. There was a light in the ward, enough to see by. I could see old Numero 57 lying crumpled up on his side, his face sticking out over the side of the bed, and towards me. He had died some time during the night, nobody knew when. When the nurses came they received the news of his death indifferently and went about their work. After a long time, an hour or more, two other nurses marched in abreast like soldiers, with a great clumping of sabots, and knotted the corpse up in the sheets, but it was not removed till some time later. Meanwhile, in the better light, I had had time for a good look at Numero 57. Indeed I lay on my side to look at him. Curiously enough he was the first dead European I had seen. I had seen dead men before, but always Asiatics and usually people who had died violent deaths. Numero 57's eyes were still open, his mouth also open, his small face contorted into an expression of agony. What most impressed me however was the whiteness of his face. It had been pale before, but now it was little darker than the sheets. As I gazed at the tiny, screwed-up face it struck me that this disgusting piece of refuse, waiting to be carted away and dumped on a slab in the dissecting-room, was an example of "natural" death, one of the things you pray for in the Litany. There you are, then, I thought, that's what is waiting for you, twenty, thirty, forty years hence: that is how the lucky ones die, the ones who live to be old. One wants to live, of course, indeed one only stays alive by virtue of the fear of death, but I think now, as I thought then, that it's better to die violently and not too old. People talk about the horrors of war, but what weapon has man invented that even approaches in cruelty some of the commoner diseases? "Natural" death, almost by definition, means something slow, smelly and painful. Even at that, it makes a difference if you can achieve it in your own home and not in a public institution. This poor old wretch who had just flickered out like a candle-end was not even important enough to have anyone watching by his deathbed. He was merely a number, then a "subject" for the students' scalpels. And the sordid publicity of dying in such a place! In the Hôpital X the beds were very close together and there were no screens. Fancy, for instance, dying like the little man whose bed was for a while foot to foot with mine, the one who cried out when the bedclothes touched him! I dare say "Je pisse!" were his last recorded words. Perhaps the dying don't bother about such things — that at least would be the standard answer: nevertheless dying people are often more or less normal in their minds till within a day or so of the end.

In the public wards of a hospital you see horrors that you don't seem to meet with among people who manage to die in their own homes, as though certain diseases only attacked people at the lower income levels. But it is a fact that you would not in any English hospitals see some of the things I saw in the Hôpital X. This business of people just dying like animals, for instance, with nobody standing by, nobody interested, the death not even noticed till the morning — this happened more than once. You certainly would not see that in England, and still less would you see a corpse left exposed to the view of the other patients. I remember that once in a cottage hospital in England a man died while we were at tea, and though there were only six of us in the ward the nurses managed things so adroitly that the man was dead and his body removed without our even hearing about it till tea was over. A thing we perhaps underrate in England is the advantage we enjoy in having large numbers of well-trained and rigidly-disciplined nurses. No doubt English nurses are dumb enough, they may tell fortunes with tealeaves, wear Union Jack badges and keep photographs of the Queen on their mantlepieces, but at least they don't let you lie unwashed and constipated on an unmade bed, out of sheer laziness. The nurses at the Hôpital X still had a tinge of Mrs. Gamp about them, and later, in the military hospitals of Republican Spain, I was to see nurses almost too ignorant to take a temperature. You wouldn't, either, see in England such dirt as existed in the Hôpital X. Later on, when I was well enough to wash myself in the bathroom, I found that there was kept there a huge packing case into which the scraps of food and dirty dressings from the ward were flung, and the wainscotings were infested by crickets.

When I had got back my clothes and grown strong on my legs
I fled from the Hôpital X, before my time was up and without
waiting for a medical discharge. It was not the only hospital I have
fled from, but its gloom and bareness, its sickly smell and, above
all, something in its mental atmosphere stand out in my memory
as exceptional. I had been taken there because it was the hospital
belonging to my arrondissement, and I did not learn till after I
was in it that it bore a bad reputation. A year or two later the celebrated swindler, Madame Hanaud, who was ill while on remand,
was taken to the Hôpital X, and after a few days of it she managed
to elude her guards, took a taxi and drove back to the prison, explaining that she was more comfortable there. I have no doubt
that the Hôpital X was quite untypical of French hospitals even at
that date. But the patients, nearly all of them working-men, were
surprisingly resigned. Some of them seemed to find the conditions almost comfortable, for at least two were destitute malingerers who found this a good way of getting through the winter.
The nurses connived because the malingerers made themselves
useful by doing odd jobs. But the attitude of the majority was: of
course this is a lousy place, but what else do you expect? It did not
seem strange to them that you should be woken at five and then
wait three hours before starting the day on watery soup, or that
people should die with no one at their bedside, or even that your
chance of getting medical attention should depend on catching
the doctor's eye as he went past. According to their traditions that
was what hospitals were like. If you are seriously ill, and if you are
too poor to be treated in your own home, then you must go into
hospital, and once there you must put up with harshness and discomfort, just as you would in the army. But on top of this I was
interested to find a lingering belief in the old stories that have now
almost faded from memory in England—stories, for instance,
about doctors cutting you open out of sheer curiosity or thinking

it funny to start operating before you were properly "under." There were dark tales about a little operating-room said to be situated just beyond the bathroom. Dreadful screams were said to issue from this room. I saw nothing to confirm these stories and no doubt they were all nonsense, though I did see two students kill a sixteen-year-old boy, or nearly kill him (he appeared to be dying when I left the hospital, but he may have recovered later) by a mischievous experiment which they probably could not have tried on a paying patient. Well within living memory it used to be believed in London that in some of the big hospitals patients were killed off to get dissection subjects. I didn't hear this tale repeated at the Hôpital X, but I should think some of the men there would have found it credible. For it was a hospital in which not the methods, perhaps, but something of the atmosphere of the nineteenth century had managed to survive, and therein lay its peculiar interest.

During the past fifty years or so there has been a great change in the relationship between doctor and patient. If you look at almost any literature before the later part of the nineteenth century, you find that a hospital is popularly regarded as much the same thing as a prison, and an old-fashioned, dungeon-like prison at that. A hospital is a place of filth, torture and death, a sort of antechamber to the tomb. No one who was not more or less destitute would have thought of going into such a place for treatment. And especially in the early part of the last century, when medical science had grown bolder than before without being any more successful, the whole business of doctoring was looked on with horror and dread by ordinary people. Surgery, in particular, was believed to be no more than a peculiarly gruesome form of sadism, and dissection, possible only with the aid of bodysnatchers, was even confused with necromancy. From the nineteenth century you could collect a large horror-literature connected with doctors and hospitals. Think of poor old George III, in his dotage, shrieking for mercy as he sees his surgeons approaching to "bleed him till he faints"! Think of the conversations of Bob Sawyer and Benjamin Allen, which no doubt are hardly parodies, or the field hospitals in *La Debâcle* and *War and Peace,* or that shocking description of an amputation in Melville's *White-Jacket*! Even the names given to doctors in nineteenth-century English fiction, Slasher, Carver, Sawyer, Fillgrave and so on, and the generic nickname "sawbones," are about as grim as they are comic. The anti-surgery tradition is perhaps best expressed in Tennyson's poem, *The Children's Hospital,* which is essentially a pre-chloroform document though it seems to have been written as late as 1880.[3] Moreover, the outlook which Tennyson records in this poem had a lot to be said for it. When you consider what an operation without anæsthetics must have been like, what it notoriously *was* like, it is difficult not to suspect the motives of people who would undertake such things. For these bloody horrors which the students so eagerly looked forward to ("A magnificent sight if Slasher does it!") were admittedly more or less useless: the patient who did not die of shock usually died of gangrene, a result which was taken for granted. Even now doctors can be found whose motives are questionable. Anyone who has had much illness, or who has listened to medical students talking, will know what I mean. But anæsthetics were a turning point, and disinfectants were another. Nowhere in the world, probably, would you now see the kind of scene described by Axel Munthe in *The Story of San Michele,* when the sinister surgeon in top hat and frock coat, his starched shirtfront spattered with blood and pus, carves up patient after patient with the same knife and flings the severed limbs into a pile beside the table. Moreover, national health insurance has partly done away with the idea that a working-class patient is a pauper who deserves little consideration. Well into this century it was usual for "free" patients at the big hospitals to have their teeth extracted with no anæsthetic. They didn't pay, so why should they have an anæsthetic — that was the attitude. That too has changed.

And yet every institution will always bear upon it some lingering memory of its past. A barrack-room is still haunted by the ghost of Kipling, and it is difficult to enter a workhouse without being reminded of *Oliver Twist*. Hospitals began as a kind of casual ward for lepers and the like to die in, and they continued as places where medical students learned their art on the bodies of the poor. You can still catch a faint suggestion of their history in their characteristically gloomy architecture. I would be far from complaining about the treatment I have received in any English hospital, but I do know that it is a sound instinct that warns people to keep out of hospitals if possible, and especially out of the public wards. Whatever the legal position may be, it is unquestionable that you have far less control over your own treatment, far less certainty that frivolous experiments will not be tried on you, when it is a case of "accept the discipline or get out." And it is a great thing to die in your own bed, though it is better still to die in your boots. However great the kindness and the efficiency, in every hospital death there will be some cruel, squalid detail, some thing perhaps too small to be told but leaving terribly painful memories behind, arising out of the haste, the crowding, the impersonality of a place where every day people are dying among strangers.

The dread of hospitals probably still survives among the very poor, and in all of us it has only recently disappeared. It is a dark patch not far beneath the surface of our minds. I have said earlier that when I entered the ward at the Hôpital X I was conscious of a strange feeling of familiarity. What the scene reminded me of, of course, was the reeking, pain-filled hospitals of the nineteenth century, which I had never seen but of which I had a traditional knowledge. And something, perhaps the black-clad doctor with his frowsy black bag, or perhaps only the sickly smell, played the queer trick of unearthing from my memory that poem of Tennyson's, *The Children's Hospital,* which I had not thought of for twenty years. It happened that as a child I had had it read aloud to me by a sick-nurse whose own working life might have stretched back to the time when Tennyson wrote the poem. The horrors and sufferings of the old-style hospitals were a vivid memory to her. We had shuddered over the poem together, and then seemingly I had forgotten it. Even its name would probably have recalled nothing to me. But the first glimpse of the ill-lit, murmurous room, with the beds so close together, suddenly roused the train of thought to which it belonged, and in the night that followed I found myself remembering the whole story and atmosphere of the poem, with many of its lines complete.

Such, Such Were the Joys[1]

1939?—June 1948?

Soon after I arrived at St. Cyprian's (not immediately, but after a week or two, just when I seemed to be settling into the routine of school life) I began wetting my bed. I was now aged eight, so that this was a reversion to a habit which I must have grown out of at least four years earlier.

Nowadays, I believe, bed-wetting in such circumstances is taken for granted. It is a normal reaction in children who have been removed from their homes to a strange place. In those days, however, it was looked on as a disgusting crime which the child committed on purpose and for which the proper cure was a beating. For my part I did not need to be told it was a crime. Night after night I prayed, with a fervour never previously attained in my prayers, "Please God, do not let me wet my bed! Oh, please God, do not let me wet my bed!," but it made remarkably little difference. Some nights the thing happened, others not. There was no volition about it, no consciousness. You did not properly speaking *do* the deed: you merely woke up in the morning and found that the sheets were wringing wet.

After the second or third offence I was warned that I should be beaten next time, but I received the warning in a curiously roundabout way. One afternoon, as we were filing out from tea, Mrs. Wilkes, the headmaster's wife, was sitting at the head of one of the tables, chatting with a lady of whom I know nothing, except that she was on an afternoon's visit to the school. She was an intimidating, masculine-looking person wearing a riding habit, or something that I took to be a riding habit. I was just leaving the room when Mrs. Wilkes called me back, as though to introduce me to the visitor.

Mrs. Wilkes was nicknamed Flip, and I shall call her by that name, for I seldom think of her by any other. (Officially, however, she was addressed as Mum, probably a corruption of the "Ma'am" used by public schoolboys to their housemasters' wives.) She was a stocky square-built woman with hard red cheeks, a flat top to her head, prominent brows and deepset, suspicious eyes. Although a great deal of the time she was full of false heartiness, jollying one along with mannish slang ("*Buck* up, old chap!" and so forth), and even using one's Christian name, her eyes never lost their anxious, accusing look. It was very difficult to look her in the face without feeling guilty, even at moments when one was not guilty of anything in particular.

"Here is a little boy," said Flip, indicating me to the strange lady, "who wets his bed every night. Do you know what I am going to do if you wet your bed again?" she added, turning to me. "I am going to get the Sixth Form to beat you."

The strange lady put on an air of being inexpressibly shocked, and exclaimed "I-should-*think*-so!" And here there occurred one of those wild, almost lunatic misunderstandings which are part of the daily experience of childhood. The Sixth Form was a group of older boys who were selected as having "character" and were empowered to beat smaller boys. I had not yet learned of their existence, and I mis-heard the phrase "the Sixth Form" as "Mrs. Form." I took it as referring to the strange lady—I thought, that is, that her name was Mrs. Form. It was an improbable name, but a child has no judgement in such matters. I imagined, therefore, that it was *she* who was to be deputed to beat me. It did not strike me as strange that this job should be turned over to a casual visi-

tor in no way connected with the school. I merely assumed that
"Mrs. Form" was a stern disciplinarian who enjoyed beating
people (somehow her appearance seemed to bear this out) and I
had an immediate terrifying vision of her arriving for the occasion in full riding kit and armed with a hunting whip. To this day
I can feel myself almost swooning with shame as I stood, a very
small, round-faced boy in short corduroy knickers, before the two
women. I could not speak. I felt that I should die if "Mrs. Form"
were to beat me. But my dominant feeling was not fear or even re-
sentment: it was simply shame because one more person, and that
a woman, had been told of my disgusting offence.

A little later, I forget how, I learned that it was not after all
"Mrs. Form" who would do the beating. I cannot remember
whether it was that very night that I wetted my bed again, but at
any rate I did wet it again quite soon, Oh, the despair, the feeling
of cruel injustice, after all my prayers and resolutions, at once again
waking between the clammy sheets! There was no chance of hiding what I had done. The grim statuesque matron, Margaret by
name, arrived in the dormitory specially to inspect my bed. She
pulled back the clothes, then drew herself up, and the dreaded
words seemed to come rolling out of her like a peal of thunder:

"REPORT YOURSELF to the headmaster after breakfast!"

I put REPORT YOURSELF in capitals because that was how it appeared in my mind. I do not know how many times I heard that
phrase during my early years at St. Cyprian's. It was only very rarely
that it did not mean a beating. The words always had a portentous
sound in my ears, like muffled drums or the words of the death
sentence.

When I arrived to report myself, Flip was doing something or
other at the long shiny table in the ante-room to the study. Her
uneasy eyes searched me as I went past. In the study Mr. Wilkes,
nicknamed Sambo, was waiting. Sambo was a round-shouldered,

curiously oafish-looking man, not large but shambling in gait, with a chubby face which was like that of an overgrown baby, and which was capable of good-humour. He knew, of course, why I had been sent to him, and had already taken a bone-handled riding crop out of the cupboard, but it was part of the punishment of reporting yourself that you had to proclaim your offence with your own lips. When I had said my say, he read me a short but pompous lecture, then seized me by the scruff of the neck, twisted me over and began beating me with the riding crop. He had a habit of continuing his lecture while he flogged you, and I remember the words "you dir-ty lit-tle boy" keeping time with the blows. The beating did not hurt (perhaps, as it was the first time, he was not hitting me very hard), and I walked out feeling very much better. The fact that the beating had not hurt was a sort of victory and partially wiped out the shame of the bed-wetting. Perhaps I was even incautious enough to wear a grin on my face. Some small boys were hanging about in the passage outside the door of the ante-room.

"D'you get the cane?"

"It didn't hurt," I said proudly.

Flip had heard everything. Instantly her voice came screaming after me:

"Come here! Come here this instant! What was that you said?"

"I said it didn't hurt," I faltered out.

"How dare you say a thing like that? Do you think that is a proper thing to say? Go in and REPORT YOURSELF AGAIN!"

This time Sambo laid on in real earnest. He continued for a length of time that frightened and astonished me — about five minutes, it seemed — ending up by breaking the riding crop. The bone handle went flying across the room.

"Look what you've made me do!" he said furiously, holding up the broken crop.

I had fallen into a chair, weakly snivelling. I remember that this was the only time throughout my boyhood when a beating actually reduced me to tears, and curiously enough I was not even now crying because of the pain. The second beating had not hurt very much either. Fright and shame seemed to have anaesthetised me. I was crying partly because I felt that this was expected of me, partly from genuine repentance, but partly also because of a deeper grief which is peculiar to childhood and not easy to convey: a sense of desolate loneliness and helplessness, of being locked up not only in a hostile world but in a world of good and evil where the rules were such that it was actually not possible for me to keep them.

I knew that the bed-wetting was (a) wicked and (b) outside my control. The second fact I was personally aware of, and the first I did not question. It was possible, therefore, to commit a sin without knowing that you committed it, without wanting to commit it, and without being able to avoid it. Sin was not necessarily something that you did: it might be something that happened to you. I do not want to claim that this idea flashed into my mind as a complete novelty at this very moment, under the blows of Sambo's cane: I must have had glimpses of it even before I left home, for my early childhood had not been altogether happy. But at any rate this was the great, abiding lesson of my boyhood: that I was in a world where it was *not possible* for me to be good. And the double beating was a turning-point, for it brought home to me for the first time the harshness of the environment into which I had been flung. Life was more terrible, and I was more wicked, than I had imagined. At any rate, as I sat snivelling on the edge of a chair in Sambo's study, with not even the self-possession to stand up while he stormed at me, I had a conviction of sin and folly and weakness, such as I do not remember to have felt before.

In general, one's memories of any period must necessarily weaken as one moves away from it. One is constantly learning new facts, and old ones have to drop out to make way for them. At twenty I could have written the history of my schooldays with an accuracy which would be quite impossible now. But it can also happen that one's memories grow sharper after a long lapse of time, because one is looking at the past with fresh eyes and can isolate and, as it were, notice facts which previously existed undifferentiated among a mass of others. Here are two things which in a sense I remembered, but which did not strike me as strange or interesting until quite recently. One is that the second beating seemed to me a just and reasonable punishment. To get one beating, and then to get another and far fiercer one on top of it, for being so unwise as to show that the first had not hurt—that was quite natural. The gods are jealous, and when you have good fortune you should conceal it. The other is that I accepted the broken riding crop as my own crime. I can still recall my feeling as I saw the handle lying on the carpet—the feeling of having done an ill-bred clumsy thing, and ruined an expensive object. *I* had broken it: so Sambo told me, and so I believed. This acceptance of guilt lay unnoticed in my memory for twenty or thirty years.

So much for the episode of the bed-wetting. But there is one more thing to be remarked. This is that I did not wet my bed again—at least, I did wet it once again, and received another beating, after which the trouble stopped. So perhaps this barbarous remedy does work, though at a heavy price, I have no doubt.

ii.

St. Cyprian's was an expensive and snobbish school which was in process of becoming more snobbish, and, I imagine, more expensive. The public school with which it had special connections was Harrow, but during my time an increasing proportion of the boys went on to Eton. Most of them were the children of rich par-

ents, but on the whole they were the unaristocratic rich, the sort
of people who live in huge shrubberied houses in Bournemouth
or Richmond, and who have cars and butlers but not country es-
tates. There were a few exotics among them—some South American boys, sons of Argentine beef barons, one or two Russians,
and even a Siamese prince, or someone who was described as a
prince.

Sambo had two great ambitions. One was to attract titled boys
to the school, and the other was to train up pupils to win scholarships at public schools, above all at Eton. He did, towards the end
of my time, succeed in getting hold of two boys with real English
titles. One of them, I remember, was a wretched, drivelling little
creature, almost an albino, peering upwards out of weak eyes, with
a long nose at the end of which a dewdrop always seemed to be
trembling. Sambo always gave these boys their titles when mentioning them to a third person, and for their first few days he actually addressed them to their faces as "Lord So-and-so." Needless
to say he found ways of drawing attention to them when any visitor was being shown round the school. Once, I remember, the
little fair-haired boy had a choking fit at dinner, and a stream of
snot ran out of his nose onto his plate in a way horrible to see.
Any lesser person would have been called a dirty little beast and
ordered out of the room instantly: but Sambo and Flip laughed it
off in a "boys will be boys" spirit.

All the very rich boys were more or less undisguisedly favoured.
The school still had a faint suggestion of the Victorian "private
academy" with its "parlour boarders," and when I later read about
that kind of school in Thackeray I immediately saw the resemblance. The rich boys had milk and biscuits in the middle of the
morning, they were given riding lessons once or twice a week, Flip
mothered them and called them by their Christian names, and
above all they were never caned. Apart from the South Americans,

whose parents were safely distant, I doubt whether Sambo ever caned any boy whose father's income was much above £2,000 a year. But he was sometimes willing to sacrifice financial profit to scholastic prestige. Occasionally, by special arrangement, he would take at greatly reduced fees some boy who seemed likely to win scholarships and thus bring credit on the school. It was on these terms that I was at St. Cyprian's myself: otherwise my parents could not have afforded to send me to so expensive a school.

I did not at first understand that I was being taken at reduced fees; it was only when I was about eleven that Flip and Sambo began throwing the fact in my teeth. For my first two or three years I went through the ordinary educational mill: then, soon after I had started Greek (one started Latin at eight, Greek at ten), I moved into the scholarship class, which was taught, so far as classics went, largely by Sambo himself. Over a period of two or three years the scholarship boys were crammed with learning as cynically as a goose is crammed for Christmas. And with what learning! This business of making a gifted boy's career depend on a competitive examination, taken when he is only twelve or thirteen, is an evil thing at best, but there do appear to be preparatory schools which send scholars to Eton, Winchester, etc. without teaching them to see everything in terms of marks. At St. Cyprian's the whole process was frankly a preparation for a sort of confidence trick. Your job was to learn exactly those things that would give an examiner the impression that you knew more than you did know, and as far as possible to avoid burdening your brain with anything else. Subjects which lacked examination-value, such as geography, were almost completely neglected, mathematics was also neglected if you were a "classical," science was not taught in any form—indeed it was so despised that even an interest in natural history was discouraged—and even the books you were encouraged to read in your spare time were chosen with one eye on

the "English paper." Latin and Greek, the main scholarship subjects, were what counted, but even these were deliberately taught
in a flashy, unsound way. We never, for example, read right through
even a single book of a Greek or Latin author: we merely read
short passages which were picked out because they were the kind
of thing likely to be set as an "unseen translation." During the last
year or so before we went up for our scholarships, most of our
time was spent in simply working our way through the scholarship papers of previous years. Sambo had sheaves of these in his
possession from every one of the major public schools. But the
greatest outrage of all was the teaching of history.

There was in those days a piece of nonsense called the Harrow History Prize, an annual competition for which many
preparatory schools entered. It was a tradition for St. Cyprian's to
win it every year, as well we might, for we had mugged up every
paper that had been set since the competition started, and the sup-
ply of possible questions was not inexhaustible. They were the
kind of stupid question that is answered by rapping out a name or
a quotation. Who plundered the Begums? Who was beheaded in
an open boat? Who caught the Whigs bathing and ran away with
their clothes? Almost all our historical teaching was on this level.
History was a series of unrelated, unintelligible but—in some way
that was never explained to us—important facts with resounding phrases tied to them. Disraeli brought peace with honour.
Hastings was astonished at his moderation. Pitt called in the New
World to redress the balance of the Old. And the dates, and the
mnemonic devices! (Did you know, for example, that the initial
letters of "A black Negress was my aunt: there's her house behind
the barn" are also the initial letters of the battles in the Wars of the
Roses?) Flip, who "took" the higher forms in history, revelled in
this kind of thing. I recall positive orgies of dates, with the keener
boys leaping up and down in their places in their eagerness to

shout out the right answers, and at the same time not feeling the faintest interest in the meaning of the mysterious events they were naming.

"1587?"

"Massacre of St. Bartholomew!"

"1707?"

"Death of Aurangzeeb!"

"1713?"

"Treaty of Utrecht!"

"1773?"

"Boston Tea Party!"

"1520?"

"Oo, Mum, please, Mum—"

"Please, Mum, please, Mum! Let me tell him, Mum!"

"Well! 1520?"

"Field of the Cloth of Gold!"

And so on.

But history and such secondary subjects were not bad fun. It was in "classics" that the real strain came. Looking back, I realise that I then worked harder than I have ever done since, and yet at the time it never seemed possible to make quite the effort that was demanded of one. We would sit round the long shiny table, made of some very pale-coloured, hard wood, with Sambo goading, threatening, exhorting, sometimes joking, very occasionally praising, but always prodding, prodding away at one's mind to keep it up to the right pitch of concentration, as one might keep a sleepy person awake by sticking pins into him.

"Go on, you little slacker! Go on, you idle, worthless little boy! The whole trouble with you is that you're bone and horn idle. You eat too much, that's why. You wolf down enormous meals, and then when you come here you're half asleep. Go on, now, put your back into it. You're not *thinking*. Your brain doesn't sweat."

He would tap away at one's skull with his silver pencil, which, in my memory, seems to have been about the size of a banana, and which certainly was heavy enough to raise a bump: or he would pull the short hairs round one's ears, or, occasionally, reach out under the table and kick one's shin. On some days nothing seemed to go right, and then it would be: "All right, then, I know what you want. You've been asking for it the whole morning. Come along, you useless little slacker. Come into the study." And then whack, whack, whack, whack, and back one would come, red-wealed and smarting—in later years Sambo had abandoned his riding crop in favour of a thin rattan cane which hurt very much more—to settle down to work again. This did not happen very often, but I do remember, more than once, being led out of the room in the middle of a Latin sentence, receiving a beating and then going straight ahead with the same sentence, just like that. It is a mistake to think such methods do not work. They work very well for their special purpose. Indeed, I doubt whether classical education ever has been or can be successfully carried on without corporal punishment. The boys themselves believed in its efficacy. There was a boy named Hardcastle, with no brains to speak of, but evidently in acute need of a scholarship. Sambo was flogging him towards the goal as one might do with a foundered horse. He went up for a scholarship at Uppingham, came back with a consciousness of having done badly, and a day or two later received a severe beating for idleness. "I wish I'd had that caning before I went up for the exam," he said sadly—a remark which I felt to be contemptible, but which I perfectly well understood.

The boys of the scholarship class were not all treated alike. If a boy were the son of rich parents to whom the saving of fees was not all-important, Sambo would goad him along in a comparatively fatherly way, with jokes and digs in the ribs and perhaps an occasional tap with the pencil, but no hair-pulling and no caning.

It was the poor but "clever" boys who suffered. Our brains were a gold-mine in which he had sunk money, and the dividends must be squeezed out of us. Long before I had grasped the nature of my financial relationship with Sambo, I had been made to understand that I was not on the same footing as most of the other boys. In effect there were three castes in the school. There was the minority with an aristocratic or millionaire background, there were the children of the ordinary suburban rich, who made up the bulk of the school, and there were a few underlings like myself, the sons of clergymen, Indian civil servants, struggling widows and the like. These poorer ones were discouraged from going in for "extras" such as shooting and carpentry, and were humiliated over clothes and petty possessions. I never, for instance, succeeded in getting a cricket bat of my own, because "Your parents wouldn't be able to afford it." This phrase pursued me throughout my school-days. At St. Cyprian's we were not allowed to keep the money we brought back with us, but had to "give it in" on the first day of term, and then from time to time were allowed to spend it under supervision. I and similarly-placed boys were always choked off from buying expensive toys like model aeroplanes, even if the necessary money stood to our credit. Flip, in particular, seemed to aim consciously at inculcating a humble outlook in the poorer boys. "Do you think that's the sort of thing a boy like you should buy?" I remember her saying to somebody—and she said this in front of the whole school; "You know you're not going to grow up with money, don't you? Your people aren't rich. You must learn to be sensible. Don't get above yourself!" There was also the weekly pocket-money, which we took out in sweets, dispersed by Flip from a large table. The millionaires had sixpence a week, but the normal sum was threepence. I and one or two others were only allowed twopence. My parents had not given instructions to this effect, and the saving of a penny a week could not conceivably have made any difference to them: it was a mark of status. Worse yet was the detail of the birthday cakes. It was usual for each boy, on his birthday, to have a large iced cake with candles, which was shared out at tea between the whole school. It was provided as a matter of routine and went on his parents' bill. I never had such a cake, though my parents would have paid for it readily enough. Year after year, never daring to ask, I would miserably hope that this year a cake would appear. Once or twice I even rashly pretended to my companions that this time I *was* going to have a cake. Then came teatime, and no cake, which did not make me more popular.

Very early it was impressed upon me that I had no chance of a decent future unless I won a scholarship at a public school. Either I won my scholarship, or I must leave school at fourteen and become, in Sambo's favourite phrase "a little office boy at forty pounds a year." In my circumstances it was natural that I should believe this. Indeed, it was universally taken for granted at St. Cyprian's that unless you went to a "good" public school (and only about fifteen schools came under this heading) you were ruined for life. It is not easy to convey to a grown-up person the sense of strain, of nerving oneself for some terrible, all-deciding combat, as the date of the examination crept nearer—eleven years old, twelve years old, then thirteen, the fatal year itself! Over a period of about two years, I do not think there was ever a day when "the exam," as I called it, was quite out of my waking thoughts. In my prayers it figured invariably: and whenever I got the bigger portion of a wishbone, or picked up a horse-shoe, or bowed seven times to the new moon, or succeeded in passing through a wishing-gate without touching the sides, then the wish I earned by doing so went on "the exam" as a matter of course. And yet curiously enough I was also tormented by an almost irresistible impulse *not* to work. There were days when my heart sickened at the labours ahead of me, and

I stood stupid as an animal before the most elementary difficulties. In the holidays, also, I could not work. Some of the scholarship boys received extra tuition from a certain Mr. Knowles, a likeable, very hairy man who wore shaggy suits and lived in a typical bachelor's "den"—booklined walls, overwhelming stench of tobacco—somewhere in the town. During the holidays Mr. Knowles used to send us extracts from Latin authors to translate, and we were supposed to send back a wad of work once a week. Somehow I could not do it. The empty paper and the black Latin dictionary lying on the table, the consciousness of a plain duty shirked, poisoned my leisure, but somehow I could not start, and by the end of the holidays I would only have sent Mr. Knowles fifty or a hundred lines. Undoubtedly part of the reason was that Sambo and his cane were far away. But in term time, also, I would go through periods of idleness and stupidity when I would sink deeper and deeper into disgrace and even achieve a sort of feeble, snivelling defiance, fully conscious of my guilt and yet unable or unwilling—I could not be sure which—to do any better. Then Sambo or Flip would send for me, and this time it would not even be a caning.

Flip would search me with her baleful eyes. (What colour were those eyes, I wonder? I remember them as green, but actually no human being has green eyes. Perhaps they were hazel.) She would start off in her peculiar, wheedling, bullying style, which never failed to get right through one's guard and score a hit on one's better nature.

"I don't think it's awfully decent of you to behave like this, is it? Do you think it's quite playing the game by your mother and father to go on idling your time away, week after week, month after month? Do you *want* to throw all your chances away? You know your people aren't rich, don't you? You know they can't afford the same things as other boys' parents. How are they to send you to a public school if you don't win a scholarship? I know how proud your mother is of you. Do you *want* to let her down?"

"I don't think he wants to go to a public school any longer," Sambo would say, addressing himself to Flip with a pretence that I was not there. "I think he's given up that idea. He wants to be a little office boy at forty pounds a year."

The horrible sensation of tears—a swelling in the breast, a tickling behind the nose—would already have assailed me. Flip would bring out her ace of trumps:

"And do you think it's quite fair to *us,* the way you're behaving? After all we've done for you? You *do* know what we've done for you, don't you?" Her eyes would pierce deep into me, and though she never said it straight out, I did know. "We've had you here all these years—we even had you here for a week in the holidays so that Mr. Knowles could coach you. We don't *want* to have to send you away, you know, but we can't keep a boy here just to eat up our food, term after term. *I* don't think it's very straight, the way you're behaving. Do you?"

I never had any answer except a miserable "No, Mum," or "Yes, Mum," as the case might be. Evidently it was *not* straight, the way I was behaving. And at some point or other the unwanted tear would always force its way out of the corner of my eye, roll down my nose, and splash.

Flip never said in plain words that I was a non-paying pupil, no doubt because vague phrases like "all we've done for you" had a deeper emotional appeal. Sambo, who did not aspire to be loved by his pupils, put it more brutally, though, as was usual with him, in pompous language. "You are living on my bounty" was his favourite phrase in this context. At least once I listened to these words between blows of the cane. I must say that these scenes were not frequent, and except on one occasion they did not take place in the presence of other boys. In public I was reminded that I was poor and that my parents "wouldn't be able to afford" this or that, but I was not actually reminded of my dependent position. It was a final unanswerable argument, to be brought forth like an instrument of torture when my work became exceptionally bad.

To grasp the effect of this kind of thing on a child of ten or twelve, one has to remember that the child has little sense of proportion or probability. A child may be a mass of egoism and rebelliousness, but it has no accumulated experience to give it confidence in its own judgements. On the whole it will accept what it is told, and it will believe in the most fantastic way in the knowledge and powers of the adults surrounding it. Here is an example.

I have said that at St. Cyprian's we were not allowed to keep our own money. However, it was possible to hold back a shilling or two, and sometimes I used furtively to buy sweets which I kept hidden in the loose ivy on the playing-field wall. One day when I had been sent on an errand I went into a sweetshop a mile or more from the school and bought some chocolates. As I came out of the shop I saw on the opposite pavement a small sharp-faced man who seemed to be staring very hard at my school cap. Instantly a horrible fear went through me. There could be no doubt as to who the man was. He was a spy placed there by Sambo! I turned away unconcernedly, and then, as though my legs were doing it of their own accord, broke into a clumsy run. But when I got round the next corner I forced myself to walk again, for to run was a sign of guilt, and obviously there would be other spies posted here and there about the town. All that day and the next I waited for the summons to the study, and was surprised when it did not come. It did not seem to me strange that the headmaster of a private school should dispose of an army of informers, and I did not even imagine that he would have to pay them. I assumed that any adult, inside the school or outside, would collaborate voluntarily in preventing us from breaking the rules. Sambo was all-powerful, and it was natural that his agents should be everywhere. When this episode happened I do not think I can have been less than twelve years old.

I hated Sambo and Flip, with a sort of shamefaced, remorseful hatred, but it did not occur to me to doubt their judgement. When they told me that I must either win a public-school scholarship or become an office-boy at fourteen, I believed that those were the unavoidable alternatives before me. And above all, I believed Sambo and Flip when they told me they were my benefactors. I see now, of course, that from Sambo's point of view I was a good speculation. He sank money in me, and he looked to get it back in the form of prestige. If I had "gone off," as promising boys sometimes do, I imagine that he would have got rid of me swiftly. As it was I won him two scholarships when the time came, and no doubt he made full use of them in his prospectuses. But it is difficult for a child to realise that a school is primarily a commercial venture. A child believes that the school exists to educate and that the schoolmaster disciplines him either for his own good, or from a love of bullying. Flip and Sambo had chosen to befriend me, and their friendship included canings, reproaches and humiliations, which were good for me and saved me from an office stool. That was their version, and I believed in it. It was therefore clear that I owed them a vast debt of gratitude. But I was *not* grateful, as I very well knew. On the contrary, I hated both of them. I could not control my subjective feelings, and I could not conceal them from myself. But it is wicked, is it not, to hate your benefactors? So I was taught, and so I believed. A child accepts the codes of behaviour that are presented to it, even when it breaks them. From the age of eight, or even earlier, the consciousness of sin was never far away from me. If I contrived to seem callous and defiant, it was only a thin cover over a mass of shame and dismay. All through my boyhood I had a profound conviction that I was no good, that I was wasting my time, wrecking my talents, behaving with monstrous folly and wickedness and ingratitude — and all this, it seemed, was inescapable, because I lived among laws which were absolute, like the law of gravity, but which it was not possible for me to keep.

iii.

No one can look back on his schooldays and say with truth that they were altogether unhappy.

I have good memories of St. Cyprian's, among a horde of bad ones. Sometimes on summer afternoons there were wonderful expeditions across the Downs to a village called Birling Gap, or to Beachy Head, where one bathed dangerously among the chalk boulders and came home covered with cuts. And there were still more wonderful midsummer evenings when, as a special treat, we were not driven off to bed as usual but allowed to wander about the grounds in the long twilight, ending up with a plunge into the swimming bath at about nine o'clock. There was the joy of waking early on summer mornings and getting in an hour's undisturbed reading (Ian Hay, Thackeray, Kipling and H. G. Wells were the favourite authors of my boyhood) in the sunlit, sleeping dormitory. There was also cricket, which I was no good at but with which I conducted a sort of hopeless love affair up to the age of about eighteen. And there was the pleasure of keeping caterpillars — the silky green and purple puss-moth, the ghostly green poplar-hawk, the privet hawk, large as one's third finger, specimens of which could be illicitly purchased for sixpence at a shop in the town — and, when one could escape long enough from the master who was "taking the walk," there was the excitement of dredging the dew-ponds on the Downs for enormous newts with orange-coloured bellies. This business of being out for a walk, coming across something of fascinating interest and then being dragged away from it by a yell from the master, like a dog jerked onwards by the leash, is an important feature of school life, and helps to build up the conviction, so strong in many children, that the things you most want to do are always unattainable.

Very occasionally, perhaps once during each summer, it was possible to escape altogether from the barrack-like atmosphere of school, when Siller, the second master, was permitted to take one or two boys for an afternoon of butterfly hunting on a common a few miles away. Siller was a man with white hair and a red face like a strawberry, who was good at natural history, making models and plaster casts, operating magic lanterns, and things of that kind. He and Mr. Knowles were the only adults in any way connected with the school whom I did not either dislike or fear. Once he took me into his room and showed me in confidence a plated, pearl-handled revolver—his "six-shooter," he called it—which he kept in a box under his bed. And oh, the joy of those occasional expeditions! The ride of two or three miles on a lonely little branch line, the afternoon of charging to and fro with large green nets, the beauty of the enormous dragon flies which hovered over the tops of the grasses, the sinister killing-bottle with its sickly smell, and then tea in the parlour of a pub with large slices of pale-coloured cake! The essence of it was in the railway journey, which seemed to put magic distances between yourself and school.

Flip, characteristically, disapproved of these expeditions, though not actually forbidding them. "And have you been catching *little butterflies?*" she would say with a vicious sneer when one got back, making her voice as babyish as possible. From her point of view, natural history ("bug-hunting" she would probably have

called it) was a babyish pursuit which a boy should be laughed out
of as early as possible. Moreover it was somehow faintly plebeian,
it was traditionally associated with boys who wore spectacles and
were no good at games, it did not help you to pass exams, and
above all it smelt of science and therefore seemed to menace classical education. It needed a considerable moral effort to accept
Siller's invitation. How I dreaded that sneer of *little butterflies*! Siller,
however, who had been at the school since its early days, had built
up a certain independence for himself: he seemed able to handle
Sambo, and ignored Flip a good deal. If it ever happened that both
of them were away, Siller acted as deputy headmaster, and on those
occasions, instead of reading the appointed lesson for the day at
morning chapel, he would read us stories from the Apocrypha.

Most of the good memories of my childhood, and up to the
age of about twenty, are in some way connected with animals. So
far as St. Cyprian's goes, it also seems, when I look back, that all
my good memories are of summer. In winter your nose ran continually, your fingers were too numb to button your shirt (this was
an especial misery on Sundays, when we wore Eton collars), and
there was the daily nightmare of football — the cold, the mud, the
hideous greasy ball that came whizzing at one's face, the gouging
knees and trampling boots of the bigger boys. Part of the trouble
was that in winter, after the age of about ten, I was seldom in good
health, at any rate during term time. I had defective bronchial
tubes and a lesion in one lung which was not discovered till many
years later. Hence I not only had a chronic cough, but running
was a torment to me. In those days however, "wheeziness," or
"chestiness," as it was called, was either diagnosed as imagination
or was looked on as essentially a moral disorder, caused by over-
eating. "You wheeze like a concertina," Sambo would say disap-
provingly as he stood behind my chair; "You're perpetually
stuffing yourself with food, that's why." My cough was referred

to as a "stomach cough," which made it sound both disgusting and reprehensible. The cure for it was hard running, which, if you kept it up long enough, ultimately "cleared your chest."

It is curious, the degree—I will not say of actual hardship, but of squalor and neglect, that was taken for granted in upper-class schools of that period. Almost as in the days of Thackeray, it seemed natural that a little boy of eight or ten should be a miserable, snotty-nosed creature, his face almost permanently dirty, his hands chapped, his nails bitten, his handkerchief a sodden horror, his bottom frequently blue with bruises. It was partly the prospect of actual physical discomfort that made the thought of going back to school lie in one's breast like a lump of lead during the last few days of the holidays.

A characteristic memory of St. Cyprian's is the astonishing hardness of one's bed on the first night of term. Since this was an expensive school, I took a social step upwards by attending it, and yet the standard of comfort was in every way far lower than in my own home, or, indeed, than it would have been in a prosperous working-class home. One only had a hot bath once a week, for instance. The food was not only bad, it was also insufficient. Never before or since have I seen butter or jam scraped on bread so thinly. I do not think I can be imagining the fact that we were underfed, when I remember the lengths we would go in order to steal food. On a number of occasions I remember creeping down at two or three o'clock in the morning through what seemed like miles of pitch-dark stairways and passages—barefooted, stopping to listen after each step, paralysed with about equal fear of Sambo, ghosts and burglars—to steal stale bread from the pantry. The assistant masters had their meals with us, but they had somewhat better food, and if one got half a chance it was usual to steal leftover scraps of bacon rind or fried potato when their plates were removed.

As usual, I did not see the sound commercial reason for this underfeeding. On the whole I accepted Sambo's view that a boy's appetite is a sort of morbid growth which should be kept in check as much as possible. A maxim often repeated to us at St. Cyprian's was that it is healthy to get up from a meal feeling as hungry as when you sat down. Only a generation earlier than this it had been common for school dinners to start off with a slab of unsweetened suet pudding, which, it was frankly said, "broke the boys' appetites." But the underfeeding was probably less flagrant at preparatory schools, where a boy was wholly dependent on the official diet, than at public schools, where he was allowed— indeed, expected—to buy extra food for himself. At some schools, he would literally not have had enough to eat unless he had bought regular supplies of eggs, sausages, sardines, etc.; and his parents had to allow him money for this purpose. At Eton, for instance, at any rate in College, a boy was given no solid meal after mid-day dinner. For his afternoon tea he was given only tea and bread and butter, and at eight o'clock he was given a miserable supper of soup or fried fish, or more often bread and cheese, with water to drink. Sambo went down to see his eldest son at Eton and came back in snobbish ecstasies over the luxury in which the boys lived. "They give them fried fish for supper!" he exclaimed, beaming all over his chubby face. "There's no school like it in the world." Fried fish! The habitual supper of the poorest of the working class! At very cheap boarding schools it was no doubt worse. A very early memory of mine is of seeing the boarders at a grammar school—the sons, probably, of farmers and shopkeepers— being fed on boiled lights.

Whoever writes about his childhood must beware of exaggeration and self-pity. I do not want to claim that I was a martyr or that St. Cyprian's was a sort of Dotheboys Hall. But I should be falsifying my own memories if I did not record that they are largely memories of disgust. The overcrowded, underfed, underwashed life that we led *was* disgusting, as I recall it. If I shut my eyes and say "school," it is of course the physical surroundings that first come back to me: the flat playing field with its cricket pavilion and the little shed by the rifle range, the draughty dormitories, the dusty splintery passages, the square of asphalt in front of the gymnasium, the raw-looking pinewood chapel at the back. And at almost every point some filthy detail obtrudes itself. For example, there were the pewter bowls out of which we had our porridge. They had overhanging rims, and under the rims there were accumulations of sour porridge, which could be flaked off in long strips. The porridge itself, too, contained more lumps, hair and unexplained black things than one would have thought possible, unless someone were putting them there on purpose. It was never safe to start on that porridge without investigating it first. And there was the slimy water of the plunge bath—it was twelve or fifteen feet long, the whole school was supposed to go into it every morning, and I doubt whether the water was changed at all frequently—and the always-damp towels with their cheesy smell; and, on occasional visits in the winter, the murky sea-water of the Devonshire Baths, which came straight in from the beach and on which I once saw floating a human turd. And the sweaty smell of the changing-room with its greasy basins, and, giving on this, the row of filthy, dilapidated lavatories, which had no fastenings of any kind on the doors, so that whenever you were sitting there someone was sure to come crashing in. It is not easy for me to think of my schooldays without seeming to breathe in a whiff of something cold and evil-smelling—a sort of compound of sweaty stockings, dirty towels, faecal smells blowing along corridors, forks with old food between the prongs, neck-of-mutton stew, and the banging doors of the lavatories and the echoing chamberpots in the dormitories.

It is true that I am by nature not gregarious, and the W.C. and dirty-handkerchief side of life is necessarily more obtrusive when great numbers of human beings are crushed together in [a] small space. It is just as bad in an army, and worse, no doubt, in a prison. Besides, boyhood is the age of disgust. After one has learned to differentiate, and before one has become hardened — between seven and eighteen, say — one seems always to be walking the tightrope over a cesspool. Yet I do not think I exaggerate the squalor of school life, when I remember how health and cleanliness were neglected, in spite of the hoo-ha about fresh air and cold water and keeping in hard training. It was common to remain constipated for days together. Indeed, one was hardly encouraged to keep one's bowels open, since the only aperients tolerated were Castor Oil or another almost equally horrible drink called Liquorice Powder. One was supposed to go into the plunge bath every morning, but some boys shirked it for days on end, simply making themselves scarce when the bell sounded, or else slipping along the edge of the bath among the crowd, and then wetting their hair with a little dirty water off the floor. A little boy of eight or nine will not necessarily keep himself clean unless there is someone to see that he does it. There was a new boy named Bachelor, a pretty, mother's darling of a boy, who came a little while before I left. The first thing I noticed about him was the beautiful pearly whiteness of his teeth. By the end of that term his teeth were an extraordinary shade of green. During all that time, apparently, no one had taken sufficient interest in him to see that he brushed them.

But of course the differences between home and school were more than physical. That bump on the hard mattress, on the first night of term, used to give me a feeling of abrupt awakening, a feeling of: "This is reality, this is what you are up against." Your home might be far from perfect, but at least it was a place ruled

by love rather than by fear, where you did not have to be perpetually on your guard against the people surrounding you. At eight
years old you were suddenly taken out of this warm nest and flung
into a world of force and fraud and secrecy, like a goldfish into a
tank full of pike. Against no matter what degree of bullying you
had no redress. You could only have defended yourself by sneaking, which, except in a few rigidly defined circumstances, was the
unforgivable sin. To write home and ask your parents to take you
away would have been even less thinkable, since to do so would
have been to admit yourself unhappy and unpopular, which a boy
will never do. Boys are Erewhonians: they think that misfortune
is disgraceful and must be concealed at all costs. It might perhaps
have been considered permissible to complain to your parents
about bad food, or an unjustified caning, or some other ill-
treatment inflicted by masters and not by boys. The fact that
Sambo never beat the richer boys suggests that such complaints
were made occasionally. But in my own peculiar circumstances I
could never have asked my parents to intervene on my behalf.
Even before I understood about the reduced fees, I grasped that
they were in some way under an obligation to Sambo, and therefore could not protect me against him. I have mentioned already
that throughout my time at St. Cyprian's I never had a cricket bat
of my own. I had been told this was because "your parents
couldn't afford it." One day in the holidays, by some casual remark, it came out that they had provided ten shillings to buy me
one: yet no cricket bat appeared. I did not protest to my parents,
let alone raise the subject with Sambo. How could I? I was dependent on him, and the ten shillings was merely a fragment of
what I owed him. I realise now of course, that it is immensely unlikely that Sambo had simply stuck to the money. No doubt the
matter had slipped his memory. But the point is that I assumed
that he had stuck to it, and that he had a right to do so if he chose.

How difficult it is for a child to have any real independence of attitude could be seen in our behaviour towards Flip. I think it would be true to say that every boy in the school hated and feared her. Yet we all fawned on her in the most abject way, and the top layer of our feelings towards her was a sort of guilt-stricken loyalty. Flip, although the discipline of the school depended more on her than on Sambo, hardly pretended to dispense strict justice. She was frankly capricious. An act which might get you a caning one day, might next day be laughed off as a boyish prank, or even commended because it "showed you had guts." There were days when everyone cowered before those deepset, accusing eyes, and there were days when she was like a flirtatious queen surrounded by courtier-lovers, laughing and joking, scattering largesse, or the promise of largesse ("And if you win the Harrow History Prize I'll give you a new case for your camera!"), and occasionally even packing three or four favoured boys into her Ford car and carrying them off to a teashop in town, where they were allowed to buy coffee and cakes. Flip was inextricably mixed up in my mind with Queen Elizabeth, whose relations with Leicester and Essex and Raleigh were intelligible to me from a very early age. A word we all constantly used in speaking of Flip was "favour." "I'm in good favour," we would say, or "I'm in bad favour." Except for the handful of wealthy or titled boys, no one was permanently in good favour, but on the other hand even the outcasts had patches of it from time to time. Thus, although my memories of Flip are mostly hostile, I also remember considerable periods when I basked under her smiles, when she called me "old chap" and used my Christian name, and allowed me to frequent her private library, where I first made acquaintance with *Vanity Fair*. The high-water mark of good favour was to be invited to serve at table on Sunday nights when Flip and Sambo had guests to dinner. In clearing away, of course, one had a chance to finish off the scraps, but one also got a servile

pleasure from standing behind the seated guests and darting def-
erentially forward when something was wanted. Whenever one had
the chance to suck up, one did suck up, and at the first smile one's
hatred turned into a sort of cringing love. I was always tremen-
dously proud when I succeeded in making Flip laugh. I have even,
at her command, written vers d'occasion, comic verses to celebrate
memorable events in the life of the school.

I am anxious to make it clear that I was not a rebel, except by
force of circumstances. I accepted the codes that I found in being.
Once, towards the end of my time, I even sneaked to Siller about
a suspected case of homosexuality. I did not know very well what
homosexuality was, but I knew that it happened and was bad, and
that this was one of the contexts in which it was proper to sneak.
Siller told me I was "a good fellow," which made me feel horribly
ashamed. Before Flip one seemed as helpless as a snake before
the snake-charmer. She had a hardly-varying vocabulary of praise
and abuse, a whole series of set phrases, each of which promptly
called forth the appropriate response. There was "*Buck* up, old
chap!," which inspired one to paroxysms of energy; there was
"Don't *be* such a fool!" (or, "It's path*et*ic, isn't it?"), which made
one feel a born idiot; and there was "It isn't very straight of you,
is it?," which always brought one to the brink of tears. And yet all
the while, at the middle of one's heart, there seemed to stand an
incorruptible inner self who knew that whatever one did—
whether one laughed or snivelled or went into frenzies of gratitude
for small favours—one's only true feeling was hatred.

iv.

I had learned early in my career that one can do wrong against
one's will, and before long I also learned that one can do wrong
without ever discovering what one has done or why it was wrong.

There were sins that were too subtle to be explained, and there were others that were too terrible to be clearly mentioned. For example, there was sex, which was always smouldering just under the surface and which suddenly blew up into a tremendous row when I was about twelve.

At some preparatory schools homosexuality is not a problem, but I think that St. Cyprian's may have acquired a "bad tone" thanks to the presence of the South American boys, who would perhaps mature a year or two earlier than an English boy. At that age I was not interested, so I do not actually know what went on, but I imagine it was group masturbation. At any rate, one day the storm suddenly burst over our heads. There were summonses, interrogations, confessions, floggings, repentances, solemn lectures of which one understood nothing except that some irredeemable sin known as "swinishness" or "beastliness" had been committed. One of the ringleaders, a boy named Cross, was flogged, according to eyewitnesses, for a quarter of an hour continuously before being expelled. His yells rang through the house. But we were all implicated, more or less, or felt ourselves to be implicated. Guilt seemed to hang in the air like a pall of smoke. A solemn, blackhaired imbecile of an assistant master, who was later to be a Member of Parliament, took the older boys to a secluded room and delivered a talk on the Temple of the Body.

"Don't you realise what a wonderful thing your body is?" he said gravely. "You talk of your motor-car engines, your Rolls-Royces and Daimlers and so on. Don't you understand that no engine ever made is fit to be compared with your body? And then you go and wreck it, ruin it—for life!"

He turned his cavernous black eyes on me and added sadly:

"And you, whom I'd always [believed] to be quite a decent person after your fashion—you, I hear, are one of the very worst."

A feeling of doom descended upon me. So I was guilty too. I too had done the dreadful thing, whatever it was, that wrecked you for life, body and soul, and ended in suicide or the lunatic asylum. Till then I had hoped that I was innocent, and the conviction of sin which now took possession of me was perhaps all the stronger because I did not know what I had done. I was not among those who were interrogated and flogged, and it was not until after the row was well over that I even learned about the trivial accident which had connected my name with it. Even then I understood nothing. It was not till about two years later that I fully grasped what that lecture on the Temple of the Body had referred to.

At this time I was in an almost sexless state, which is normal, or at any rate common, in boys of that age; I was therefore in the position of simultaneously knowing and not knowing what used to be called the Facts of Life. At five or six, like many children, I had passed through a phase of sexuality. My friends were the plumber's children up the road, and we used sometimes to play games of a vaguely erotic kind. One was called "playing at doctors," and I remember getting a faint but definitely pleasant thrill from holding a toy trumpet, which was supposed to be a stethoscope, against a little girl's belly. About the same time I fell deeply in love, a far more worshipping kind of love than I have ever felt for anyone since, with a girl named Elsie at the convent school which I attended. She seemed to me grown up, so I suppose she must have been fifteen. After that, as so often happens, all sexual feeling seemed to go out of me for many years. At twelve I knew more than I had known as a young child, but I understood less, because I no longer knew the essential fact that there is something pleasant in sexual activity. Between roughly seven and fourteen, the whole subject seemed to me uninteresting and, when for some reason I was forced to think of it, disgusting. My knowledge of the so-called Facts of Life was derived from animals, and was therefore distorted, and in any case was only intermittent. I knew that animals copulated and that human beings had bodies resembling those of animals: but that human beings also copulated I only knew, as it were, reluctantly, when something, a phrase in the Bible, perhaps, compelled me to remember it. Not having desire, I had no curiosity, and was willing to leave many questions unanswered. Thus, I knew in principle how the baby gets into the woman, but I did not know how it gets out again, because I had never followed the subject up. I knew all the dirty words, and in my bad moments I would repeat them to myself, but I did not know what the worst of them meant, nor want to know. They were abstractly wicked, a sort of verbal charm. While I remained in this state, it was easy for me to remain ignorant of any sexual misdeeds that went on about me, and to be hardly wiser even when the row broke. At most, through the veiled and terrible warnings of Flip, Sambo and all the rest of them, I grasped that the crime of which we were all guilty was somehow connected with the sexual organs. I had noticed, without feeling much interest, that one's penis sometimes stands up of its own accord (this starts happening to a boy long before he has any conscious sexual desires), and I was inclined to believe, or half-believe, that *that* must be the crime. At any rate, it was something to do with the penis—so much I understood. Many other boys, I have no doubt, were equally in the dark.

After the talk on the Temple of the Body (days later, it seems in retrospect: the row seemed to continue for days), a dozen of us were seated at the long shiny table which Sambo used for the scholarship class, under Flip's lowering eye. A long, desolate wail rang out from a room somewhere above. A very small boy named Duncan, aged no more than about ten, who was implicated in some way, was being flogged, or was recovering from a flogging. At the sound, Flip's eyes searched our faces, and settled upon me.

"*You see,*" she said.

I will not swear that she said, "You see what you have done," but that was the sense of it. We were all bowed down with shame. It was *our* fault. Somehow or other we had led poor Duncan astray: *we* were responsible for his agony and his ruin. Then Flip turned upon another boy named Clapham. It is thirty years ago, and I cannot remember for certain whether she merely quoted a verse from the Bible, or whether she actually brought out a Bible and made Clapham read it; but at any rate the text indicated was:

"Whoso shall offend one of these little ones that believe in me, it were better for him that a millstone were hanged about his neck, and that he were drowned in the depth of the sea."

That, too, was terrible. Duncan was one of these little ones; we had offended him; it were better that a millstone were hanged about our necks and that we were drowned in the depth of the sea.

"Have you thought about that, Clapham — have you thought what it means?" Flip said. And Clapham broke down into snivelling tears.

Another boy, Hardcastle, whom I have mentioned already, was similarly overwhelmed with shame by the accusation that he "had black rings round his eyes."

"Have you looked in the glass lately, Hardcastle?" said Flip. "Aren't you ashamed to go about with a face like that? Do you think everyone doesn't know what it means when a boy has black rings round his eyes?"

Once again the load of guilt and fear seemed to settle down upon me. Had *I* got black rings round my eyes? A couple of years later I realised that these were supposed to be a symptom by which masturbators could be detected. But already, without knowing this, I accepted the black rings as a sure sign of depravity, *some* kind of depravity. And many times, even before I grasped the supposed meaning, I have gazed anxiously into the glass, looking for the first hint of that dreaded stigma, the confession which the secret sinner writes upon his own face.

These terrors wore off, or became merely intermittent, without affecting what one might call my official beliefs. It was still true about the madhouse and the suicide's grave, but it was no longer acutely frightening. Some months later it happened that I once again saw Cross, the ringleader who had been flogged and expelled. Cross was one of the outcasts, the son of poor middle-class parents, which was no doubt part of the reason why Sambo had handled him so roughly. The term after his expulsion he went on to Eastbourne College, the small local public school, which was hideously despised at St. Cyprian's and looked on as "not really" a public school at all. Only a very few boys from St. Cyprian's went there, and Sambo always spoke of them with a sort of contemptuous pity. You had no chance if you went to a school like that: at the best your destiny would be a clerkship. I thought of Cross as a person who at thirteen had already forfeited all hope of any decent future. Physically, morally and socially he was finished. Moreover I assumed that his parents had only sent him to Eastbourne College because after his disgrace no "good" school would have him.

During the following term, when we were out for a walk, we passed Cross in the street. He looked completely normal. He was a strongly-built, rather good-looking boy with black hair. I immediately noticed that he looked better than when I had last seen him—his complexion, previously rather pale, was pinker—and that he did not seem embarrassed at meeting us. Apparently he was not ashamed either of having been expelled, or of being at Eastbourne College. If one could gather anything from the way he looked at us as we filed past, it was that he was glad to have escaped from St. Cyprian's. But the encounter made very little im-

pression on me. I drew no inference from the fact that Cross, ruined in body and soul, appeared to be happy and in good health.
I still believed in the sexual mythology that had been taught me by
Sambo and Flip. The mysterious, terrible dangers were still there.
Any morning the black rings might appear round your eyes and
you would know that you too were among the lost ones. Only it
no longer seemed to matter very much. These contradictions can
exist easily in the mind of a child, because of its own vitality. It accepts—how can it do otherwise?—the nonsense that its elders
tell it, but its youthful body, and the sweetness of the physical
world, tell it another story. It was the same with Hell, which up to
the age of about fourteen I officially believed in. Almost certainly
Hell existed, and there were occasions when a vivid sermon could
scare you into fits. But somehow it never lasted. The fire that
waited for you was real fire, it would hurt in the same way as when
you burnt your finger, and *for ever,* but most of the time you could
contemplate it without bothering.

v.

The various codes which were presented to you at St. Cyprian's—
religious, moral, social and intellectual—contradicted one another
if you worked out their implications. The essential conflict was
between the tradition of nineteenth-century asceticism and the
actually existing luxury and snobbery of the pre-1914 age. On the
one side were low-church Bible Christianity, sex puritanism, insistence on hard work, respect for academic distinction, disapproval of self-indulgence: on the other, contempt for "braininess"
and worship of games, contempt for foreigners and the working
class, an almost neurotic dread of poverty, and, above all, the assumption not only that money and privilege are the things that
matter, but that it is better to inherit them than to have to work for

them. Broadly, you were bidden to be at once a Christian and a social success, which is impossible. At the time I did not perceive that the various ideals which were set before us cancelled out. I merely saw that they were all, or nearly all, unattainable, so far as I was concerned, since they all depended not only on what you did but on what you *were*.

Very early, at the age of only ten or eleven, I reached the conclusion—no one told me this, but on the other hand I did not simply make it up out of my own head: somehow it was in the air I breathed—that you were no good unless you had £100,000. I had perhaps fixed on this particular sum as a result of reading Thackeray. The interest on £100,000 would be £4,000 a year (I was in favour of a safe 4 percent), and this seemed to me the minimum income that you must possess if you were to belong to the real top crust, the people in the country houses. But it was clear that I could never find my way into that paradise, to which you did not really belong unless you were born into it. You could only *make* money, if at all, by a mysterious operation called "going into the City," and when you came out of the City, having won your £100,000, you were fat and old. But the truly enviable thing about the top-notchers was that they were rich while young. For people like me, the ambitious middle-class, the examination passers, only a bleak, laborious kind of success was possible. You clambered upwards on a ladder of scholarships into the Home Civil Service or the Indian Civil Service, or possibly you became a barrister. And if at any point you "slacked" or "went off" and missed one of the rungs in the ladder, you became "a little office boy at forty pounds a year." But even if you climbed to the highest niche that was open to you, you could still only be an underling, a hanger-on of the people who really counted.

Even if I had not learned this from Sambo and Flip, I would have learned it from the other boys. Looking back, it is astonish-

ing how intimately, intelligently snobbish we all were, how knowledgeable about names and addresses, how swift to detect small
differences in accents and manners and the cut of clothes. There
were some boys who seemed to drip money from their pores even
in the bleak misery of the middle of a winter term. At the beginning and end of the term, especially, there was naively snobbish
chatter about Switzerland, and Scotland with its ghillies and grouse
moors, and "my uncle's yacht," and "our place in the country,"
and "my pony" and "my pater's touring car." There never was, I
suppose, in the history of the world a time when the sheer vulgar
fatness of wealth, without any kind of aristocratic elegance to re-
deem it, was so obtrusive as in those years before 1914. It was the
age when crazy millionaires in curly top hats and lavender waist-
coats gave champagne parties in rococo houseboats on the
Thames, the age of diabolo and hobble skirts, the age of the
"knut" in his grey bowler and cutaway coat, the age of *The Merry
Widow,* Saki's novels, *Peter Pan* and *Where the Rainbow Ends,* the age
when people talked about chocs and cigs and ripping and topping
and heavenly, when they went for divvy weekends at Brighton and
had scrumptious teas at the Troc. From the whole decade before
1914 there seems to breathe forth a smell of the more vulgar, un-
grown-up kinds of luxury, a smell of brilliantine and creme de
menthe and soft-centre chocolates, —an atmosphere, as it were,
of eating everlasting strawberry ices on green lawns to the tune of
the Eton Boating Song. The extraordinary thing was the way in
which everyone took it for granted that this oozing, bulging wealth
of the English upper and upper-middle classes would last for ever,
and was part of the order of things. After 1918 it was never quite
the same again. Snobbishness and expensive habits came back,
certainly, but they were self-conscious and on the defensive. Before the war the worship of money was entirely unreflecting and
untroubled by any pang of conscience. The goodness of money

was as unmistakeable as the goodness of health or beauty, and a glittering car, a title or a horde of servants was mixed up in people's minds with the idea of actual moral virtue.

At St. Cyprian's, in term time, the general bareness of life enforced a certain democracy, but any mention of the holidays, and the consequent competitive swanking about cars and butlers and country houses, promptly called class distinctions into being. The school was pervaded by a curious cult of Scotland, which brought out the fundamental contradiction in our standard of values. Flip claimed Scottish ancestry, and she favoured the Scottish boys, encouraging them to wear kilts in their ancestral tartan instead of the school uniform, and even christened her youngest child by a Gaelic name. Ostensibly we were supposed to admire the Scots because they were "grim" and "dour" ("stern" was perhaps the key word), and irresistible on the field of battle. In the big schoolroom there was a steel engraving of the charge of the Scots Greys at Waterloo, all looking as though they enjoyed every moment of it. Our picture of Scotland was made up of burns, braes, kilts, sporrans, claymores, bagpipes and the like, all somehow mixed up with the invigorating effects of porridge, Protestantism and a cold climate. But underlying this was something quite different. The real reason for the cult of Scotland was that only very rich people could spend their summers there. And the pretended belief in Scottish superiority was a cover for the bad conscience of the occupying English, who had pushed the Highland peasantry off their farms to make way for the deer forests, and then compensated them by turning them into servants. Flip's face always beamed with innocent snobbishness when she spoke of Scotland. Occasionally she even attempted a trace of Scottish accent. Scotland was a private paradise which a few initiates could talk about and make outsiders feel small.

"You going to Scotland this hols?"

"Rather! We go every year."

"My pater's got three miles of river."

"My pater's giving me a new gun for the twelfth. There's jolly good black game where we go. Get out, Smith! What are you listening for? You've never been in Scotland. I bet you don't know what a black-cock looks like."

Following on this, imitations of the cry of a black-cock, of the roaring of a stag, of the accent of "our ghillies," etc., etc.

And the questionings that new boys of doubtful social origin were sometimes put through—questionings quite surprising in their mean-minded particularity, when one reflects that the inquisitors were only twelve or thirteen!

"How much a year has your pater got? What part of London do you live in? Is that Knightsbridge or Kensington? How many bathrooms has your house got? How many servants do your people keep? Have you got a butler? Well, then, have you got a cook? Where do you get your clothes made? How many shows did you go to in the hols? How much money did you bring back with you?" etc., etc.

I have seen a little new boy, hardly older than eight, desperately lying his way through such a catechism:

"Have your people got a car?"

"Yes."

"What sort of car?"

"Daimler."

"How many horse-power?"

(Pause, and leap in the dark.) "Fifteen."

"What kind of lights?"

The little boy is bewildered.

"What kind of lights? Electric or acetylene?"

(A longer pause, and another leap in the dark.) "Acetylene."

"Coo! He says his pater's car's got acetylene lamps. They went out years ago. It must be as old as the hills."

"Rot! He's making it up. He hasn't got a car. He's just a navvy. Your pater's a navvy."

And so on.

By the social standards that prevailed about me, I was no good, and could not be any good. But all the different kinds of virtue seemed to be mysteriously interconnected and to belong to much the same people. It was not only money that mattered: there were also strength, beauty, charm, athleticism and something called "guts" or "character," which in reality meant the power to impose your will on others. I did not possess any of these qualities. At games, for instance, I was hopeless. I was a fairly good swimmer and not altogether contemptible at cricket, but these had no prestige value, because boys only attach importance to a game if it requires strength and courage. What counted was football, at which I was a funk. I loathed the game, and since I could see no pleasure or usefulness in it, it was very difficult for me to show courage at it. Football, it seemed to me, is not really played for the pleasure of kicking a ball about, but is a species of fighting. The lovers of football are large, boisterous, nobbly boys who are good at knocking down and trampling on slightly smaller boys. That was the pattern of school life — a continuous triumph of the strong over the weak. Virtue consisted in winning: it consisted in being bigger, stronger, handsomer, richer, more popular, more elegant, more unscrupulous than other people — in dominating them, bullying them, making them suffer pain, making them look foolish, getting the better of them in every way. Life was hierarchical and whatever happened was right. There were the strong, who deserved to win and always did win, and there were the weak, who deserved to lose and always did lose, everlastingly.

I did not question the prevailing standards, because so far as I could see there were no others. How could the rich, the strong, the elegant, the fashionable, the powerful, be in the wrong? It was their world, and the rules they made for it must be the right ones. And yet from a very early age I was aware of the impossibility of any *subjective* conformity. Always at the centre of my heart the inner self seemed to be awake, pointing out the difference between the moral obligation and the psychological *fact*. It was the same in all matters, worldly or other-worldly. Take religion, for instance. You were supposed to love God and I did not question this. Till the age of about fourteen I believed in God, and believed that the accounts given of him were true. But I was well aware that I did not love him. On the contrary, I hated him, just as I hated Jesus and the Hebrew patriarchs. If I had sympathetic feelings towards any character in the Old Testament, it was towards such people as Cain, Jezebel, Haman, Agag, Sisera: in the New Testament my friends, if any, were Ananias, Caiaphas, Judas and Pontius Pilate. But the whole business of religion seemed to be strewn with psychological impossibilities. The Prayer Book told you, for example, to love God and fear him: but how could you love someone whom you feared? With your private affections it was the same. What you *ought* to feel was usually clear enough, but the appropriate emotion could not be commanded. Obviously it was my duty to feel grateful towards Flip and Sambo; but I was not grateful. It was equally clear that one ought to love one's father, but I knew very well that I merely disliked my own father, whom I had barely seen before I was eight and who appeared to me simply as a gruff-voiced elderly man for ever saying "Don't." It was not that one did not want to possess the right qualities or feel the correct emotions, but that one could not. The good and the possible never seemed to coincide.

There was a line of verse that I came across not actually while I was at St. Cyprian's, but a year or two later, and which seemed to strike a sort of leaden echo in my heart. It was: "The armies of unalterable law." I understood to perfection what it meant to be Lucifer, defeated and justly defeated, with no possibility of revenge. The schoolmasters with their canes, the millionaires with their Scottish castles, the athletes with their curly hair—these were the armies of the unalterable law. It was not easy, at that date, to realise that in fact it *was* alterable. And according to that law I was damned. I had no money, I was weak, I was ugly, I was unpopular, I had a chronic cough, I was cowardly, I smelt. This picture, I should add, was not altogether fanciful. I was an unattractive boy. St. Cyprian's soon made me so, even if I had not been so before. But a child's belief in its own shortcomings is not much influenced by facts. I believed, for example, that I "smelt," but this was based simply on general probability. It was notorious that disagreeable people smelt, and therefore presumably I did so too. Again, until after I had left school for good I continued to believe that I was preternaturally ugly. It was what my schoolfellows had told me, and I had no other authority to refer to. The conviction that it was *not possible* for me to be a success went deep enough to influence my actions till far into adult life. Until I was about thirty I always planned my life on the assumption not only that any major undertaking was bound to fail, but that I could only expect to live a few years longer.

But this sense of guilt and inevitable failure was balanced by something else: that is, the instinct to survive. Even a creature that is weak, ugly, cowardly, smelly and in no way justifiable still wants to stay alive and be happy after its own fashion. I could not invert the existing scale of values, or turn myself into a success, but I could accept my failure and make the best of it. I could resign myself to being what I was, and then endeavour to survive on those terms.

To survive, or at least to preserve any kind of independence, was essentially criminal, since it meant breaking rules which you yourself recognized. There was a boy named Cliffy Burton who for some months oppressed me horribly. He was a big, powerful, coarsely handsome boy with a very red face and curly black hair, who was forever twisting somebody's arm, wringing somebody's ear, flogging somebody with a riding crop (he was a member of Sixth Form), or performing prodigies of activity on the football field. Flip loved him (hence the fact that he was habitually called by his Christian name), and Sambo commended him as a boy who "had character" and "could keep order." He was followed about by a group of toadies who nicknamed him Strong Man.

One day, when we were taking off our overcoats in the changing-room, Burton picked on me for some reason. I "answered him back," whereupon he gripped my wrist, twisted it round and bent my forearm back upon itself in a hideously painful way. I remember his handsome, jeering red face bearing down upon mine. He was, I think, older than I, besides being enormously stronger. As he let go of me a terrible, wicked resolve formed itself in my heart. I would get back on him by hitting him when he did not expect it. It was a strategic moment, for the master who had been "taking" the walk would be coming back almost immediately, and then there could be no fight. I let perhaps a minute go by, walked up to Burton with the most harmless air I could assume, and then, getting the weight of my body behind it, smashed my fist into his face. He was flung backwards by the blow, and some blood ran out of his mouth. His always sanguine face turned almost black with rage. Then he turned away to rinse his mouth at the washing-basins.

"*All right!*" he said to me between his teeth as the master led us away.

For days after this he followed me about, challenging me to fight. Although terrified out of my wits, I steadily refused to fight. I said that the blow in the face had served him right, and there was an end of it. Curiously enough he did not simply fall upon me there and then, which public opinion would probably have supported him in doing. So gradually the matter tailed off, and there was no fight.

Now, I had behaved wrongly, by my own code no less than his. To hit him unawares was wrong. But to refuse afterwards to fight, knowing that if we fought he would beat me — that was far worse: it was cowardly. If I had refused because I disapproved of fighting, or because I genuinely felt the matter to be closed, it would have been all right; but I had refused merely because I was afraid. Even my revenge was made empty by that fact. I had struck the blow in a moment of mindless violence, deliberately not looking far ahead and merely determined to get my own back for once and damn the consequences. I had had time to realise that what I did was wrong, but it was the kind of crime from which you could get some satisfaction. Now all was nullified. There had been a sort of courage in the first act, but my subsequent cowardice had wiped it out.

The fact I hardly noticed was that though Burton formally challenged me to fight, he did not actually attack me. Indeed, after receiving that one blow he never oppressed me again. It was perhaps twenty years before I saw the significance of this. At the time I could not see beyond the moral dilemma that is presented to the weak in a world governed by the strong: Break the rules, or perish. I did not see that in that case the weak have the right to make a different set of rules for themselves; because, even if such an idea had occurred to me, there was no one in my environment who could have confirmed me in it. I lived in a world of boys, gregarious animals, questioning nothing, accepting the law of the stronger and avenging their own humiliations by passing them down to someone smaller. My situation was that of countless other boys, and if potentially I was more of a rebel than most, it was only because, by boyish standards, I was a poorer specimen. But I never did rebel intellectually, only emotionally. I had nothing to help me except my dumb selfishness, my inability—not, indeed, to despise myself, but to *dislike* myself—my instinct to survive.

It was about a year after I hit Cliffy Burton in the face that I left St. Cyprian's for ever. It was the end of a winter term. With a sense of coming out from darkness into sunlight I put on my Old Boy's tie as we dressed for the journey. I well remember the feeling of that brand-new silk tie round my neck, a feeling of emancipation, as though the tie had been at once a badge of manhood and an amulet against Flip's voice and Sambo's cane. I was escaping from bondage. It was not that I expected, or even intended, to be any more successful at a public school than I had been at St. Cyprian's. But still, I was escaping. I knew that at a public school there would be more privacy, more neglect, more chance to be idle and self-indulgent and degenerate. For years past I had been resolved—unconsciously at first, but consciously later on—that when once my scholarship was won I would "slack off" and cram no longer. This resolve, by the way, was so fully carried out that between the ages of thirteen and twenty-two or three I hardly ever did a stroke of avoidable work.

Flip shook hands to say good-bye. She even gave me my Christian name for the occasion. But there was a sort of patronage, almost a sneer, in her face and in her voice. The tone in which she said good-bye was nearly the tone in which she had been used to say *little butterflies*. I had won two scholarships, but I was a failure, because success was measured not by what you did but by what you *were*. I was "not a good type of boy" and could bring no credit on the school. I did not possess character or courage or health or strength or money, or even good manners, the power to look like a gentleman.

"Good-bye," Flip's parting smile seemed to say; "it's not worth quarrelling now. You haven't made much of a success of your time at St. Cyprian's, have you? And I don't suppose you'll get on awfully well at a public school either. We made a mistake, really, in wasting our time and money on you. This kind of education hasn't much to offer to a boy with your background and your outlook. Oh, don't think we don't understand you! We know all about those ideas you have at the back of your head, we know you disbelieve in everything we've taught you, and we know you aren't in the least grateful for all we've done for you. But there's no use in bringing it all up now. We aren't responsible for you any longer, and we shan't be seeing you again. Let's just admit that you're one of our failures and part without ill-feeling. And so, good-bye."

That at least was what I read into her face. And yet how happy I was, that winter morning, as the train bore me away with the gleaming new silk tie (dark green, pale blue and black, if I remember rightly) round my neck! The world was opening before me, just a little, like a grey sky which exhibits a narrow crack of blue. A public school would be better fun than St. Cyprian's, but at bottom equally alien. In a world where the prime necessities were money, titled relatives, athleticism, tailor-made clothes, neatly-brushed hair, a charming smile, I was no good. All I had gained was a breathing-space. A little quietude, a little self-indulgence, a little respite from cramming—and then, ruin. What kind of ruin I did not know: perhaps the colonies or an office stool, perhaps prison or an early death. But first a year or two in which one could "slack off" and get the benefit of one's sins, like Doctor Faustus. I believed firmly in my evil destiny, and yet I was acutely happy. It is the advantage of being thirteen that you can not only live in the moment, but do so with full consciousness, fore-seeing the future and yet not caring about it. Next term I was going to Wellington. I had also won a scholarship at Eton, but it was uncertain whether there would be a vacancy, and I was going to Wellington first. At Eton you had a room to yourself—a room which might even have a fire in it. At Wellington you had your own cubicle, and could make yourself cocoa in the evenings. The privacy of it, the grown-upness! And there would be libraries to hang about in, and summer afternoons when you could shirk games and mooch about the countryside alone, with no master driving you along. Meanwhile there were the holidays. There was the .22 rifle that I had bought the previous holidays (the Crack-shot, it was called, costing twenty-two and sixpence), and Christ-mas was coming next week. There were also the pleasures of over-eating. I thought of some particularly voluptuous cream buns which could be bought for twopence each at a shop in our town. (This was 1916, and food-rationing had not yet started.) Even the detail that my journey-money had been slightly miscalculated, leav-ing about a shilling over—enough for an unforeseen cup of cof-fee and a cake or two somewhere on the way—was enough to fill me with bliss. There was time for a bit of happiness before the fu-ture closed in upon me. But I did know that the future was dark. Failure, failure, failure—failure behind me, failure ahead of me— that was by far the deepest conviction that I carried away.

vi.

All this was thirty years ago and more. The question is: Does a child at school go through the same kind of experiences nowadays?

The only honest answer, I believe, is that we do not with cer-tainty know. Of course it is obvious that the present-day *attitude* to-wards education is enormously more humane and sensible than that of the past. The snobbishness that was an integral part of my own education would be almost unthinkable today, because the society that nourished it is dead. I recall a conversation that must have taken place about a year before I left St. Cyprian's. A Russian boy, large and fair-haired, a year older than myself, was questioning me.

"How much a year has your father got?"

I told him what I thought it was, adding a few hundreds to make it sound better. The Russian boy, neat in his habits, produced a pencil and a small notebook and made a calculation.

"My father has over two hundred times as much money as yours," he announced with a sort of amused contempt.

That was in 1915. What happened to that money a couple of years later, I wonder? And still more I wonder, do conversations of that kind happen at preparatory schools now?

Clearly there has been a vast change of outlook, a general growth of "enlightenment," even among ordinary, unthinking middle-class people. Religious belief, for instance, has largely vanished, dragging other kinds of nonsense after it. I imagine that very few people nowadays would tell a child that if it masturbates it will end in the lunatic asylum. Beating, too, has become discredited, and has even been abandoned at many schools. Nor is the underfeeding of children looked on as a normal, almost meritorious act. No one now would openly set out to give his pupils as little food as they could do with, or tell them that it is healthy to get up from a meal as hungry as you sat down. The whole status of children has improved, partly because they have grown relatively less numerous. And the diffusion of even a little psychological knowledge has made it harder for parents and schoolteachers to indulge their aberrations in the name of discipline. Here is a case, not known to me personally, but known to someone I can vouch for, and happening within my own lifetime. A small girl, daughter of a clergyman, continued wetting her bed at an age when she should have grown out of it. In order to punish her for this dreadful deed, her father took her to a large garden party and there introduced her to the whole company as a little girl who wetted her bed: and to underline her wickedness he had previously painted her face black. I do not suggest that Flip and Sambo would actually have done a thing like this, but I doubt whether it would have much surprised them. After all, things do change. And yet—!

The question is not whether boys are still buckled into Eton collars on Sunday, or told that babies are dug up under gooseberry bushes. That kind of thing is at an end, admittedly. The real question is whether it is still normal for a schoolchild to live for years amid irrational terrors and lunatic misunderstandings. And here one is up against the very great difficulty of knowing what a child really feels and thinks. A child which appears reasonably happy may actually be suffering horrors which it cannot or will not reveal. It lives in a sort of alien under-water world which we can only penetrate by memory or divination. Our chief clue is the fact that we were once children ourselves, and many people appear to forget the atmosphere of their own childhood almost entirely. Think for instance of the unnecessary torments that people will inflict by sending a child back to school with clothes of the wrong pattern, and refusing to see that this matters! Over things of this kind a child will sometimes utter a protest, but a great deal of the time its attitude is one of simple concealment. Not to expose your true feelings to an adult seems to be instinctive from the age of seven or eight onwards. Even the affection that one feels for a child, the desire to protect and cherish it, is a cause of misunderstandings. One can love a child, perhaps, more deeply than one can love another adult, but it is rash to assume that the child feels any love in return. Looking back on my childhood, after the infant years were over, I do not believe that I ever felt love for any mature person except my mother, and even her I did not trust, in the sense that shyness made me conceal most of my real feelings from her. Love, the spontaneous, unqualified emotion of love, was something I could only feel for people who were young. Towards people who were old—and remember that "old" to a child means over thirty, or even over twenty-five—I could feel reverence, respect, admiration or compunction, but I seemed cut off from them by a veil of fear and shyness mixed up with physical distaste. People are too ready to forget the child's *physical* shrinking from the adult. The enormous size of grown-ups, their ungainly, rigid bodies, their coarse, wrinkled skins, their great relaxed eyelids, their yellow teeth, and the whiffs of musty clothes and beer and sweat and tobacco that disengage from them at every movement! Part of the reason for the ugliness of adults, in a child's eyes, is that the child is usually looking upwards, and few faces are at their best when seen from below. Besides, being fresh and unmarked itself, the child has impossibly high standards in the matter of skin and teeth and complexion. But the greatest barrier of all is the child's misconception about age. A child can hardly envisage life beyond thirty, and in judging people's ages it will make fantastic mistakes. It will think that a person of twenty-five is forty, that a person of forty is sixty-five, and so on. Thus, when I fell in love with Elsie I took her to be grown-up. I met her again, when I was thirteen and she, I think, must have been twenty-three; she now seemed to me a middle-aged woman, somewhat past her best. And the child thinks of growing old as an almost obscene calamity, which for some mysterious reason will never happen to itself. All who have passed the age of thirty are joyless grotesques, endlessly fussing about things of no importance and staying alive without, so far as the child can see, having anything to live for. Only child life is real life. The schoolmaster who imagines that he is loved and trusted by his boys is in fact mimicked and laughed at behind his back.

An adult who does not seem dangerous nearly always seems ridiculous.

I base these generalisations on what I can recall of my own childhood outlook. Treacherous though memory is, it seems to me the chief means we have of discovering how a child's mind works. Only by resurrecting our own memories can we realise how incredibly distorted is the child's vision of the world. Consider this, for example. How would St. Cyprian's appear to me now, if I could go back, at my present age, and see it as it was in 1915? What should I think of Sambo and Flip, those terrible, all-powerful monsters? I should see them as a couple of silly, shallow, ineffectual people, eagerly clambering up a social ladder which any thinking person could see to be on the point of collapse. I would no more be frightened of them than I would be frightened of a dormouse. Moreover, in those days they seemed to me fantastically old, whereas—though of this I am not certain—I imagine they must have been somewhat younger than I am now. And how would Cliffy Burton appear, with his blacksmith's arms and his red, jeering face? Merely a scruffy little boy, barely distinguishable from hundreds of other scruffy little boys. The two sets of facts can lie side by side in my mind, because those happen to be my own memories. But it would be very difficult for me to see with the eyes of any other child, except by an effort of the imagination which might lead me completely astray. The child and the adult live in different worlds. If that is so, we cannot be certain that school, at any rate boarding school, is not still for many children as dreadful an experience as it used to be. Take away God, Latin, the cane, class distinctions and sexual taboos, and the fear, the hatred, the snobbery and the misunderstanding might still all be there. It will have been seen that my own main trouble was an utter lack of any sense of proportion or probability. This led me to accept outrages and believe absurdities, and to suffer torments

over things which were in fact of no importance. It is not enough
to say that I was "silly" and "ought to have known better." Look
back into your own childhood and think of the nonsense you used
to believe and the trivialities which could make you suffer. Of
course my own case had its individual variations, but essentially it
was that of countless other boys. The weakness of the child is that
it starts with a blank sheet. It neither understands nor questions
the society in which it lives, and because of its credulity other
people can work upon it, infecting it with the sense of inferiority
and the dread of offending against mysterious, terrible laws. It may
be that everything that happened to me at St. Cyprian's could happen in the most "enlightened" school, though perhaps in subtler
forms. Of one thing, however, I do feel fairly sure, and that is that
boarding schools are worse than day schools. A child has a better
chance with the sanctuary of its home near at hand. And I think
the characteristic faults of the English upper and middle classes
may be partly due to the practice, general until recently, of sending children away from home as young as nine, eight or even
seven.

I have never been back to St. Cyprian's. Reunions, old boys'
dinners and such-like leave me something more than cold, even
when my memories are friendly. I have never even been down to
Eton, where I was relatively happy, though I did once pass through
it in 1933 and noted with interest that nothing seemed to have
changed, except that the shops now sold radios. As for St.
Cyprian's, for years I loathed its very name so deeply that I could
not view it with enough detachment to see the significance of the
things that happened to me there. In a way, it is only within the last
decade that I have really thought over my schooldays, vividly
though their memory has always haunted me. Nowadays, I believe, it would make very little impression on me to see the place
again, if it still exists. (I remember hearing a rumour some years

ago that it had been burnt down.) If I had to pass through East-bourne I would not make a detour to avoid the school: and if I happened to pass the school itself I might even stop for a moment by the low brick wall, with the steep bank running down from it, and look across the flat playing field at the ugly building with the square of asphalt in front of it. And if I went inside and smelt again the inky, dusty smell of the big schoolroom, the rosiny smell of the chapel, the stagnant smell of the swimming bath and the cold reek of the lavatories, I think I should only feel what one invariably feels in revisiting any scene of childhood: How small everything has grown, and how terrible is the deterioration in myself!

NOTES

The Spike

1. "And there is nothing left remarkable / Beneath the visiting moon"; Cleopatra's response to Antony's death, *Antony and Cleopatra*, 4.15.67–68.

Clink

1. Clink is a cant word for a prison, from the Clink, one-time prison in the London borough of Southwark dating from the sixteenth century.

2. Lord Kylsant (1863–1937), a Conservative MP, Chairman of the Royal Mail Steam Package Company, and with large shipbuilding interests, was sentenced to twelve months' imprisonment in 1931 for circulating a false prospectus. His personal guilt was never entirely established in the public mind.

3. His lodgings at 2 Windsor Street, Paddington, near St. Mary's Hospital. The house has been demolished.

My Country Right or Left

1. The title of the essay adopts Stephen Decatur's "Toast Given at Norfolk" (Virginia, 1816), "My country, right or wrong."

2. The slogan dates from 1909.

3. On August 23, 1939, Germany and the Soviet Union signed, in the persons of Ribbentrop and Molotov, a nonaggression pact in Moscow, completely reversing the balance of relationships in Europe. A secret protocol provided for the partition of Poland between the signatories. Hitler was informed of the signing of an Anglo-Polish agreement at 4:30 P.M. on August 25 and three hours later cancelled an order given at 3:00 P.M. for his troops to invade Poland. The invasion was postponed until September 1, 1939.

War-time Diary

1. There were at this time three London evening papers: *Star, Evening News,* and *Evening Standard.*

2. British Expeditionary Force, the troops in France at the time of that country's fall to the Germans.

3. Eileen Blair, Orwell's wife.

4. Alfred Duff Cooper (1890–1954; Viscount Norwich, 1952) was a Conservative politician, diplomat, and author.

5. A Socialist weekly to which Orwell contributed many reviews and essays.

6. The Communist Party's daily newspaper in Britain.

7. The journal of the British Union of Fascists.

8. In May, Max Aitken, first Baron Beaverbrook (1879–1964), the Canadian newspaper proprietor, had been made minister of aircraft production by Churchill.

9. Dr. Franz Borkenau (1900–1957), Austrian sociologist and political writer, born in Vienna, was from 1921 to 1929 a member of the German Communist Party. For his conversations with Orwell at the time of Dunkirk, see above and Orwell's War-time Diary, *65, 6.6.40*.

10. Cyril Connolly (1903–1974) was with Orwell at St. Cyprian's and Eton. They met again in 1935, and were associated in a number of literary activities, particularly *Horizon*, which Connolly edited.

11. Unidentified.

12. "Eric," abbreviated from his second name, was the name by which Eileen Blair's much-loved brother, Laurence Frederick O'Shaughnessy, was known. He was a distinguished chest and heart surgeon, joined the Royal Army Medical Corps at the outbreak of war, and was killed tending the wounded on the beaches of Dunkirk.

13. Eamon de Valera (1882–1975), Irish political leader, was at this time prime minister of the Irish Free State.

14. A popular Sunday newspaper.

15. Margot Asquith (1864–1945) was the widow of Herbert Henry Asquith, Earl of Oxford and Asquith, who was prime minister 1906–1916.

16. These figures were, in fact, correct. Although most of their equipment was lost, 198,000 British and 140,000 mainly French and Belgian soldiers were evacuated. Of the forty-one naval vessels involved, six were sunk and nineteen damaged. About 220,000 servicemen were evacuated from ports in Normandy and Brittany.

17. "Suppressed" implies censorship; such posters were forbidden simply to conserve raw materials and economize on imports, thereby saving shipping space.

18. Sir Stafford Cripps (1889–1952), lawyer and labour politician, was ambassador to the Soviet Union, 1940–1942, and minister of aircraft production, 1942–1945.

19. Orwell eventually did so, in "As I Please," 42, *Tribune*, September 15, 1944.

20. Local Defence Volunteers, later the Home Guard. Orwell joined on June 12 what became C Company, 5th County of London Battalion, and was soon promoted to sergeant, with ten men to instruct. He took his duties very seriously.

21. Marylebone Cricket Club, the body that then controlled national and international cricket.

22. A working-class constituency in the East End of London.

23. George Lansbury (1859–1940), leader of the Labour Party, 1931–1935, was a pacifist and resigned as leader on that issue.

24. Juan Negrín (1889–1956) was Socialist prime minister of the Republic of Spain, September 1936–March 1938. He fled to France where he died in exile.

25. Milton, *Paradise Lost,* iv, 110.

26. Orwell had signed the contract for publication of *Coming Up for Air* just three days before war broke out; the book remained unpublished by Albatross.

27. Victor William (Peter) Watson (1908–1956), a rich young man who, after much travel, decided, about 1939, to devote his life to the arts, was cofounder with his friend Cyril Connolly of the magazine *Horizon,* which he financed and also provided all the material for the art section. He was always an admirer of Orwell's writing.

28. The Hon. Unity Valkyrie Mitford (1914–1948), fourth daughter of the second Lord Redesdale, was, from 1934, when she first met Hitler, his admirer. In January 1940 she was brought back to England from Germany suffering from bullet wounds in the head. Thereafter she lived in retirement.

29. Possibly Michael, the owner of the small clothing factory mentioned in Orwell's diary entry of *3.9.40*; see *95.*

30. Gwen O'Shaughnessy, Eileen's sister-in-law. In the early stages of the war, there was a government-sponsored scheme to evacuate children to Canada and the United States. Gwen's son, Laurence, nineteen months old in June 1940, went to Canada on one of the last ships to take evacuees before the evacuee ship *City of Benares* was sunk in the Atlantic.

31. "*New Statesman*" seems probable here.

32. Probably Richard Crossman (1907–1974), scholar, intellectual, journalist, and left-wing politician, who was assistant editor of *The New Statesman,* 1938–1955, and Labour MP, 1945–1970.

33. The British 146th Infantry Brigade landed at Namsos, Norway, on the coast some 300 miles north of Oslo, on April 16–17, 1940. They withdrew May 2–3. The last Allied forces left Norway on June 9.

34. Aneurin (Nye) Bevan (1897–1960) was a Labour MP and a director of *Tribune* when Orwell wrote for that journal, and allowed Orwell complete freedom to say what he wished against current party policy. G. R. Strauss (1901–1993, Life Peer, 1979) was a Labour MP and codirector of *Tribune.*

35. Neville Chamberlain (1869–1940). Conservative prime minister associated with the appeasement of Hitler, though he initiated the rearmament of Britain. Chamberlain's government fell on May 10, 1940, and a coalition government under Winston Churchill was formed. Magnanimously, Churchill included Chamberlain in his cabinet.

36. Rayner Heppenstall.

37. "Unblimping" was a frequent concern of Orwell's. See, for example, "War-time Diary," *92, 23.8.40.*

38. Not certainly identified. Possibly Richard Crossman again (see *n. 32* above) or Cyril Connolly.

39. See "My Country Right or Left," *52–58.*

40. Jean Chiappe (1878–1940), Corsican head of the Paris police, 1927–1934, was pro-Fascist and responsible for severely repressive measures against the left. For Orwell on Chiappe's death, see *107.*

41. Henri Philippe Pétain (1856–1951), successful defender of Verdun in 1916, which led to his being regarded as a national hero, was created a marshal of France in 1918. He became premier in 1940, presided over the defeat and dismemberment of France by the Germans, and led the occupied zone's Vichy government until war's end. He was tried for collaboration with the Nazis and sentenced to death. President De Gaulle commuted his sentence to solitary confinement for life.

42. Pierre Laval (1883–1945) held various offices in French governments and was premier 1931–1932 and 1935–1936. He left the Socialist Party in 1920 and gradually moved to the extreme right. On January 7, 1935, as foreign minister, he signed an agreement with Mussolini that backed Italian claims to areas of Abyssinia (Ethiopia) in return for Italian support against German intervention in Austria. Italy invaded Abyssinia on October 3, 1935, and on December 18 the British foreign secretary, Sir Samuel Hoare (1880–1959, Viscount Templewood, 1944), was forced to resign when it was revealed that he had entered into a pact with Laval appeasing Mussolini. After the fall of France, Laval came to represent treacherous collaboration. He even provided Frenchmen for work in German industry. Tried in 1945, he was executed after failing in a suicide attempt.

43. Pierre-Étienne Flandin (1889–1958) held numerous offices in French governments. He was premier 1934–1935, and foreign minister in Pétain's government in 1940, but attempted to resist German demands and was replaced by Laval. He was forbidden to participate in public life after the war.

44. Eileen Blair and Gwen O'Shaughnessy, her sister-in-law.

45. Probably Mrs. Anderson, who cleaned for the Orwells in Wallington. Although Orwell had, by the time this was written, been living in London for five or six weeks, he still visited Wallington.

46. Ministry of Information, which was responsible for wartime propaganda. It had offices in the Senate House of the University of London, the city's tallest new building of the interwar years. It suggested Minitrue of *1984.*

47. R. A. Butler (1902–1984; Life Peer, 1965) was Under-Secretary of State for Foreign Affairs, 1938–1941, Chancellor of the Exchequer, and later Foreign Secretary in the Conservative government of 1951–1964.

48. Sir Samuel Hoare (see *n. 42,* above) was at this time British Ambassador to Spain.

49. L. H. Myers was a novelist and good friend to Orwell.

50. Weekly newspaper of the Independent Labour Party, which Orwell had joined in June 1938, having fought with the ILP contingent in Spain. He left the party at the beginning of the war.

51. Charles de Gaulle (1890–1970) was at this time leader of the Free French and the inspiration for continuing French resistance to Germany after the fall of France. After the war, he was interim president 1945–1946. He returned to power in 1958 as a result of the crisis in Algeria, and, as architect and president of the Fifth Republic, 1959–1969, maintained France's military and strategic independence.

52. Italo Balbo (1896–1940), head of the Italian Air Force, was responsible for the bombing of Ethiopians during the Italo-Ethiopian War, 1935–1936.

53. Cyril Connolly.

54. Unidentified. Probably not L. H. Myers and his wife, for whom the description "all but pure pacifists" is inappropriate.

55. The home of Gwen O'Shaughnessy in Greenwich.

56. In June 1939 the British submarine *Thetis* failed to surface on its trials. Only four of the complement of 103 were saved, owing to faulty escape apparatus. The submarine was recovered and entered active service as HMS *Thunderbolt* in November 1940. All the crew were told of the submarine's history and given the opportunity to decline to serve in her. After a successful career, she was depth-charged and lost with all hands in March 1943. The non sequitur here is a result of Orwell's cut.

57. Werner von Fritsch (1880–1939), an old-guard general on the German Army General Staff, never concealed his contempt for Hitler. His death in action in 1939 was always thought to have been engineered by the Führer.

58. Buenaventura Durruti (1896–1936), a gunman who became a general and popular leader. He was killed in the defense of Madrid, possibly by Communists. His funeral gave rise to a great popular demonstration in Barcelona. Emilio Mola Vidal (1887–1937), an equal colleague of Franco, was killed in the early stages of the civil war, before the question of primacy with Franco could arise.

59. On July 3, the Royal Navy under the command of Vice-Admiral Sir John Somerville attacked French warships at Oran and Mers el-Kébir, in Algeria. Among the French ships sunk or damaged were the battleships *Provence* and *Bretagne* and the fast battle-cruiser *Dunkerque;* 1,300 French seamen were killed. Several ships, including the battle-cruiser *Strasbourg* and the aircraft carrier *Commandant Teste,* escaped to Toulon. French ships at Portsmouth and Plymouth were also seized, including two battleships, two cruisers, eight destroyers, some two hundred small craft, and a number of submarines. Crews had the option of joining the Allies or being repatriated.

60. On July 8, 1940, Royal Navy torpedo-boats attacked and seriously damaged the *Richelieu* at Dakar and the *Jean Bart* at Casablanca.

61. Vernon Bartlett (1894–1983), author of many books of political affairs, was at this

time a leading liberal political journalist. He won a sensational by-election in 1938 as an Independent MP opposing the Munich Agreement.

62. Edward, Duke of Windsor (1894–1972), had, as Prince of Wales, been extremely popular, and had expressed sympathy with the unemployed and those living in depressed areas. He ascended the throne, as Edward VIII, on January 20, 1936, but his decision to marry a twice-divorced woman, Mrs. Wallis Simpson, caused a crisis that led to his abdication on December 10, 1936. He and Mrs. Simpson married and lived in France thereafter except for the war years, when he acted as governor of the Bahamas. Ill-feeling and controversy about "the Abdication Crisis" and his association with Nazi Germany have not entirely evaporated.

63. Unidentified; possibly Tosco Fyvel (1907–1985). He was Jewish; his parents had emigrated from Vienna to what was then Palestine, where he was associated with the Zionist movement and had worked with Golda Meir. Orwell and he met in January 1940, with Fredric Warburg and others. The outcome of a series of further meetings was Searchlight Books, of which *The Lion and the Unicorn* (1941) was the first; see *306, n. 1.*

64. Unidentified; possibly Fredric Warburg.

65. See *71, 17.6.40* regarding evacuation of children to Canada.

66. David Lloyd George (1863–1945, Earl Lloyd George of Dwyfor, 1945), Liberal prime minister 1916–1922, had, like Pétain, been cast as a heroic leader during World War I, when he proved an effective prime minister. He was in a minority in seeking a conciliatory peace treaty with Germany after the war.

67. Unidentified.

68. On July 16, 1940, Hitler had said, in Directive 16: "I have decided to prepare a landing operation against England, and, if necessary, to carry it out. The aim . . . will be to eliminate the English homeland . . . and, if necessary, to occupy it completely" (*Hitler's War Directives 1939–45*, edited by Hugh Trevor-Roper, 1964).

69. William Joyce (1908–1946), known as Lord Haw-Haw supposedly from his way of speaking, was an American citizen who never acquired British nationality, although he spent most of his life in England and was a rabid nationalist. In August 1939 he went to Germany and in 1940 became a naturalized German. Throughout the early part of the war he broadcast propaganda to England. He was hanged by the British, January 3, 1946.

70. Sir Oswald Mosley, Bt. (1896–1980) was successively a Conservative, Independent, and Labour MP. In 1931 he broke away from the Labour Party to form the "New Party." Later he became fanatically pro-Hitler and turned his party into the British Union of Fascists. He was interned early in the war.

71. Jacques Doriot (1898–1945), a Communist who had turned to Fascism, was leader of the Parti Populaire Français, which was financed by the Germans. He was behind the formation of La Légion des volontaires français contre bolchevisme (the LVF)—a first step in military collaboration with Germany during the occupation.

72. Gaston Bergery, a French deputy and intellectual, moved from the extreme right to the extreme left, and after the fall of France collaborated with the Germans.

73. Philip Cunliffe-Lister, Viscount Swinton (1884–1972; Earl, 1955), entered Parliament as a Unionist (allied closely with the Conservatives) in 1918. He was Secretary of State for the Colonies, 1931–1935; Secretary of State for Air, 1935–1938; Chairman of the United Kingdom Commercial Corporation, 1940–1942; Cabinet Minister Resident in West Africa, 1942–1944; and Minister of Civil Aviation, 1944–1945.

74. Fewer planes were actually shot down than British and German air forces claimed at the time. On August 14 the Royal Air Force claimed to have shot down 144 German planes; this was revised to 71 after the war, when German records could be examined. On that day the RAF lost 16 planes, but eight pilots were saved. On September 15, 185 German planes were claimed; this proved to be 56; 26 RAF planes were lost, but half the pilots were rescued. This was the largest number claimed for any day of the Battle of Britain. From July to the end of October, the claim was 2,698 German planes shot down; the correct number was 1,733. The Germans claimed 3,058 RAF planes, but only 915 were lost. To what extent this was deliberate official exaggeration and to what degree overenthusiastic reporting by pilots is difficult to assess.

75. The Orwells' dog, a large poodle.

76. This is probably George Mason, a medical consultant and friend of the O'Shaughnessy family.

77. Leon Trotsky (1879-1940), a leader of the October 1917 revolution in Russia, and Commissar for Foreign Affairs and for War, 1917–1924, was instrumental in the creation of the Red Army. In the power struggle that followed the death of Lenin in 1924, he lost to Stalin and was exiled. He was assassinated in Mexico because he and those who followed him continued to oppose Stalin. His death was attributed to the Soviet secret police, the OGPU.

78. David Low (1891–1963) was a political cartoonist of left-wing views.

79. Unidentified.

80. Passed over for promotion.

81. "Art of Knowing What Gives One Pleasure," *Further Extracts from the Note-Books of Samuel Butler,* chosen and edited by A. T. Bartholomew (1934), 165–66. This book was reviewed by Orwell in 1934.

82. In this raid, the first bombs fell on central London; St. Giles's Church, Cripplegate, was hit. Although 11-ton blockbuster bombs were later dropped by the RAF, at this stage of the war 2,000-pound bombs were not available. In the attack on Woolwich Arsenal and the London docks on September 7, 1940, some three hundred German bombers dropped 337 tons of bombs—an average of 2,500 pounds per plane. Orwell may have had parachute mines, or their effect, in mind here. Churchill wrote General Ismay a memorandum on September 19, 1940 noting that the Germans had dropped thirty-six parachute mines. He wanted an appropriate response—1,000-pound bombs if parachute mines were not available. The disadvantage of the parachute mine, except as a weapon of terror, was that, released at five thousand feet, anything might be hit.

83. A suburb of London about a mile from where Orwell was living in Chagford Street.

84. Richard Rees.

85. Unidentified.

86. The number killed in air raids in September was 6,954; 10,615 were seriously injured. The figures during the ensuing winter throughout Britain were:

	Killed	Injured
October 1940	6,334	8,695
November	4,588	6,202
December	3,793	5,244
January 1941	1,500	2,012
February	789	1,068
March	4,259	5,557

In the devastation of Coventry on November 16 (code-named "Moonlight Sonata" by the Germans), 554 people were killed of a population of a quarter of a million; only one German plane was shot down. Throughout the war, 60,595 civilians were killed by enemy action. This stands in contrast to 30,248 members of the Merchant Marine; 50,758 Royal Navy; 69,606 RAF; and 144,079 Army. Of some 36,500 civilians killed in air raids to the end of 1941, more than 20,000 died in London, more than 4,000 in Liverpool, more than 2,000 in Birmingham, and nearly 2,000 in Glasgow.

87. Probably the "M" mentioned in diary entry of *16.6.40,* see *70.* Fifty pounds would be about a week's wages for a total of ten to twelve people.

88. See "My Country Right or Left," *55.*

89. South and east of the Thames, often regarded as if it was an East End community, this area is well known in Cockney tradition.

90. Holborn is in the City of London; Marylebone Railway Station, a London terminus, was only two hundred to three hundred yards from where Orwell was living in Chagford Street.

91. Madame Tussaud's Waxworks Exhibition was in Marylebone Road, a couple of hundred yards from where Orwell lived, in the opposite direction from Marylebone station.

92. Woolwich, some two to three miles east of Greenwich, where the O'Shaughnessys lived, was the location of a Royal Artillery depot, the Royal Military Academy, and the Royal Arsenal.

93. In Piccadilly Circus. The Windmill Theatre, as it proudly boasted, also "never closed"; it was a little to the northeast of Piccadilly Circus.

94. The Elephant and Castle, a public house, gave its name to this major working-class residential area, shopping center, and meeting point of several important roads.

95. Stephen Spender's flat, and the *Horizon* office, in Lansdowne Terrace, WC1. Orwell originally typed "S.S's place" but the first *S* was crossed out.

96. On September 22, 1940, Churchill wrote to President Roosevelt saying that 250,000 rifles "are most urgently needed, as I have 250,000 trained and uniformed men [the Home Guard] into whose hands they can be put." If they could be made available, it would "enable us to take 250,000 .303 rifles from the Home Guard and transfer them to the Regular Army, leaving the Home Guard armed with about 800,000 American rifles."

97. When the Germans first bombed London, there appeared to be no anti-aircraft defense. Sometimes a single plane could be cruising above and people could only wait anxiously, often for seemingly long periods, for a bomb to be dropped. At other times there would be a concentrated attack of incendiary bombs, high explosives, or both. After all the anti-aircraft guns available had been regrouped around London, quite unexpectedly they all opened up on the night of September 10. Orwell is absolutely correct about the effect on morale. See also *98, 12.9.40.*

98. Air Raid Precautions.

99. A department store.

100. In September 1940 a British expedition, cooperating with Free French forces under General de Gaulle, made an attempt to recapture the port of Dakar, West Africa, from the Vichy government. The expedition was a failure.

101. Unidentified.

102. Unidentified.

103. Unidentified.

104. J. B. Priestley (1894–1984) was a prolific popular novelist, dramatist, and man of letters. During 1940 and 1941 he gave a series of weekly radio talks urging the nation to determination and unity against Hitler, so as to make the country more democratic and egalitarian.

105. David R. Margesson (1890–1965; Viscount, 1942), Conservative MP for Rugby, 1924–1942; Government Chief Whip, 1931–1940, was loyal to each prime minister he served. Under Churchill he continued as Joint Government Whip, and after six months was Secretary of State for War.

106. Probably Tosco Fyvel, with whom Orwell was then working; see *302, n. 63.*

107. Editor and journal not identified.

108. Hitler's New Order for Europe — Nazism.

109. It is possible that Orwell's animosity toward Sir Samuel Hoare (see last sentence of the paragraph and *n. 42,* above) led him to retail H.P.'s assertion.

110. Unidentified.

111. Pierre Comert, French journalist and former diplomat, went to England after the fall of France.

112. Mrs. Wallis Simpson, by this time married to the Duke of Windsor; see *302, n. 62.*

113. For Pierre Laval, see *300, n. 42.*

114. Coventry was attacked during the night of November 14, 1940.

115. See *300, n. 40,* above.

116. See *301, n. 52,* above.

England Your England

1. Searchlight Books, of which *The Lion and the Unicorn* was the first, were planned by Fredric Warburg, Tosco Fyvel, and Orwell during the summer of 1940. Orwell was persuaded, rather against his will, to write the first book—in effect, a sixty-four-page pamphlet. Having agreed, he wrote at speed, delivering the manuscript in November 1940. *The Lion and the Unicorn* was published by Secker & Warburg on February 19, 1941.

2. The June Purge, or Night of the Long Knives, led to the execution, without trial, of Hitler's close friend Ernst Röhm (head of the S.A., the Brownshirts) and seventy-seven leading Nazis plus many others, prompted initially by Göering and Himmler, later by Hitler, in June 1934.

3. Orwell is not quite correct. He overlooks, for example, "A Ballad of Waterloo" by Thomas Hood (1799–1845), a poem sardonic in words and illustration. Byron wrote a notable, and anthologized, poem, "The Eve of Waterloo."

4. Orwell is indirectly referring to the poem by Charles Wolfe (1791–1823), "The Burial of Sir John Moore after Corunna," much anthologized and often set, in the first decades of the twentieth century, for schoolboys to learn.

5. William Richard Morris (1877–1963; Viscount Nuffield) was largely responsible for the establishment of an automobile-manufacturing industry in Cowley, Oxford, following the success of his Morris-Oxford car in 1913. He devoted much of his wealth to philanthropic purposes.

6. Baron Montagu Norman (1871–1950) was governor of the Bank of England, 1920–44. He was decorated for service in the Boer War. For Orwell's grouping of him with those who supported Fascism, see "Looking Back on the Spanish War," *163.*

7. Anthony Eden (1897–1977, Earl of Avon, 1961) Conservative MP, was then Secretary of State for War in Churchill's war cabinet. The Local Defence Volunteers became the Home Guard.

8. For Pierre Laval, see *300, n. 42.* Vidkun Quisling (1887–1945), Norwegian Fascist who led the puppet government of Norway under the Germans, was executed for treason. His name has been applied generally to collaborators.

9. Half of the extracts abstracted by Orwell for his Diary of Events Leading Up to the War were taken from the *Daily Telegraph.*

10. Lord Halifax (1881–1959), Edward Frederick Lindley Wood (Lord Irwin, 1925; 3rd Viscount Halifax, 1934; Earl of Halifax, 1944), was a Conservative politician.

11. Stanley Baldwin (1867–1947, Earl Baldwin 1937), thrice Conservative prime minister, was blamed for Britain's failure to prepare for war.

12. Fashionable "society" magazines; the *Tatler* was founded in 1901 and amalgamated with the *Bystander* (founded 1903) in November 1940.

13. John Simon (1873–1954, Viscount 1940), Chancellor of the Exchequer, 1937–40, was a supporter of Neville Chamberlain. Samuel Hoare, a close associate of Chamberlain, served in several Conservative-led administrations; see *300, n. 42*. For Neville Chamberlain, see *299, n. 35*.

14. John Nicholson (1821–1857), soldier and administrator, played an important role in the Indian Mutiny, 1857. He effected the Relief of Delhi but was mortally wounded after leading an assault on the Kashmir Gate.

15. "Lawrence of Arabia" (1888–1935) led the Arab Revolt against the Turks, 1916–18; see his *Seven Pillars of Wisdom* (1922), abridged by Lawrence as *Revolt in the Desert* (1927).

16. Founded by Edward Hulton, October 1, 1938, it ran until June 1, 1957. Its marriage of illustrations, captions, and text, coupled with its social and political concerns, especially in its early days, showed how effectively popular interest could be aroused.

Looking Back on the Spanish War

1. The Oxford Union's motion in 1933 supporting the refusal to fight "for King and Country" initiated a series of alternating demands that Britain abstain from and engage in military action.

2. The source of this quotation has not been traced.

3. "A resolution, / To fight to the end"

4. *Homage to Catalonia.*

5. Orwell possibly had in mind Gerald Heard (1889–1971), whom he mentions in his September 1943 review in *Horizon* of Lionel Fielden's *Beggar My Neighbour;* also Aldous Huxley, and possibly Christopher Isherwood, all of whom settled in Los Angeles just before the war. In California, Isherwood developed an interest in Yoga and Vedanta (though whether Orwell knew this is uncertain), edited and introduced *Vedanta for the Western World* (Hollywood, 1945; London, 1948), and with Swami Prabhavananda translated *The Bhagavad-Gita* (1944) and other related works. It is possible that this reference was inspired by Orwell's preliminary arrangements for G. V. Desani to talk on the *Bhagavad-Gita* in his BBC series "Books that Changed the World."

6. From Auden, "Sir, No Man's Enemy" (1930): "New styles of architecture, a change of heart."

As I Please, 1

1. Robin Maugham (Robert Cecil Romer Maugham, 2nd Viscount Maugham, 1916–1981), barrister, prose writer, and dramatist.

2. Orwell probably had in mind Major-General J. F. C. Fuller (1878–1966). He wrote a pamphlet, *Back to Sanity,* which was published by the British Union of Fascists in the thir-

ties. He was listed by British Intelligence (MI5) as a prospective gauleiter if the Germans had successfully occupied Britain (although in 1943 Orwell would not have known that).

3. The passages will be found on pages 168–69 and 208–9 of the second, corrected, edition of 1888.

As I Please, 2

1. Thomas Edmund Dewey (1902–1971), governor of New York for three successive terms (1942–54), was Republican Party's presidential candidate in 1944 and 1948; he lost both elections.

2. *Burmese Days* (1944).

As I Please, 3

1. See "As I Please," 1, December 3, 1943, *167*.

2. Reviewed by Orwell, December 9, 1943. Philip Jordan was a well-known wartime correspondent for the *News Chronicle*.

3. John Lemprière (d. 1824) produced his *Bibliotheca Classica* in 1788. It was revised many times and became known by the title given it here.

As I Please, 16

1. The spelling is *Inprecor* in *Homage to Catalonia*. *Inprecor*'s title varied. It was published from Vienna and Berlin in the 1920s as *Internationale Press, Korrespondenz*, and French and Swiss versions were issued. Its frequency was at least weekly, but there was some irregularity in its publication. It was a Communist news sheet opposed to the POUM when Orwell was in Barcelona.

The Sporting Spirit

1. The Moscow Dynamos, a Russian soccer team, toured Britain in the autumn of 1945 and played a number of leading British clubs. "Guest players" were allowed into teams at this time because of wartime conditions, but, even allowing for that, it was claimed that Britain's Arsenal team had been unduly strengthened.

In Front of Your Nose

1. Roger Charles Tichborne (1829–1854), heir to a large estate in Hampshire, was lost at sea in 1854. His mother refused to accept that her son was dead and, when she learned that a butcher working in Wagga Wagga, Australia, claimed to be the heir, she recognized his claim. This led to a trial in 1871–1872, marked by conflicting evidence, which resulted in his being declared an impostor. His true identity was said to be Arthur Orton, of Wapping (a dockland area of London). In 1874 he was found guilty of perjury and imprisoned. He was released in 1884 and died a pauper in 1898.

A Good Word for the Vicar of Bray

1. John Overall (1560–1618) was Regius Professor of Theology, University of Cambridge, 1596–1607, and Dean of St. Paul's Cathedral, 1602. Oliver Lawson Dick in his *Aubrey's Brief Lives* (1949) notes that "He was not given to preaching, because he found he had spoken Latin so long as it was troublesome to him to speak English in a continued oration." His wife Aubrey described as "not more beautifull than she was obliging and kind . . . the loveliest Eies that were ever seen, but wondrous wanton." The Dean "knew well enough that he was horned" but loved her infinitely "in so much that he was willing she should enjoy what she had a mind to." This was Orwell's favourite "life," as he told Anthony Powell when sent a complimentary copy of Powell's edition. Powell had evidently considered omitting it. It has not been possible to identify the source of Orwell's text. Powell's follows that of Andrew Clark (1898, vol. 2, 116–18). Orwell's differs from these, and from Dick's, in capitalisation, although it retains most of the seventeenth-century spellings. Orwell may have known Clark's edition, but most probably Powell had sent him a typed copy of this "life" when deciding whether or not to include it.

2. Orwell miscounted the verses; his text has six. In Clark's, Powell's, and Dick's editions there are eight stanzas, of which Orwell reproduces the first, third, and eighth.

Why I Write

1. Lines 1021–22 of Book II of *Paradise Lost.* "He" is Satan, "Sin and Death amain / Following his track."

2. These are the last three stanzas of the nine making up "A happy vicar I might have been," *The Adelphi,* December 1936.

How the Poor Die

1. The admission records of the Hôpital Cochin show that Orwell was admitted to the Salle Lancereaux "pour une grippe" on March 7, 1929 and discharged on March 22. This essay, therefore, though based on experience, is not strictly autobiographical. See *n. 2.* (Information supplied to Sonia Orwell by le Directeur-Adjoint, Hôpital Cochin, November 25, 1971.)

2. Orwell was evidently seriously ill with a bad attack of influenza–une grippe — rather than pneumonia; and the month was March, not February. Had Orwell been ill with pneumonia he would hardly have recovered in two weeks after the treatment he described — if he recovered at all. The essay, as indicated in *n. 1,* is a literary rather than a documentary account.

3. Tennyson's "In the Children's Hospital: Emmie" was published in 1880.

Such, Such Were the Joys

1. Earlier printings of "Such, Such Were the Joys" have shown changes of names to avoid giving offense to those then living. The text given here is that revised by Orwell but with the original names.